Timeless
BOWHUNTING

What Others are Saying:

"Has the potential to be one of the best books ever written for serious bowhunters."
Mike Strandlund, Editor, BOWHUNTING WORLD Magazine

"In a word: Wonderful!—I really enjoyed it. I've been bowhunting for a long time and I still learned a lot."
Fred Richter; Former President, National Bowhunter Education Foundation, Professional Bowhunters Society, and West Virginia Bowhunters Association

"A whale of a bunch of useful information.... has no equal in breadth of coverage... A tribute to the writer's years of experience and knowledge."
Norb Mullaney; Archery Engineer; Chairman, ASTM Archery Products Sub-Committee and ATA Safety and Standards Committee; Director of Bow Testing, BOWHUNTING WORLD Magazine

"It's about time! ... a valuable and pleasantly refreshing read [that] fills an obvious void in the archery literature. A well written, well researched book that candidly, factually, and completely examines [all bowhunting] tackle..."
M.R. James; Founder and Editor-Emeritus, BOWHUNTER Magazine

"A must-read for every bowhunter, whether a modern or a traditional archer."
T.J. Conrads; Founder and Editor, TRADITIONAL BOWHUNTER Magazine

"Superb... rich in detail and coverage... Jammed full of practical wisdom and hard technical data..."
C.L., Texas

"I tried your 'tricks.' They work. 100% they work! Thanks so much."
P.K., Florida

"An enticing blend of old and new..."
L.P., South Dakota

"I've been shooting a bow since the 1930s. Your easy to understand explanations of bow and arrow weight tradeoffs, trajectory, and penetration were great. It's about time that someone put the facts straight."
J.C., Pennsylvania

"Insightful and hard hitting. [The author] presents his case powerfully... he backs up his points with irrefutable logic and examples..."
D.S., New Jersey

"Cuts through the chaff and tells it like it is... What a refreshing approach..."
J.S., California

"Has information that every bowhunter should know with the sport under increasing attack by anti-hunters"
N.S, Michigan

Timeless
BOWHUNTING

the Art, the Science, the Spirit

Roy S. Marlow

STACKPOLE
BOOKS

Published by
STACKPOLE BOOKS
5067 Ritter Road
Mechanicsburg, PA 17055
www.stackpolebooks.com

Printed in the United States

10 9 8 7 6 5 4 3 2 1

First edition

Originally published in 2003 by Strikepoint Technologies

Cover design by Caroline Stover

Library of Congress Cataloging-in-Publication Data

on file with the Library of Congress

Dedication

I owe a huge debt to the following people and dedicate this book to them:

- ❖ My father, an occasional rifle hunter, who supported my desire to hunt with a bow without fully understanding it, and for introducing me to those early hunting camps.
- ❖ Joe Fillinger, my uncle, for teaching me a love of wild places and wild things without ever realizing it.
- ❖ Bonnie Marlow, for her constant support and "reminders" that since I've introduced her to the healthful benefits of wild meat, I need to keep providing it.
- ❖ Charles Lenz, my longtime friend and hunting partner, for his constant good cheer in hunting camp and his creativity with *Hamburger Helper*, but most importantly, for modeling in many bowhunting photos over the years.

Acknowledgements

To the following people (in alphabetical order) who took time away from their own hunting to review this book and offer many helpful suggestions, I owe a hearty thanks:

- ❖ G. Fred Asbell, Former Bowhunting Editor, *Bowhunter* Magazine; Former President, Pope and Young Club
- ❖ T.J. Conrads, Editor/Publisher/Founder, *Traditional Bowhunter* Magazine
- ❖ M.R. James, Founder/Editor Emeritus, *Bowhunter* Magazine
- ❖ Bill Krenz, Editor, *Inside Archery* and *Bowhunt America* Magazines
- ❖ Norb Mullaney, Director of Bow Testing, *Bowhunting World* Magazine
- ❖ Tim Poole, Former Executive Director, *National Bowhunter Education Foundation*
- ❖ Fred Richter, Former President, *Professional Bowhunters Society* and the *National Bowhunter Education Foundation*
- ❖ John Simpson, Ph.D., Professor Emeritus (Ret.), Eastern Illinois University; President, Kudu Quest, Inc.
- ❖ Mike Strandlund, Editor, *Bowhunting World* Magazine

Finally, I owe an extra-special thanks to M.R. James for his ongoing support of this project and for his kindly agreeing to write the Foreword to the book.

Foreword

During the two-plus decades that I have known Roy Marlow, I've grown increasingly impressed with his ability to examine complex archery topics and communicate his discoveries in layman's language. His writing talent always made my job as a professional magazine editor much easier, but even more important is the fact that Roy consistently strives to provide all archers and bowhunters with an objective source of accurate information. His well researched magazine articles have always reflected an inquisitive nature combined with a professional engineer's eye for analytical detail; his new book carries on that well established tradition.

TIMELESS BOWHUNTING fills an obvious void in archery literature. This is not a book that simply advocates traditional equipment over modern tackle because its author favors hunting and shooting with stickbows. Neither is it a book that stresses the benefits and convenience of using of modern equipment while offering shortcuts to archery or bowhunting success. So exactly what is it? It's a well written, well researched book that candidly, factually, and completely examines advantages and disadvantages of using both traditional and modern tackle. Best of all, it's a book that presents facts and urges readers to choose and use what's best for them and their personal bowhunting endeavors and preferences. This is what makes Roy Marlow's new book a valuable and pleasantly refreshing read.

Bows and arrows. Techniques and tricks of the archery trade. Proper preparation and mental conditioning. It's all here. While some writers piously present their personal biases while relating chest-thumping tales of past hunting adventures, Roy Marlow has created a balanced and thought provoking book that answers questions and provides considerable food for thought. I, for one, say, "It's about time!"

M. R. James
BOWHUNTER Magazine
Founder/Editor Emeritus

Preface

Why
Another
Bowhunting
Book?

In the past decade I've written more than one-hundred magazine articles on archery and bowhunting. During this time, many readers called or wrote and asked me to compile them into a book for easy reference. While I haven't exactly done that here, I've addressed many of the topics that they expressed the greatest interest in.

The original articles took three basic forms. First was my coverage of technical topics such as trajectory, penetration, bow performance, or aiming techniques that are of interest to all archers. As a practicing engineer, I'm an incurable data collector and analyzer of technical problems, both in archery and other fields. I want to prove to myself the things that work and don't work and find the practical tradeoffs involved before I use them.

These mental exercises led me to discover some unknown or little used ways of doing things more effectively or more simply. For instance, they led me to discover a simple technique that largely eliminates the need to estimate shooting distance when using sights. They also allowed me to determine—in hard technical terms—the relative pros and cons involved for different shooting alternatives. An example is arrow speed versus weight. It's commonly known that light arrows have flatter trajectories that improve accuracy at unknown distances for sight-shooters. What isn't generally known is that when you factor in normal range estimation and shooting errors, most weight arrows will perform just about as well. In their quest for speed, many archers give up arrow penetration, durability, and other advantages unnecessarily.

Most bowhunting books don't address the sport in this technical way. I wanted to write a book that presented these *data* so that readers could make their own decisions based on well documented scientific *facts*.

I've also written about traditional archery topics in the past. The practice of traditional and modern archery have diverged so much in recent years that many contemporary books treat one subject but not the other. They treat them as separate sports. I wanted to write a book that included all types of archery equipment but that concentrated on their similarities—the brotherhood of all archers—more than their differences.

I wanted to blur the distinction between traditional and modern archery a bit and encourage archers to make their shooting decisions based on what works best for them rather than on marketing hype or what their buddies do. I wanted to remind "modern" shooters of some traditional techniques that they might find useful; and to remind "traditional" shooters of some useful modern techniques. I wanted to remind them, for instance, that traditional bows can be shot very well with sights and that compounds can be shot very well instinctively, as many people did in bygone eras and some still do today.

I also wanted to show that shooting modern or traditional archery isn't an either/or decision. Both have advantages and disadvantages and many archers do both. I wanted to encourage people to expand their archery horizons by trying all types of equipment, or just to read and learn about their fellow archers if they don't use something themselves right now.

Lastly, some of my original articles addressed difficult philosophical or ethical issues in the sport. Most authors avoid these topics. I wanted to write a book that talked about a few major issues openly and encouraged people to discuss them. These "problems" are debated in hushed tones at archery gatherings and loudly in closed industry committee meetings. I wanted to air them publicly for all archers to read about and decide upon. While they have no "right" or "wrong" answers, they may well determine the way in which we practice bowhunting in the future.

A Note About Photos & Graphics

As mentioned, my archery writings over the years have covered the gamut of equipment, from primitive to modern. In some cases, file photos that best supported a particular discussion point happened to show recurves or longbows. In almost every case, if a recurve or longbow is shown in a photo, the main points being made are equally valid for modern equipment as well. Similarly, I've tended to show compounds in line-art graphics but in most cases the points made are also valid for traditional shooters. Don't dismiss a chapter simply because of the photos or graphics used.

Contents

Part 1. The Arrow   1

Introduction

This is a book of the *hows* and *whys* of contemporary archery and bowhunting. It isn't meant to help you find more deer or larger bucks. There are plenty of other good books available that cover these topics. But it *will* help you to tag more animals by making you a much better, and a much more knowledgeable archer!

I say this because the single most important factor determining a hunter's success is his ability to put an arrow in a deer's boiler room. Despite the wealth of information that's written every year on finding big deer or elk, the fact is that in good hunting country you're going to get your share of opportunities if you just spend enough time in the woods. The difference between consistently successful hunters and those who only end the season with stories to tell is that good hunters make the most of their shots. A wealth of data support this and I've seen it over and over again myself.

How This Book Will Help You

This book will show you how to score more often by describing:
- ❖ The reasons why your equipment performs the way it does
- ❖ How to evaluate equipment performance tradeoffs
- ❖ How to choose the best equipment for your style of shooting and the animals that you hunt
- ❖ How different equipment factors, such as bow style, bow weight, and arrow weight affect performance
- ❖ How wind, shooting angle, and terrain affect arrow flight and aiming requirements
- ❖ How to determine the best aiming method(s) for you
- ❖ How to develop good shooting form
- ❖ How to practice effectively and continually improve your shooting skills
- ❖ How to conquer the significant mental demands of the sport, includ-

ing the dreaded demons—target panic and buck fever
- ❖ How to perform efficiently and ethically in all of your bowhunting activities
- ❖ And many other important topics.

Who This Book Is For

The book discusses all types of archery equipment (from speed bows and laser range finders to primitive all-wood bows) but much of the discussion centers on moderate technology and moderate shooting distances that have historically defined bowhunting. Studies show that most bowhunters experience the greatest *long term* satisfaction with the sport by seeking to balance the opposing goals of challenge and success, and the book emphasizes this "timeless" approach.

I've addressed the sport, or made suggestions, that avid maximum-technology or avid minimum-technology proponents may take issue with. Most hunters fall in between these extremes. They want to use effective equipment—and use it well—but also want to learn some simple tricks that will reduce their dependence on ever-advancing technology. They want to employ *both* the art and the science of bowhunting. They want to romantically experience a bit of the simple lives of their hunting ancestors and still score. Mostly, they just want archery and bowhunting to be fun.

If you fall into this category, then this book is for you.

A Different Approach

While I've included information that both beginners and experts will find useful, I haven't addressed many elementary concepts such as broadhead sharpening, bow tuning, choosing minor accessories, or other similar topics that have been covered elsewhere many times. Except in a few cases, I've avoided mentioning specific equipment makes and models (by the time you read this, they will have changed) and have simply given you some general points to consider when making your equipment decisions.

When discussing basic equipment or technique, I've tried to add a new twist or two, a new way of thinking about things, or have included technical points to consider that most books don't address.

In short, I've tried to cover common topics in a little different way and to add some uncommon ones for your consideration.

Tables & Graphs— Yuck!

Part of this book is technical and part is non-technical in nature. Over the years, some magazine readers have called or written to say that they loved my articles for the rich level of technical detail they provided. Others wrote (usually to my editors) to say that they disliked them for the same reason.

I've tried to provide interesting information for both groups while keeping the technical discussion simple. My advise to non-technical readers: If all or part of a chapter doesn't interest you, just skip over it. There are many other parts of the book that you should enjoy and find useful. At the same time, don't automatically dismiss a technical discussion before giving it a chance. These concepts are fairly straight forward and are often important to discussions that follow. Study the tables and graphics. They often present information that can't be appreciated from the text.

He Said, She Said

While bowhunting is drawing an increasing number of females into its folds, most of this book's readers are likely males. For this reason, and for ease of presentation, I've used the masculine *he* or *him* throughout the book when referring to a person. I ask my female readers to forgive me this sin of political incorrectness.

Unless otherwise noted for a specific example, I've also used the word *deer* to refer to any big game animal that you might hunt.

How To Read This Book

Despite my goal of treating both modern and traditional archery as one sport, I wrestled with the writing mechanics of how to do that. Yes, they have a number of overlapping techniques and skills. At the same time, there are enough differences so that they need to be addressed separately at times.

My initial solution was to add a symbol tag at the top of each chapter indicating who would gain the most from it. In the end, I rejected that as just another way to increase divisiveness. So, how should you read this book?

My recommendation is this: If you're either a die-hard modern archer or a die-hard traditional archer, simply skip over the sections that obviously don't pertain to you. You will quickly recognize what they are. But don't get too hung up over these distinctions. Most of the chapters are equally valid for all archers and *everyone*, regardless of their equipment choices, can gain something from them. For maximum benefit, and to gain an appreciation for the sport as a whole, read the entire book from start to finish.

Part 1. The Arrow

The arrow is the most important equipment item in bowhunting! It's the thing that ultimately gets the job done. For all of the anguish that surrounds choosing a new bow, the incessant tinkering that we subject it to, and all of the loving attention that we lavish on it, the fact remains that once an arrow is in the air it's on its own. It doesn't know if it was launched by a bow, a sling shot, or an air cannon.

Throughout the centuries, archers have experimented with a wide variety of shaft materials. Today, shaft choices have been narrowed down to three main categories—aluminum, carbon/graphite, and wood—each having their own particular advantages and disadvantages.

Then, there are arrow weight decisions. Faster arrows have better trajectory but heavy arrows penetrate better. What are the tradeoffs? Next come fletching and broadhead choices. Small fletching is faster but larger fletching stabilizes an arrow better; two-blade broadheads penetrate deeper but multi-blade broadheads do more cutting.

Finally, there's the important issue of arrow spine. The most expensive arrow in the world won't do the job unless it's carefully matched to your bow and tuned to your particular shooting style.

For all of these reasons, we'll start our quest for shooting perfection with the arrow.

1. Carbon Arrows

One of the most exciting arrow materials to come along in years—for modern and traditional shooters alike—is carbon (also referred to as graphite, or carbon/graphite).

I was late coming to carbon arrows. Perhaps the early soda-straw thin shafts just didn't look like arrows to me. I first considered them after the grudging admission that it's getting harder and harder for me to pull my heavy bows with each passing year. Carbon's stiff, deep penetrating properties promised some relief.

After seeing two high-speed films showing their awesome capabilities[*], I was totally sold. When released perfectly using a shooting machine, an aluminum arrow bent more than a carbon arrow in flight, buckled more severely upon impact, and then drove into the target in a fishtailing, corkscrew fashion. The carbon arrow's oscillations quickly damped out in flight and it penetrated deeply with barely a flicker of sideways movement. When shot into a cinder block, the aluminum arrow buckled at impact and bounced off while the carbon arrow cracked the block in two.

Then, there are the growing number of hunting testimonials. One friend of mine shot a quartering antelope from 30-yards using a 47-pound bow and carbon arrow. The arrow entered its hind quarter, traversed the entire length of its body, and exited through its brisket. Others tell of getting penetration to the fletching on moose using 50-pound recurves and 26-inch draw lengths. My own initial field test was just as impressive. Shot from a 55-pound bow, the arrow sliced through an elk's chest and shattered the off-side femur. It piled up just 30-yards away.

All of this is pretty impressive stuff.

---

[*] *Bowhunting on the Edge* and *Shoot Instinctively Better Then Ever-II*, Great Outdoors Multi-Media Productions

Aluminum Arrow at
Impact, Soft Target

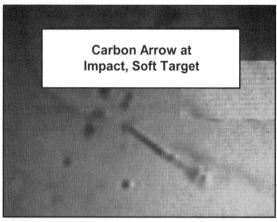

Carbon Arrow at
Impact, Soft Target

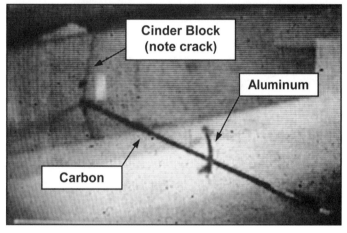

Cinder Block
(note crack)

Aluminum

Carbon

HIGH SPEED PHOTOS OF ALUMINUM AND CARBON ARROWS. When shot into a soft target, the aluminum arrow buckled on impact and cork-screwed its way in. The carbon arrow penetrated with barely a flicker. When shot into a cinder block, the aluminum arrow bounced off while the carbon arrow cracked the block in two.

Advantages   The main advantages of carbon arrows are their high strength (the carbon fibers themselves have several-times the tensile strength of aluminum), their improved accuracy, and their greater penetration.

Thick-walled shafts are extremely durable on big game. A bowhunting buddy shot a Colorado elk a few years ago that ran 40-yards and stopped on top of a hill. He quickly put two more insurance shots into the bull and then watched as it went down and rolled over three times against the still-protruding arrows, without breaking a single one.

Most converts also report improved accuracy since the arrows bend less when they leave the bow. This smoothes out ragged releases and reduces "flyers." The small diameter pultruded designs fly especially well from non-center-shot recurves and longbows.

The biggest advantage of carbon arrows is their tremendous penetrating ability. Compared to other arrow materials, they lose less energy due to flexing when they leave the bow and this increases their launch speed (differences are small but every little bit helps). And they flex less upon impact which concentrates more of their downrange energy directly behind the point.

This gives you two options. You can improve penetration on very large animals without increasing bow weight. Or, you can drop down in bow weight, shoot the bow more accurately, and maintain the penetration that you're getting now.

Another nice carbon arrow feature: They have a wide spine range—twenty-pounds or more—so that finding a precise spine is not as critical as with other arrows. This means that you can probably shoot them from several different bows.

Arrow Weight Options

For light arrow proponents, a variety of carbon shafts are available off-the-shelf. For those favoring heavier arrows, the options are more limited. A few manufacturers are currently marketing heavy "African" shafts but they are the exception.

Other manufacturers sell internal weighting systems to boost mass weight. *Gold Tip's* system is particularly interesting. Internal, modular weights can be attached to both ends of the arrow, in equal or unequal amounts. This clever feature allows you to add up to 120-grains of weight and micro-tune spine and balance-point at the same time.

Disadvantages

Despite all of their advantages, carbon arrows do have two major concerns compared to other arrows.

Specialty Preparation. Where wood or aluminum shafts can be sized to length with a knife, hacksaw, or tubing cutter, an expensive abrasive cut-off wheel is needed for fibrous carbon shafts. And, while a loose nock or point on other arrows might be easily repaired using quick-curing *Fletch-Tite* or *Ferrule-Tite* adhesives, slow drying epoxies and special surface preparations are needed for carbon shafts. (I've had excellent results with slow-curing epoxy but very poor results with quick-curing epoxy). This can make field-repairs difficult or impossible.

Once you've got a good bond, arrow components are hard to remove and this makes it difficult to alter arrow length or fine tune internal weighting systems later. Solve these problems by securing nocks with masking tape during your trial shots and bond them firmly in place only after you're satisfied with the result. Or consider one of the new removable nock designs.

Light Arrow Safety. Tests show that small-diameter, thick-walled pultruded shafts (all the fibers run directly down the shaft) are extremely durable, even if they sustain minor damage while shooting. It takes a severe impact to fracture them and when this happens the entire shaft often "un-zips" instantly. The weak points of this design are the exposed fibers at the two ends of the arrow. This is solved using "outsert" adapters to attach nocks and points. Early carbon shafts were all pultruded. Their thick walls, which are needed to achieve stiffness for their small diameters, restricted archers to mid-weight arrows.

Many archers disliked the look of these arrows, the outserts caused them problems with some arrow rests, and offset or helical fletching was difficult to apply. They also wanted lighter shafts. As a result, the recent

CARBON ARROWS. Carbon arrow come in a variety of styles and diameters. Shown at top are Gold Tip's full diameter shafts and its unique internal weighting system which allows weight to be added at both the nock and broadhead ends of the arrow in equal or unequal mounts (note the removable nock and Allen wrench). Thin, pultruded shafts (bottom) use outserts and have proved to be exceptionally strong in impact tests due to their thicker walls which are needed to achieve the proper stiffness.

trend has been towards full diameter shafts that use standard nock and broadhead adapters. To reduce the hoop-stress imposed by these internal components, manufacturers have added bias-wound carbon fibers.

These are fine designs but problems can arise with light, thin-walled shafts that many archers want for greater arrow speed. According to archery engineer and industry consultant, Norb Mullaney, these shafts have a tendency to break if they've sustained previous shooting damage—damage so small that it can't be easily seen.

As an expert witness, Mullaney has been involved in a number of court cases where plaintiffs were injured when light carbon shafts fractured upon release. In practically all of these cases, it was shown that the shafts were damaged previously. The problem, he notes, is that aluminum arrows permanently bend before they break (in engineering parlance, their yield stress is much lower than their ultimate stress) and this can easily be seen. The yield stress and ultimate stress of carbon fibers lie very close together and they can break suddenly with no apparent damage.

Mullaney is quick to point out that these are isolated instances and that not all light-weight carbon arrows are equally susceptible to breakage. Still, this is an important point to consider. A wise approach might be to forgo the use of light, thin-walled shafts in favor carbon's many other advantages.

Inspect all of your carbon arrows regularly (whatever their design and weight) for any signs of dents, dings, or other potential safety problems. *Always* inspect them after high-impact hits or when they slam into one another in a target.

One More Tool

Am I going to give up my other arrows? No way. But I *am* going to add more carbon shafts to my personal hunting arsenal. They're just one more tool in my bag of shooting tricks. You should consider doing the same for a new level of shooting performance.

2. Aluminum Arrows

Aluminum arrows have been around for almost six decades. You likely started with them and still use them.

While other entrepreneurs experimented with aluminum shafts, Doug Easton was the first to successfully commercialize them on a large scale, over a decade before Fred Bear developed the modern fiberglass laminated bow!

Early shafts were made of soft alloys which "bent on sight" according to some critics. Still, they endured due to their many desirable qualities. They were inherently straight; and while they might bend during use, they were easily straightened.

Modern Alloys

Today's aluminum arrows, made from higher strength alloys, don't bend as easily as earlier products. They are also manufactured to much more exacting tolerances. They come out of the factory straight and stay that way unless they're abused.

Versatility Galore

Another advantage of aluminum arrows is their tremendous versatility. A huge number of shaft sizes, weights, points, nock inserts, and broadhead adapters are available. They come in many grades and many indelible surface-art patterns to meet the discriminating needs of any user.

An Intermediate Choice

Aluminum arrows have long resided on the high-tech end of archery equipment. Today, they fill a middle-of-the-road niche between wood and carbon arrows. In contrast to wood, they don't require initial straightening, but require more in-use straightening than carbon. They're more durable than wood but are less durable than carbon. They penetrate on par with wood but not as deeply as carbon. Top-quality shafts often cost less than carbon or wood. For these reasons, aluminum arrows will always remain an excellent choice for any archer.

Aluminum/ Carbon Hybrids

Can't decide between aluminum and carbon? Try one of the new generation of arrows that combine the benefits of both materials. Using a thin-walled aluminum core to handle the stress of full-sized nock and broadhead adapters, and a carbon fiber over-winding, shafts can be made that combine high-spine and low weight. In addition, the aluminum core provides a nice safety feature in case of surface damage.

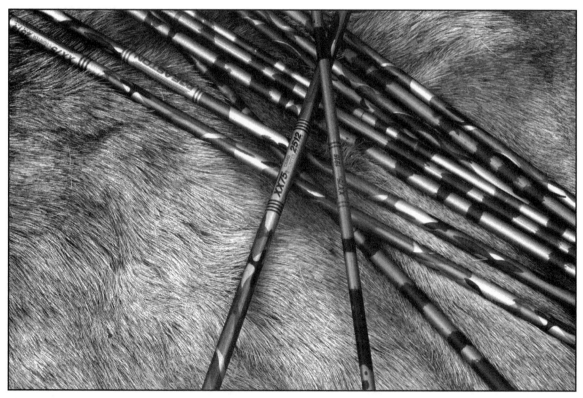

ALUMINUM ARROW VERSATILITY. The dependability, uniformity, straightness, and consistency of aluminum arrows, plus the wide variety of available shaft sizes—from the behemoth 2514 to the diminutive 1813—have made them a top choice among bowhunters for over 50-years. They remain an excellent choice for any bowhunter today.

3. Wood Arrows

For over ten-thousand years, wood arrows were the near-universal choice of all archers. They only lost favor in the mid-twentieth-century when straighter, more durable manmade arrow materials entered the scene.

Along with traditional archery's strong growth in recent years has come a resurgence in the use of wooden arrows. Aluminum or graphite arrows are certainly as traditional as fiberglass bows, carbon bow laminations, plastic nocks, and synthetic arm guards and tabs. Still, there's something special about wood that's hard to describe. Aluminum or carbon arrows are tools meant solely to do a job. A good wood arrow often goes beyond this.

A Soul of Its Own

For anyone who savors the rich tradition and unparalleled sweet-shooting properties of wood arrows, they remain an excellent choice. Unlike manmade materials, a finely crafted wood arrow seems to have a soul of its own. It's made from a living thing—something that we can identify with. Using it just feels good. Wood also has a soothing, natural sound when shot and a soft, lively spring from a bow.

Finely crafted wood arrows can also be works of art. Some Native Americans believed that their animal-brothers appreciated the effort made in crafting beautiful equipment and responded by willingly offering themselves up to the hunter. Many painted their arrows with extraordinary artwork, going far beyond what was needed to simply kill an animal. Many contemporary archers continue this practice.

Wood Arrow Faults

Wood arrows *do* have their faults. They can require frequent straightening to keep them in tip-top hunting condition. Individual shaft weights can vary by five grains or so on matched sets, and much more on unmatched sets. A premium set of matched shafts can cost an arm and a leg. And they have a nasty habit of shattering on rocks and trees rather than simply bending.

Arrow Woods

If it were possible to make a perfect wood arrow, it would be naturally straight and even-grained, made of readily available woods, have high strength, durability and shock resistance, and come in a variety of mass weights according to need. Archers throughout history have experimented with hundreds of different types of wood in their search for the perfect one.

Forest Nagler, a well known archery-writer in the 1930s, tested many arrow woods and settled on Sitka Spruce and Douglas Fir. After extensive testing, Saxton Pope chose birch as his personal favorite. Howard Hill liked cedar. Other favorites are almost as numerous as the archers who used them.

A few of today's popular arrow woods are:

Cedar. Port Orford cedar has been the undisputed king of arrow woods for over fifty years. It's readily available, fine-grained, and easy to manufacture. Curiously, it wasn't widely used until Howard Hill popularized it.

Perhaps cedar's most enticing quality is its fragrance. Until the 1970s, every archery shop smelled sweetly of freshly cut cedar shavings. The fleeting smell of a Port Orford shaft still unleashes a flood of wistful memories for many older archers. If for no other reason then this, cedar will always be high on many people's list of favorites.

One problem with cedar today is the increasing scarcity of high quality raw shafting. When timber companies cut down cedar trees, they aren't replanting them. Even when good cedar can be found, it isn't as dense and heavy as earlier stocks since younger trees are being harvested.

Despite this problem, it's hard to go wrong with a good quality Port Orford cedar shaft. It's a thoroughly time-tested wood that should serve any archer well.

Hardwoods. Although popular, cedar isn't for everybody. Fortunately for some, the growing shortage of good cedar is forcing many arrow suppliers to turn to alternative woods. Some common choices are fir, larch, spruce, poplar, maple, cherry, birch, ash, and ramin. Other historical woods can be found with a little looking around. There's an on-going discussion over which of these woods is the best. Like preferences in cars,

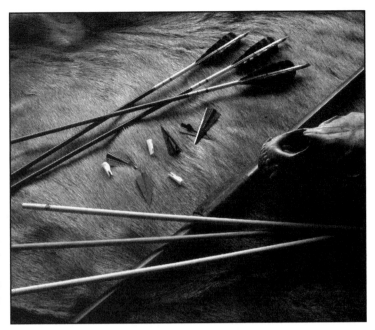

THE ENDURING LURE OF WOOD ARROWS. Although wood arrows don't have the durability or consistency of man-made materials (a premium matched set can come close), their rich history and sweet-shooting properties make them the arrow of choice among many traditional shooters.

this question can probably never be answered. All will make good arrows with proper care.

Most of these species are denser and heavier than cedar, and this improves their penetration with lower energy stick bows. Some woods, like poplar, are only slightly heavier than cedar (about 10% on the average) and are being marketed as a cedar-substitute. Two popular woods are ash and ramin. A full length shaft in either will weigh about 100-grains more than cedar.

Gabriella Cosgrove of *Kustom King Traditional Archery* recommends ash and cedar—the cedar for its natural straightness and the ash for its superior durability. Cherry is another top seller. According to Bill Bonczal, owner of *Allegheny Mountain Arrow Woods*, cherry is fairly straight grained for a hardwood, is easy to straighten, and is very durable. Bonczal's personal favorite is birch, which can weigh up to 750-grains.

None of these woods are clear winners for everyone, but all of them offer a different and pleasing alternative to cedar. They're all well worth experimenting with.

Wood arrows come in a variety of construction styles. Consider these alternatives.

Footed Shafts. Softwood shafts are not particularly durable. To overcome this problem, many arrow makers foot them with dense hardwoods to strengthen the tip. The footing also moves the balance-point forward a bit which can improve arrow flight for some shooters. Utility arrows are usually footed with tough, inexpensive woods like hickory. Higher quality shafts are often footed with exotic rosewood, purpleheart, bubinga, and others. These make for a unique and very attractive arrow.

Tapered Shafts. Wood arrows can also be doweled in non-cylindrical shapes. Tapered, barreled, or breasted shafts are the most common. These features are starting to be seen on some alternative woods but tend to be found more on cedar shafts due to cedar's higher demand.

The most common technique is to take a standard cylindrically doweled (parallel) shaft of 11/32" or 23/64" diameter and taper the nock end down to 5/16" over the first six- to nine-inches. This removes weight from the nock end and moves the arrow's balance-point forward slightly. It also helps the nock clear a traditional arrow shelf.

Other manufacturers taper the entire shaft, typically from 5/8" at the tip to 3/8" at the nock. This process is more expensive but makes for a beefier tip. It also results in a more forward balance-point for archers who like this feature.

Barreled shafts are tapered over equal lengths on both ends while leaving the center section parallel. The result is a lighter shaft with a balance-point similar to untapered shafts. Archers who like a little more speed tend to favor these arrows.

Breasting is similar to barreling except that the shaft's point-end is tapered over a longer length than its nock end. This lightens the shaft further and, according to some proponents, makes the arrow more aerodynamic.

Compressed Shafts. One clever method used to improve straightness and increase shaft density is to compress the shaft. This is done in two ways. The first is to dowel the shaft and then force it through a circular die having a slightly smaller diameter. The resulting radial compression is

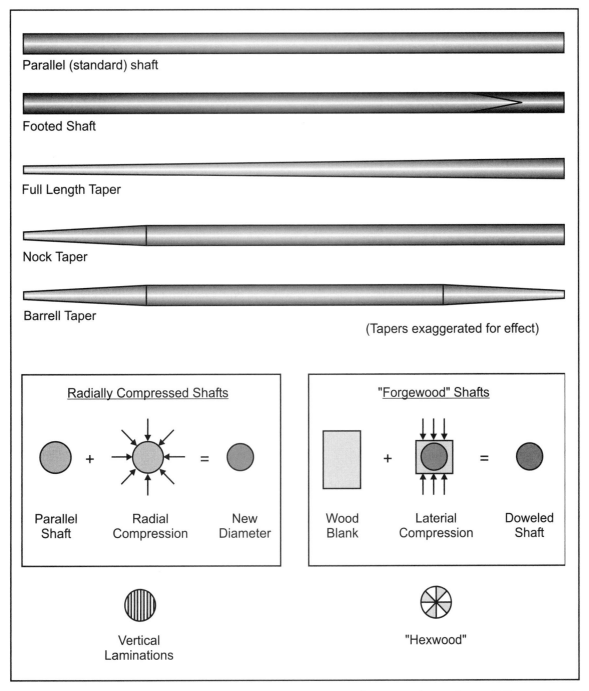

Parallel (standard) shaft

Footed Shaft

Full Length Taper

Nock Taper

Barrell Taper

(Tapers exaggerated for effect)

Radially Compressed Shafts

Parallel
Shaft

Radial
Compression

New
Diameter

Vertical
Laminations

"Forgewood" Shafts

Wood
Blank

Lateral
Compression

Doweled
Shaft

"Hexwood"

WOOD ARROW CONSTRUCTION. Wood arrows come in a variety of construction styles to fit the needs of any archer.

minor and is limited to the outermost fibers, but this can be enough to dramatically improve straightness.

The second method is to heat a wood blank, compress it using several tons of pressure, and then dowel it in the standard manner. This is the method used on the famous *Sweetland Forgewoods*. This process not only maintains the natural straightness of cedar, but actually improves it. This more radical compression makes the arrow heavier, harder hitting, and more resistant to breakage. Spine is controlled by varying the amount of compression (typically 2-to-1 or 3-to-1). Using a maximum 4-to-1 compression, shafts can be made in very high spine weights. Some are so hard that they spark when sanded.

Another nice Forgewood feature is internal footing. Where conventional footed shafts have a piece of spliced hardwood, Forgewoods can be made more dense at the point end by simply leaving one end of the blank a little thicker than the other before compressing it.

Other Possibilities. One exciting new arrow shaft is made from vertically laminated maple, the same technology that has been used for years to make *Actionwood* bow laminations and risers. Thin maple veneers are bonded together and cut across the layers to make arrow blanks for doweling. The arrows are stronger than cedar, weigh more, are very consistent from one to another, and resist bending over time.

Another option is *Hexwood* shafting. These are made by gluing six wedge-shaped pieces of slow-growth pine together, similar to the construction of premium split-bamboo fly rods. This process has many of the same advantages as vertically laminated wood. Unlike vertical laminating, however, each wood wedge can be oriented so that the arrow has flat grain exposed on the surface. Most wood arrows vary slightly in spine depending on the orientation of the nock to the grain. The hexwood process eliminates this problem and helps keep the arrow straight.

Wanted: A Sense of Adventure

Unlike modern arrow materials, wood arrows have quirks that require them to be approached with a sense of adventure. Yet, for a growing number of today's history conscious shooters, they are the preferred choice.

4. Fletching

Arrow fletching serves two major purposes. It grabs the rear of the shaft as it passes through the air and holds the point on line, and if mounted at an angle, it causes the shaft to spin. Spinning stabilizes the arrow gyroscopically in flight and minimizes planing. As a byproduct, fletching also slows an arrow down as it moves downrange, hurting trajectory and penetration.

In the modern quest for arrow speed, air friction (called *drag*) is often viewed as a bad thing. In reality, it's a good thing. It's what causes the arrow to stay on line and drive into the target with its full weight behind the point.

The trick is to find the optimum combination of accuracy, trajectory, and impact properties that you need. What are the tradeoffs involved here?

Vanes or Feathers?

Feathers have been archers' favored choice throughout history and they remain an excellent choice today. They are lighter than equivalent-sized rubber vanes and this gives the arrow slightly more launch speed. Their rough, veined surface grabs the passing air better than smooth-surfaced vanes and straightens an arrow out more quickly as it leaves the bow. And, unless damaged, they resist bending under aerodynamic forces better than flexible vanes.

Their rougher surface *does* slow the arrow down more as it moves downrange, but in most cases the arrow's lighter weight and higher initial speed offsets this so that it will still have a flatter trajectory at normal bowhunting distances. Feathers are also more fragile than vanes and more easily damaged when shooting in rough terrain or through targets.

Being naturally water repellent, vanes hold the advantage in wet weather (although feathers can be effectively waterproofed with a variety of substances.) Lastly, feathers are easier to cut into unique shapes using die-cutters or feather burners for people with special technical or aesthetic needs.

Large or Small?

Larger fletching grips the air better and stabilizes an arrow better throughout its flight path. It's especially effective from short range when shooting with fingers. With a mechanical release and true center-shot bow, this is not as important. Smaller fletching can work well here, but larger is still better.

Large fletching also provides some factor of safety when damaged or, in the case of feathers, when it's matted down due to moisture. If you damage large fletching on a hunt, it still provides some measure of stability; small fletching may provide very little. Small fletching has less surface area and may drift or fishtail less in strong cross winds; however, this situation isn't normal and shouldn't figure into your choice.

With all of its advantages, large fletching does come at a cost in speed and trajectory. There's no quick answer here. At normal bowhunting distances, the cost will be small and large fletching is worth the advantages it has in quick recovery from a bow and greater in-flight stability. At longer distances, trajectory and penetration can be hurt slightly.

Fast or Slow Arrow?

An arrow's in-flight stability is affected by its speed. A 250-fps arrow will be 25% faster than a 200-fps arrow but will have 56% more stabilizing drag (drag increases in proportion to speed *squared,* not speed itself). This means that you can reduce fletching size on faster arrows and still have good stability.

If you shoot slower speed equipment, stay with larger fletching. If you shoot faster equipment, you can get by with smaller fletching. When in doubt, opt for larger rather than smaller fletching.

Straight- or Helical- Fletch?

A frequent question is whether straight or helical fletching is better for hunting. In my opinion, helical fletching is the clear choice. Helical fletching, or straight fletching that is set at a significant angle on the shaft, causes an arrow to spin faster than straight fletching with no angle, and has a miniscule effect on trajectory. Chronograph tests of identical machine-released shafts, one with five-inch helical fletching and the other with five-inch straight fletching, showed a difference in impact speed of less than one foot-per-second at 60-yards.

For this small cost, helical fletching pays rich dividends in arrow flight. A

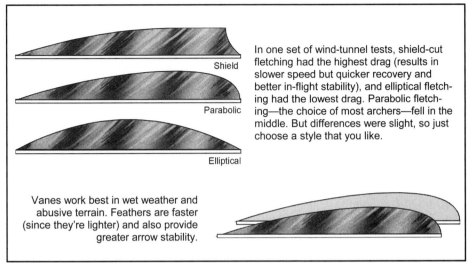

In one set of wind-tunnel tests, shield-cut fletching had the highest drag (results in slower speed but quicker recovery and better in-flight stability), and elliptical fletching had the lowest drag. Parabolic fletching—the choice of most archers—fell in the middle. But differences were slight, so just choose a style that you like.

Shield

Parabolic

Elliptical

Vanes work best in wet weather and abusive terrain. Feathers are faster (since they're lighter) and also provide greater arrow stability.

FLETCHING TRADEOFFS. Although differences are minor, fletching shape and material can can affect your equipment's performance.

fast spinning arrow is much more stable than a slow spinning arrow. This is similar to the way in which a fast spinning child's top stays upright better than one that's spinning slowly. If the fletching on an arrow is set at twice the angle of another arrow, it will spin twice as fast, but will have four times the stabilizing effect. If it's set at four times the angle, it will have *sixteen* times the stabilizing effect.

High or Low Profile?

Due to an aerodynamic phenomenon called a *boundary-layer*, the air passing closest to an arrow is slower than the air traveling farther from it. As a result, high-profile fletching will have more stabilizing drag than low-cut fletching.

If you have two feathers, one 4½" long and one five-inches long, both with equal surface area, the shorter one will provide more control because it reaches higher into the air stream. For equal heights, the longer one will provide more control since it has more surface area.

As a practical matter, most die-cut feathers are about 5/8" high. Higher ones provide more control, but if cut higher than ¾" or so they can whistle when shot. Find the maximum height that shoots quietly.

Three- or Four-Fletch?

This is an extension of the large versus small fletching question. Adding a fourth feather or vane will create more drag but it can make an arrow shoot

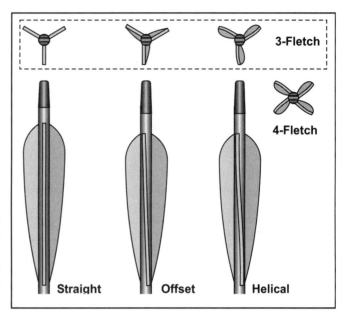

MORE SPIN IS BETTER. Feathers or vanes that are set at some angle to the shaft like offset- or helical-fletching (middle two sketches) rotate a shaft in flight and provide better shooting stability with only a miniscule loss in trajectory. Adding a fourth feather (right) is even better.

more accurately and improve short range penetration. It may also require a little extra tuning effort to insure that the arrow properly clears the bow's arrow rest.

Color

Fletching color is largely personal, with one exception. Choose a color that will not draw attention to you but one that you can see well in low light. This will help you to pinpoint the exact location of your hit. I like orange. Orange looks grayish to a deer but I can still see it well at dawn or dusk. Experiment for yourself.

Practical Decisions

In most common bowhunting situations, 4½- to 5½-inch offset or helical feathers provide the greatest shooting accuracy and stability, with only a miniscule cost in speed and downrange trajectory. Adding a fourth feather is even better. For higher-speed bows, 3½ - to 4½-inch straight-fletch arrows will work, but they're more fragile and less reliable under adverse conditions.

Vanes are easier to keep dry and are more durable than feathers but will cost you a little in speed and stability. If you spend a lot of time hunting in wet conditions, or drag your quiver through a lot of heavy brush, they may be the way to go.

5. Broadheads

We could talk all day long about arrow materials and fletching, but when all that's said, it's still the broadhead that actually does the job. Choosing an effective broadhead involves a variety of factors. The "correct" choice is the one that gives you the best combination of accuracy, penetration, durability, and reliability for your shooting style and the animals you hunt.

Accuracy

The first consideration is accuracy. Poorly constructed heads may cause inconsistent shots. Use a top quality make and model for all of your serious hunting. Economy models will work fine for plinking or small game.

Choose a head that's *consistently* accurate with your equipment. Spin each arrow on a table or across your fingernails after mounting your broadhead to check for wobble. If it appears straight, shoot it a few times to check it for accuracy and planing. Also check for whistling if you use vented broadheads.

Ideally, your broadheads and field points should shoot consistently into the same group. This makes it easier to practice without destroying an expensive 3-D target or mat. All of the good quality broadheads I've tried will group together but only a few of them will group consistently with my field points. These are the ones I use. Experiment to find the designs that will do this with your equipment.

Finally, test your arrows under the actual conditions where they'll be used. I once field tested a prototype, large-profile head on an Alaskan caribou hunt. The heads did fine at home but planed hopelessly in the strong North Slope winds. Switching back to my regular heads solved the problem.

Durability

Durability refers to a head's ability to withstand abuse. All of today's top-selling broadheads are made of high quality materials, but their overall

BROADHEAD SAMPLER. Shown here are just a few of the many dozens of broadhead models and types that are available to meet different bowhunting needs. In Africa field tests, the *Grizzly* (lower left) had the best penetration and the least number of malfunctions on large animals. The 1970s vintage *Little Shaver* (upper right) was the first commercial replacement-blade head and is shown here for its historical interest. It used Shick injector blades that were inserted into slots.

strength and durability can vary according to their construction.

Traditional, fixed-blade heads are generally more durable than modular, replacement-blade heads. The blades are thicker and are rigidly attached to the ferrule. The strongest heads are two-bladed and have a brazed or spot-welded steel reinforcing layer overlaying the ferrule and tip. Vented heads have less blade attachment area and may not be as strong as unvented heads.

Vented, unreinforced heads work fine and have stood the test of time on light boned, thin skinned animals like deer; but sturdy, reinforced, unvented heads are a wise choice when hunting large animals such as elk and moose.

In one African field test of nearly three dozen common broadhead makes and models, a number of replaceable-blade broadheads came apart at impact and resulted in lost or hard-to-recover animals. If this possibility concerns you, then stay with fixed blade broadheads.

Screw-on broadheads are not as durable as glue-on heads. The small threaded portion of the adapter just doesn't have the strength of a full-diameter glue-in shank. If your heads tend to bend at this weak point, think about switching to glue-on heads.

Whatever your final choice, it's wise to test shoot a few of your arrows into rocks or cinder blocks before hunting with them. Do the blades stay intact? Does the head fracture or bend? Does the adapter bend? And so forth.

Waste a few dollars and find this out now. Eliminate any heads that might cause you problems later.

Reliability

Reliability refers to a head's ability to function properly. Fixed-blade, brazed-and-welded heads score highest in this category. They're strong and there's nothing to come apart. Slightly lower on the list are replacement-blade heads since the blades can come off occasionally and reduce their cutting ability. Mechanical broadheads that are designed to open at impact score lower still. No mechanical device having moving parts has ever been invented that's one-hundred percent reliable. Many early mechanical heads were notorious for their poor reliability and this caused some bowhunting outfitters to ban them from their camps due to instances of lost animals. Newer designs

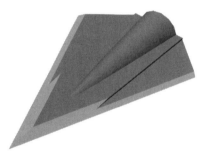

Two-blade, cut-on-impact broadheads are stronger and penetrate better than multi-blade heads. Choose one without vents and with a reinforced tip for best performance on large, tough animals.

While multi-blade heads don't penetrate as well as two-blade heads (the differences are small), they may do more actual cutting in the process. Vented heads may not be as strong as non-vented heads and may whistle when shot.

Replacement-blade broadheads are easy to use and keep sharp but come with a slight loss in reliability. Chisel points penetrate slightly better than cone points. Screw-in adapters (on any broadhead type) can bend on high impact hits.

BROADHEAD CONSTRUCTION. All broadheads have advantages and disadvantages. Choose the one that works best for the animal that you're hunting.

perform better but even as they continue to improve, mechanical heads will always fail some percentage of the time, even if that percentage is small.

The main advantage of mechanical heads is their ease of tuning and their long range accuracy with fast arrows. While real, this advantage should be balanced against reliability concerns. Most bows, regardless of speed, can be made to shoot a conventional broadhead accurately. It just takes a little extra work or slightly larger fletching.

Penetration

In both laboratory and field tests, two-blade, cut-on-impact heads penetrated slightly better than multi-blade or modular cone-point heads, but multi-blade heads actually did more cutting. More on this important subject in a later chapter.

Sharpening

Replacement-blade heads are popular since they don't require sharpening. Simply replace the blades with new ones after a shot. Although this solves the problem, it can be expensive.

Fixed-blade heads must be sharpened before their first use but can be sharpened again and again as needed (as can some replacement-blade heads). This is a handy feature on remote hunts. And where sharpening was an arduous process thirty years ago, a variety of excellent sharpening systems are now available to put razor edges on heads in a quick, easy manner.

All broadheads can become dull over time from riding in a quiver. Self-sharpened heads just require a few licks with a sharpening stone or steel to bring their edge back to razor sharp. If you use a modular head, choose one that can be easily re-sharpened.

In short, all broadheads require work to keep them in top hunting condition. The activities are just a little different. Again, the choice here is a personal one.

Practical Decisions

For most hunting situations on thin-skinned animals, any well-made broadhead will work as long as it's kept razor sharp. If ruggedness and maximum penetration on large animals is your goal, then stay with reinforced, two-bladed, cut-on-impact heads.

6. Depth-of-Kill

The most important trajectory concept for people who guess target distance and aim mechanically is *depth-of-kill* (also called *shooting window*). This refers to the number of yards in front of and behind an animal where the arrow will pass vertically through the kill zone. Faster arrows allow you to miss-guess the range more and still hit solidly in the boiler room.

Some Examples

The table on the following page gives some examples. Note two important things. First, depth-of-kill is greatest at short range where arrow trajectory is flattest; and it declines sharply as distance increases. This is true for all arrow speeds. Aim at the center of a deer's chest with your 20-yard pin and your depth-of-kill using a 250-fps arrow is about 25-yards. Aim with your 30-yard pin and it's seven-yards; use your 40-yard pin and it's just four-yards.

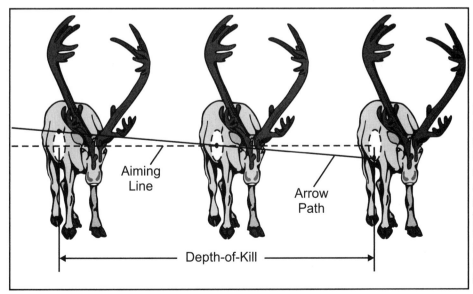

Aiming Line

Arrow Path

Depth-of-Kill

DEPTH-OF-KILL DEFINED. Your arrow's depth-of-kill is the yardage spread, in front of and behind an animal, where you will still hit the kill zone if you misjudge the shooting distance.

Second, note that higher arrow speeds help, but the advantage they provide is smaller than many people realize. With a 225-fps arrow, you'd have to guess the distance correctly to within plus or minus two-yards at 40-yards. With a 275-fps arrow, you'd have to guess correctly to within plus or minus three-yards. This one-yard advantage is minor since most people can't guess range that accurately.

Measuring Depth-of-Kill

The depth-of-kill for your equipment will differ from these examples. To determine it, take a large piece of cardboard or other material (three- by five-foot panels sold by packing supply companies work well), and draw an aiming spot in the center.

Now aim at the spot from different distances with each of your sight pins and see where the arrow hits. For example, using your 30-yard pin, find the distance (closer than 30-yards) where your arrow hits three-inches above the spot, and the distance (farther than 30-yards) where it hits three-inches below it. These will be the extremes where you can aim for 30-yards on a whitetail and hit solidly within the kill zone. For larger or smaller animals, you can adjust these values to correspond to the different size kill zones.

	Arrow Speed (fps)	Shot Distance (yards)			
		20	**25**	**30**	**40**
Depth-of-Kill (yards)	175	16.3 - 22.6	22.5 - 27.0	28.1 - 31.7	38.7 - 41.3
	200	10 - 23.5	21.5 - 27.6	27.4 - 32.2	38.3 - 41.6
	225	0 - 24.1	18.5 - 28.5	26.6 - 32.7	37.9 - 42.0
	250	0 - 25.1	17.5 - 28.9	25.6 - 33.2	37.3 - 42.4
	275	0 - 25.9	0 - 29.6	24.5 - 33.8	36.8 - 42.7
Depth-of-Kill Spread (yards)	175	6.3	4.5	3.6	2.6
	200	13.5	6.1	4.8	3.3
	225	24.1	10.0	6.1	4.1
	250	25.1	11.4	7.6	5.1
	275	25.9	29.6	9.3	5.9

ACTUAL DEPTHS-OF-KILL FOR VARIOUS ARROW SPEEDS AND SHOT DISTANCES (TYPICAL ARROW). Depth-of-kill is greatest at short range and declines sharply as distance increases (for all arrow speeds). The shaded values are cases where even an expert range estimator (+/- 15% of true distance) will have trouble placing consistent killing shots.

Practical
Decisions
If you hunt mainly from tree stands and routinely pace off distances to surrounding markers, depth-of-kill shouldn't concern you. You'll know the distance to your targets fairly closely and any speed arrow will work.

In situations where you don't know the shooting distance—when stalking or still hunting, for instance—your chances of guessing the range correctly go down sharply as distance increases. Studies show that skilled range estimators can guess correctly to within plus or minus 15% of the true distance 90% of the time. Average range estimators can do no better than plus or minus 30% (see *Part 7, Compound Accuracy*). This means that your effective range is pretty much restricted to 25-yards and under for whitetails. Any common arrow speed will work almost as well here (unhighlighted values in the lower portion of the table).

Calculating Depth-of-Kill

An arrow's actual depth-of-kill at different distances and atmospheric conditions is determined by a number of complex technical factors. If all that you're interested in is comparing different arrow speeds, however, then the following simple expression can be used to calculate approximate depths-of-kill:

Impact point (inches) above or below your aiming point =
$$\text{1739 x (Actual Distance) x (Sighting Distance - Actual Distance) / (Launch Speed)}^2$$

where the actual distance and the sighting distance to the target are measured in yards and launch speed is measured in feet-per-second.

Example:
If you used your 30-yard pin to aim at a target 26-yards away using a 240-fps arrow, the arrow would hit about +3-inches [above] your aiming point:

$$\text{Impact point = 1739 x 26 x (30 - 26) / 240}^2$$
$$= \text{+3 inches}$$

If the target was 33-yards away, the arrow would hit -3-inches [below] your aiming point. Your depth-of-kill would be 7-yards (33-yards minus 26-yards) for a 6-inch high kill zone.

7. Arrow Weight

Y our choice of arrow weight is a major contributor to your hunting success. Consider the following factors when making your decision.

Heavy or Light?

Lighter arrows have flatter trajectories that minimize range estimation errors for sight-shooters. Heavier arrows, while having a higher arc, win in most other categories of comparison. They make a bow shoot more efficiently, are quieter when shot, lose less of their punch traveling through the air, hit harder and penetrate deeper, and are generally more durable.

Efficiency

All bows shoot heavier arrows with higher efficiently than lighter arrows. This is one of the reasons that solid fiberglass arrows are so effective for bowfishing. Their ultra-high launch efficiency causes them to penetrate deeply into water. Normal hunting arrows would be stopped at much shallower depths than fishing arrows.

Noise

So where does the lost launch energy of lighter arrow go? It goes mainly into bow vibration and noise. The reduced shooting noise of heavier arrows translates into fewer string-jumping deer, a prime cause of misses.

Downrange Punch

Air resists a moving arrow and causes it to continuously slow down throughout its flight path. Heavier, slower arrows have less air rushing past them and have more mass to resist aerodynamic forces to boot. As a result, they retain more of their initial speed and punch as they travel downrange. Heavier arrows also drift off line less in cross winds.

Penetration

With higher energy and momentum throughout their flight path, heavier arrows penetrate deeper than lighter arrows. This could spell the difference between a spine-hit deer that drops in its tracks and one with only a minor wound. Or it might result in a quick trailing job from a pass-through hit compared to an animal that is lost due to a poor blood trail from a high, non-exiting wound.

Durability

Heavier arrows are beefier and resist the nasty effects of misses better than lighter arrows. Consider a 2219 and a 2315 aluminum shaft, both of which have spine ratings for the same bow. The 2219 has almost 20% more cross-sectional area to resist impact, bending, and metal shear. Thick-walled

Arrow Weight* (grains)		300	500	700
Launch	Speed (fps)	263	217	190
	Energy (foot-pounds)	46.1	52.3	56.1
	Momentum (grain-sec)	2,453	3,374	4,136
20-yards	Speed (fps)	248	209	185
	Energy (foot-pounds)	41.0	48.5	53.2
	Momentum (grain-sec)	2,313	3,249	4,027
40-yards	Speed (fps)	234	202	185
	Energy (foot-pounds)	48.6	49.8	53.2
	Momentum (grain-sec)	2,191	3,455	4,027
60-yards	Speed (fps)	220	195	181
	Energy (foot-pounds)	32.2	42.2	50.9
	Momentum (grain-sec)	2,052	3,032	3,940
Lost Energy (%)		34.3%	21.6%	9.2%
Lost Momentum (%)		29.8%	15.6%	4.7%

* 60# @ 30" compound; 21xx-series aluminum arrows with 5" feathers

BALLISTIC DATA FOR THREE ARROWS SHOT FROM THE SAME BOW. Heavy arrows have higher trajectories but punch through the air and into the target better than light arrows. Note that the 700-grain arrow arrives *at the target* with more energy and momentum than the 300-grain arrow had *when first launched.* Mid-weight arrows lie between these extremes and provide good tradeoffs for most hunting situations. (The numbers for traditional bows would be a little different but the general trends would be the same.)

carbon arrows are safer and more durable than thin-walled arrows. Wood arrows made from dense species are more durable than less dense species.

Bow Problems

As you move to lighter and lighter arrows, you are moving towards a dry-fire condition. If you shoot arrows that are *too* light, you are likely to experience bow problems in time, including possible bow breakage and injury.

The *Archery Trade Association* (*ATA*, formerly the *Archery Manufacturers and Merchants Association, AMO*) has developed a chart showing minimum recommended arrow weights for different types of bows and different draw lengths. These range from about 3½ grains-per-pound to about 8½ grains-per-pound of peak bow weight. A good rule-of-thumb for normal setups is to stay with arrows weighing at least six grains-per-pound. Check with your arrow vendor or bow manufacturer for your equipment before making a final selection.

Practical Decisions

If you shoot a heavy bow and light arrows give you the penetration that you want on the animals you hunt, you can give up some performance in other areas to improve trajectory. If you hunt large, thick-skinned animals, or shoot lower weight equipment, heavy arrows will give you better penetration.

If you're an instinctive shooter, trajectory is a non-issue since your mind will calculate trajectory for you. In this case, any arrow weight will work. Chose a heavier arrow for its many non-trajectory advantages.

Finally, keep in mind that your choice is usually not between wafer thin 300-grain and behemoth 800-grain shafts. In most cases, mid-weight arrows in your appropriate spine range strike a good balance between trajectory and downrange performance. It's hard to go wrong with this balanced approach.

8. Penetration Simplified

In 1923, Saxton Pope performed some of the first modern penetration tests on arrows. Many archer-researchers followed suit throughout the century. In recent years, this issue has become increasingly complex, with different people coming to different conclusions on what's important in different situations. Fortunately, the question is easily answered for most archers.

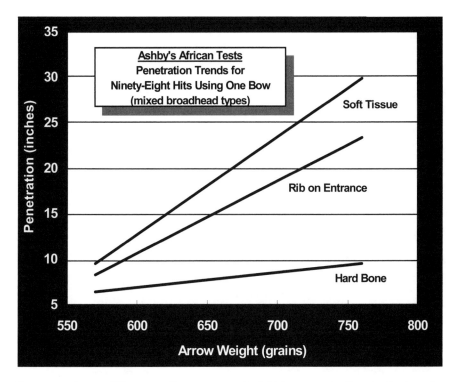

EFFECT OF ARROW WEIGHT ON PENETRATION. In African penetration tests, heavier arrows tended to penetrate better for all types of hits. Note that the most dramatic improvement in penetration was for rib and soft tissue hits—the chest shots that you're looking for.

A Single Bow

Penetration is caused by an arrow's energy and momentum at impact. Experts disagree over the actual importance of each factor, but both laboratory and field tests clearly show that both play a part.

These disagreements vanish when an archer uses a favorite hunting bow and just wants to find an arrow that does the best job with it. *Any bow* will launch heavier arrows with more energy *and* momentum than lighter arrows. It doesn't matter which is more important. As we saw in the previous chapter, heavy arrows win on both counts.

Arrow Weight

These points were demonstrated in extensive African field testing conducted by Dr. Ed Ashby. Ashby shot 154 animals (54 using an 80-pound compound and 100 using a 94-pound longbow) and measured penetration in each animal for different hits. Penetration varied according to the hit location, but, on average, heavier arrows clearly penetrated better than lighter arrows.

Broadhead Style

Similar questions surround broadhead penetration. Dave Holt, a popular book author and magazine writer, performed a series of tests a few years ago that sheds some light on this subject. Holt shot like-energy arrows with different broadheads into several different target materials and found that each penetrated similarly.

Two-blade, cut-on-impact heads penetrated better in all targets except for cardboard, but only by small amounts. When shooting into meat slabs, they penetrated just three-percent better than two-blade and three-blade cone-point heads. Holt also pointed out that for a small cost in lost penetration, multi-blade heads did more cutting since they had more cutting surfaces.

These conclusions are supported by Ed Ashby's field tests. Ashby's main goal was to compare penetration with different broadheads and he concluded that broadhead style had a major effect on penetration. But he inadvertently used heavier arrows (on average) for his two-blade, cut-on-impact heads and this likely affected the results.

After mathematically adjusting his reported data so that all arrows had the same launch energy, different broadheads penetrated similarly for similar hits. Like Holt's tests, the two-blade, cut-on-impact heads tended to penetrate better than multi-blade or modular heads, but the effect was not dramatic.

Practical
Decisions

If your equipment gives you the penetration that you want on the animals you hunt, then stay with it. If you want to improve penetration, the single most important thing you can do is shoot a heavier arrow. To improve penetration further, shoot a cut-on-impact head.

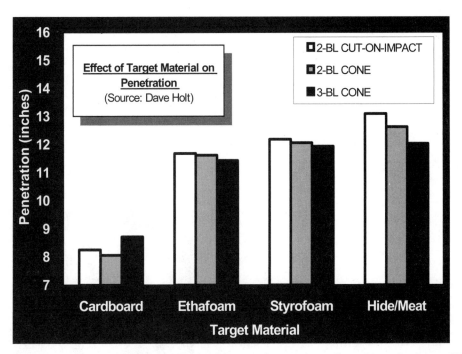

BROADHEAD TYPE VS. PENETRATION. In this set of tests, broadhead type had very little effect on penetration in different target materials. In everything but cardboard, two-blade, cut-on-impact heads penetrated deeper, but only slightly. And, with an extra blade, three-blade heads actually did more cutting.

9. Understanding Spine

If you had to pick the single most misunderstood subject in archery, what would it be? According to Bob Ragsdale, a longtime PSE technical service rep, it's arrow spine. "Perhaps 40% of the calls we get are spine related," he told me once when I once asked him this question. "They're either about spine directly or about problems that are caused by using inadequately spined arrows."

The problem is that spine is a relative thing. It's dependent on a whole host of shooting style and equipment factors. What works for one person may not work for another.

In the next few chapters, we'll take a brief look at the different types of arrow spine, the different things that can affect them, and give you information that you can use to make arrow tuning easier.

The Archer's Paradox

Before doing that, let's first review the well-known *archer's paradox*. When an arrow is released, the string and arrow nock roll left for a right-handed shooter. This puts the string force outside of the arrow and causes it to bend inward toward the bow handle. As the arrow continues forward, it springs back and bends in the direction opposite to the first bend.

A properly spined arrow reaches its maximum bending

(Photo from video, courtesy of Easton Company)

HIGH SPEED PHOTO OF AN ARROW MOMENTS AFTER RELEASE. The arrow has reached its maximum outward bending as it passes the bow handle. It will then bend inward by almost the same amount to allow the nock to pass the rest.

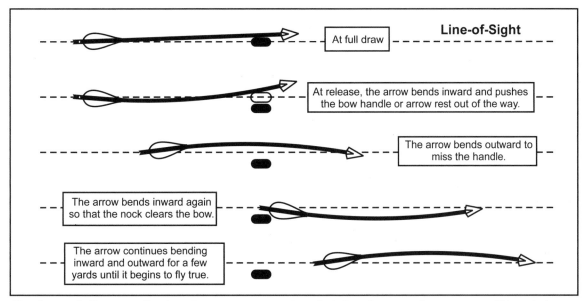

Line-of-Sight

At full draw

At release, the arrow bends inward and pushes
the bow handle or arrow rest out of the way.

The arrow bends outward to
miss the handle.

The arrow bends inward again
so that the nock clears the bow.

The arrow continues bending
inward and outward for a few
yards until it begins to fly true.

THE ARCHER'S PARADOX. Static spine measurements only tell us how much an arrow will bend. As this sketch shows, an arrow also has to bend at the right *times* during launch. Known as "dynamic spine," this can only be determined on the practice range.

away from the bow as the center of the shaft passes the rest. As the fletching nears the bow, the arrow bends again in the opposite direction which moves the nock away from the rest as it passes. In effect, the arrow has bent around the bow without touching it.

After clearing the bow, the arrow continues oscillating right and left, each time bending a little less than before, until it stops and the arrow is flying true. For nocking points that are set above perpendicular on the string, the arrow also bends upward slightly when shot. This allows it to clear the arrow rest as it passes. The effect using center-shot compounds and mechanical releases is less than for finger shooting, but is still there.

Two Types of Spine

From this, we can see that for an arrow to fly properly, it needs to do two things. It needs to bend by the *right amount*, and it needs to bend at the *right times*.

An arrow's stiffness when it's bent sideways with a weight is called *static spine* (not "spline" as some people incorrectly refer to it). Its stiffness when actually shot from a bow is called *dynamic spine*.

10. Static Spine

Static spine is what we measure on a spine tester. It's determined solely by the arrow material (its *elastic modulus* in engineering parlance) and by its cross-sectional dimensions (its *moment-of-inertia*). These two properties, acting together, determine how much it will bend when a weight is applied to its center.

For a specific material, spine rating is most affected by an arrow's outside diameter. A 2216 aluminum shaft (22/64" diameter with a .016" wall thickness) is one-third stiffer than a 2016 shaft (20/64" diameter and 016" wall thickness) on a standard spine tester; but it has a fifty-percent greater spine rating.

Wall thickness also affects spine, but not as greatly. The wall thickness of a 2219 is sixteen percent greater than a 2216, and the arrow has a seventeen-percent higher spine rating.

Arrow manufacturers use different materials, diameters, and wall thickness to provide a wide range of shaft weights and sizes to archers. Light, stiff shafts are made with large diameters and thin walls. Heavy, weak-spine shafts are made with small diameters and thick walls.

Arrow length doesn't figure into static spine since testers use fixed-width support points. If one arrow is longer than another, it just hangs over the ends more and doesn't affect the readings.

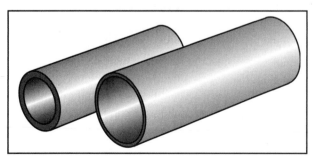

THICKNESS AND DIAMETER. Shaft diameter generally affects stiffness more than wall thickness. Light, stiff shafts have larger diameters and thinner walls. Heavy, flexible shafts have smaller diameters and thicker walls. Arrow length or weight doesn't figure into static spine measurements.

11. Dynamic Spine

Since static spine is the only stiffness property that we can measure without shooting an arrow, it's very useful in narrowing down your shaft choices. However, it doesn't account for the many equipment and shooting variables that can affect arrow flight. You can only find the best arrow for your bow and your shooting style by shooting it. Here are some things to consider.

Arrow Length

The longer an arrow is, the more easily it will bend when shot. If you placed the point of a 26" long 2016 shaft on a bathroom scale and pushed down on the nock (this is dangerous, so don't do it yourself), it wouldn't bend until you reached about 24-pounds of force. Then, it would suddenly start bending and would continue bending as you increased the force. A 30" long 2016 shaft would start bending with about 18-pounds of force. Since they're weaker, long arrows need to be stiffer than short arrows to shoot properly.

Balance-Point

An arrow's center of mass lies at the point where you can balance it across a sharp edge and it doesn't tip over. This is called its *balance-point*.

When an arrow is shot, the nock doesn't push against the arrow point as it did in the bathroom scale experiment. Instead, it pushes against the arrow's center of mass as it accelerates. If two arrows are identical except for balance-point, the one with the forward most balance-point will act like it's longer and will bend more. This will give it a lower dynamic spine. This is really what arrow spine charts are measuring for different length arrows.

Arrow Weight

To understand why weight is important, imagine that you've supported a horizontal arrow at its two ends. If you bent the shaft downward by an inch at the center, balanced a 100-grain weight on top of it, and then released the shaft, the weight would jump some distance into the air. This is a measure of the shaft's dynamic recovery characteristics. Now imagine that you did the same thing using a 500-grain weight. The heavier weight wouldn't jump as high.

Shaft weight affects how an arrow bends around the bow in much the same way. A light arrow doesn't have as much weight to move as it bends around a bow and this causes it to react differently than a heavy arrow. Two arrows can have the same static spine and the same balance-point but can have two different dynamic spines.

Arrow Offset

If your bow is *center-cut* (the edge of the sight window is in line with the undrawn string), the arrow will point to the left for a right-handed shooter and the string will push on it at an angle. If your bow is *center-shot* (cut past center so that the arrow lies directly in front of the string), the string will push from directly behind it. An arrow that lies at an angle to the string will have a lower dynamic spine.

If your bow has an adjustable arrow rest (most compounds do), fine tune spine by moving the rest in or out. Longbows and recurves are usually center-cut and have non-adjustable rests. The rests can be shimmed outward which will correct some spine problems. But they can't be moved in, so you may have to change arrows shafts to correct problems.

Bow Type

The amount of energy that a bow stores, and the way it transfers that energy to the arrow, affects spine. Compounds push on an arrow with low energy when released, then hit it with higher energy after it already has some speed. Recurves and longbows hit the arrow with high energy out of the starting gate. As a result, stick bows usually need stiffer arrows than identical weight compounds.

Bows that store more energy, pound-for-pound, need higher spined arrows than lower energy bows. A 60# cam bow may need a stiffer arrow than a 60# round-wheel bow. And a 60# recurve may need a stiffer arrow than a 60# longbow.

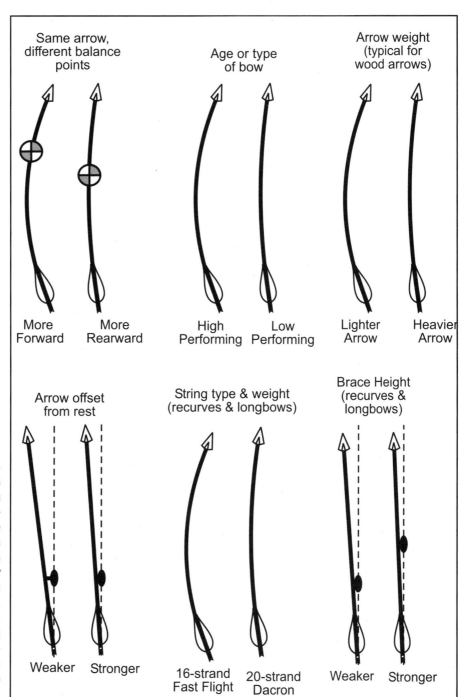

DYNAMIC SPINE. Dynamic spine is affected by a number of shooting factors. Here are a few things that spine charts don't normally mention (or list in the small print). There are others. The only way you can know what arrow flies best from your bow is to shoot it.

Same arrow, different balance points

More Forward   More Rearward

Age or type of bow

High Performing   Low Performing

Arrow weight (typical for wood arrows)

Lighter Arrow   Heavier Arrow

Arrow offset from rest

Weaker   Stronger

String type & weight (recurves & longbows)

16-strand Fast Flight   20-strand Dacron

Brace Height (recurves & longbows)

Weaker   Stronger

As a general rule, older, less efficient bows need spines that are three- to five-pounds lighter than newer ones, even if they're designed similarly.

Brace Height (Recurves & Longbows)

Variable brace heights on recurves and longbows affect spine in two ways. First, bows that are braced lower have longer power strokes and store more energy. This will require more arrow spine. Second, unless the arrow rest is adjusted inward, lower braced bows will point the arrow more off-line when shot. This will require weaker spined arrows. The bow's setup and the amount of adjustment needed will govern which of these conditions dominate. The opposite effect would occur by raising brace height.

String Type (Recurves & Longbows)

With a compound, you're pretty much tied to the manufacturer's cable and string harness. Recurve and longbow shooters have a choice of strings. Dacron strings weigh more for equal strength than Fast Flight strings and also stretch more. Both factors take available energy away from the arrow and this means that you can get by with a lower spined arrow. In general, changing from dacron to Fast-Flight usually requires a three- to five-pound spine increase.

Adding string silencers or brush buttons to a string will slow it down and will lower arrow spine requirements.

12. Balance-Point

Balance-point was mentioned briefly in the last chapter. This is an extremely important—but often overlooked—element of arrow tuning.

Why It's Important

If you ever made a paper airplane as a kid, you probably figured out that adding a paperclip to the front end made it fly better. This is due to a principle called *aerodynamic stability*. It states that the center of gravity of a flying object needs to lie forward of its major wind catching surfaces. If you add weight to the rear end of a paper airplane, its in-flight stability is destroyed and it's likely to do flip-flops in the air. Some early archery pioneers found that they could actually make an arrow turn around in flight when its back end was heavier than its front end.

How It's Measured

Balance-point is expressed as the distance in inches, or the percentage of total length, that an arrow's center of balance lies forward of its mid-point. To find it, first measure the length of your arrow, from the bottom of the nock groove to the back of the point and any *visible* broadhead adapters. This is normally referred to as the arrow's *cut-length*. For swaged aluminum shafts or tapered wood shafts, measure to where the taper starts. On arrows having outserts, subtract ¾" from the cut-length. (These procedures were adopted in 1994 to eliminate the effect of different commercial broadhead components.)

Divide your measurement in half, measure down the shaft, and mark the center point on it. Next, balance the arrow across a sharp edge and mark this location.

If the balance-point lies 18" forward of the nock groove on a 30" arrow, it is said to lie *3" FOC* (Front-Of-Center) or *10% FOC* (3" divided by 30" times 100 = 10%).

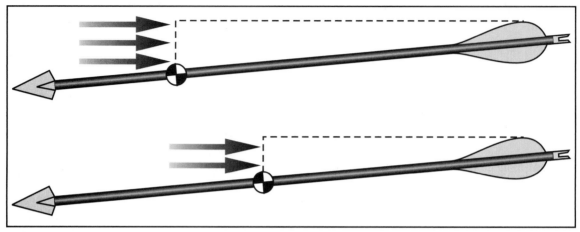

BALANCE POINT IN FLIGHT. Arrows tend to rotate around their balance-point if they move off-line in flight. A more forward balance-point gives them greater steering leverage to right themselves. If the balance-point is moved too far forward, though, the arrow can over-correct and start "wagging."

What Should It Be?

For good flight, the balance-point on a hunting arrow should be between 10% and 20% FOC. Olympic archers routinely use target arrows with balance-points of 18% FOC or greater for maximum flight stability.

Broadheads act like a forward wing that catches air and tries to move the point off line. The larger the head, the more forward balance-point that's required to give the arrow the in-flight steering leverage that it needs. If it's moved *too far* forward, the leverage may be too large which can cause the arrow to over-correct and start "wagging."

On arrows over 28" long, 10-15% FOC will work fine for most setups. On shorter arrows 15-20% FOC works better since it increases the distance from the balance-point to the fletching and gives the arrow more steering leverage.

What Affects It?

Balance-point is affected by everything that you add to a bare shaft. This includes the weight of the point and inserts as well as the weight and location of the fletching, crown dipping paint, tracking "fluffs," internal weights, and so forth.

As long as your arrow has normal components it will have a normal balance-point and standard arrow weight charts should work well. If you use non-standard components, the charts may not work for you. The better charts show the effect of adding different point weights, but not other components.

A Real World Example

Many people today are turning to light broadheads to improve trajectory. Then they have accuracy problems and don't know why. Let's look at an example of one archer's problems.

His arrows were 31-inch long, 2217s fitted with five-inch vanes and a 75-grain broadhead. They were spined correctly to his bow and dynamically tuned for proper short range flight. But he was getting poor accuracy at longer distances.

When measured, one of his arrows had a balance point that was 4% FOC. Switching to a 100-grain broadhead raised it to 6% FOC. Replacing the vanes with lighter feathers raised it to 9%. This was still inadequate, so a 125-grain broadhead was substituted. This gave the arrow a balance-point of 11% and put it in the acceptable range. The heavier head cost him a little in trajectory but greatly improved his down range accuracy and shooting consistency.

Point Weight (grains)	Total Arrow Weight (grains)	Balance Point, FOC	Accuracy	Launch Speed (fps)	Depth-of-Kill at 40-yards (yards)
75	450	4%	Poor	230	4.4
100	475	6%	Better	225	4.1
125	500	11%	Excellent	220	4.0

For only a half-yard loss in depth-of-kill at 40-yards, this archer was able to greatly improve his accuracy by using heavier broadheads. This made his arrows more stable and forgiving in flight.

13. Spine Charts & Testers

Spine charts and testers provide a starting point in your search for that *perfect* shaft, but they should be used with some caution. Here are some tips for getting the most out of them.

Charts

The spine charts published by arrow manufacturers are generally excellent but they're changing constantly due to ever more efficient bows and evolving shooting styles. Old charts don't always agree with new ones and this can cause confusion.

One example: I recently went through ten different charts from one manufacturer and they recommended anywhere from a 35-pound to a 50-pound bow for a particular shaft size and draw length. When I put this same shaft on a popular commercial spine tester, it recommended a 60-pound bow. Yet, the arrow shoots fine for me out of a 72-pound bow. None of these recommendations are wrong. They're based on different bows and different shooting styles.

Better spine charts consider factors such as arrow length, bow type, bow weight, and point weight. They usually don't consider non-standard component weights or any internal weighting that you might want to add.

They're also based on different bow efficiencies. If you've got a new bow, use a new spine chart. If you've got an old bow, use an older chart. At the minimum, read the small print before using any chart. This should show the assumptions that went into developing it or the types of equipment it's based on.

Testers

Like charts, the spine values shown on testers are based on averages which may or may not be right for you. Some testers are for compounds and others are for longbows and recurves; some are for wood arrows and some are for aluminum or carbon arrows. Newer testers might be accurate for today's high-performance bows but not the older model that you have. Know which one you're using.

Deflection readings can also be different on different testers. Some testers use two-pound weights while others use 880-gram (1.94-pound) metric weights; some have a fixed 26- or a 28-inch spacing while others are variable. All will measure accurate deflections, but each will give you different number depending on its setup.

When ordering arrows, tell the vendor what spine tester you used or what spacing and weight you used to determine spine or deflection values. Also, tell him your draw length and what kind of bow you shoot so that he can give you an intelligent recommendation.

Most pro shops or mail-order houses that sell arrows as one of their main products will be knowledgeable in this area and will work with you.

Get a Sample Pack

Whether you base your decision on spine charts or spine testers, be sure to make adjustments to the recommended spine rating based on the factors discussed in the previous chapter.

If you're still unsure about a particular shaft, or just want to experiment to find the best one for you, ask your arrow vendor if he'll sell you a sampling

RECURVE BOW¹ BOW WEIGHT² (LBS)				COMPOUND BOW — PEAK BOW WEIGHT⁶ (LBS.)												22½"- 23" -23½"			23½"- 24" -24½"			24½
				Round Wheel³				Energy Wheel⁴				Speed Cam⁵									
Broadhead or Field Point Weight Only				Broadhead or Field Point Weight Only				Broadhead or Field Point Weight Only				Broadhead or Field Point Weight Only				Shaft Size	Shaft Model	Shaft Weight	Shaft Size	Shaft Model	Shaft Weight	Shaft Size
75 (grains) 65-85	100 (grains) 90-110	125 (grains) 115-135	150 (grains) 140-160	75 (grains) 65-85	100 (grains) 90-110	125 (grains) 115-135	150 (grains) 140-160	75 (grains) 65-85	100 (grains) 90-110	125 (grains) 115-135	150 (grains) 140-160	75 (grains) 65-85	100 (grains) 90-110	125 (grains) 115-135	150 (grains) 140-160							
35 to 39	32 to 36	29 to 33	26 to 30	41 to 46	38 to 43	35 to 40	32 to 37	35 to 40	32 to 37	29 to 34	26 to 31								1813	XX75	189 A	1913
																						1816
40 to	37 to	34 to	31	41	38	41	35	32	35	32	29	26				1813	XX75	181 A	1913	XX75	200 A	XX75.E

KEY ELEMENTS TO LOOK FOR. A good spine chart, like this one from Easton, should show the effects of bow type, cam type, point weight, draw weight, and draw length. Read the fine print for any assumptions used to develop it.

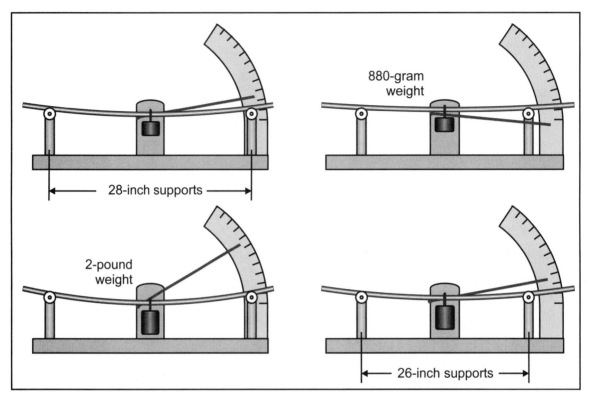

NOT ALL SPINE TESTERS ARE EQUAL. In this sketch, the same arrow has four different deflection readings on four different testers. All are correct for that tester. Know which one you're using.

of shafts having different diameters and spine ratings. I did this ten years ago and it was one of the best moves I ever made. I don't worry about charts or testers any more. If I want to go to a heavier or lighter arrow, or a longer or shorter one, I just choose the one in my arrow bin that works the best.

Bow Weight Not Critical

Finally, don't get too hung up on precise bow weight when picking a shaft. With the huge variety of bows available today, and the different ways in which they launch an arrow, the difference between a 50-pound and a 60-pound bow means very little any more. Many people get into trouble by rigidly following charts or using testers without really understanding the information they provide.

Don't be afraid to try something out of the ordinary just because your dealer or your buddy says it won't work.

Part 2. The Bow

When I started bowhunting seriously in the early 1960s, I had one practical choice in bows—a fiberglass laminated recurve. No one I knew still used a longbow. And certainly no one used an all-wood bow, or at least wouldn't own up to it in public.

Then, in 1969, came compounds. They were slow to catch on, but when they did they took the archery world by storm. Within a few years, it was virtually impossible to find anything else for sale. Some folks took to compounds like ducks to water. Others tried them for a while and then migrated back to traditional equipment when it started making a comeback in the 1980s. A small but growing number of today's bowhunters are also experimenting with primitive all-wood or sinew backed bows for their greater sense of challenge and hunting heritage.

In short, today's hunting archer has more bow choices than at any other time in history. Any of them will do the job if you stay within their limitations. The challenge is finding one that meets your own personal wants and needs.

In this section, we'll look at the choices available. You'll learn how to find the best bow for you, evaluate its pros and cons, and set it up for maximum hunting performance.

14. Compounds

Compounds are the undisputed king of arrow launchers. They're easy to use and have unparalleled technical performance. Over 90% of all bowhunters today use them, either full-time or part-time.

Holless Allen's original compounds were rather ugly, poor performing affairs compared to modern designs. They did have the archer-friendly weight let-off (only fifteen-percent in his first models) that all compounds are known for, but they offered little real downrange performance advantage. They were also prone to frequent mechanical problems.

(Photo courtesy of Ohio bowhunter Mike Dickess.)

COMPOUNDS ARE KING. Over 90% of all bowhunters today use compound bows, either full-time or part-time, due to their easy-use and unparalleled technical performance.

Allen's patent shows a non-circular cam but this was hard to perfect so early production models had round ("eccentric") cams. These came to be known as *wheel-bows*. They remained the standard into the 1980s. Top performing compounds in 1978 shot a 540-grain hunting arrow at about 170-fps. By 1985, let-offs had increased to about 50% and rating speeds (60-pound bow pulled 30-inches and 540-grain arrow) had been extended to about 200-fps, barely more than top performing recurves of the time. Archers didn't use compounds for their blistering speed; they used them for their easy shooting qualities.

In the intervening years, the usability, durability, and technical performance of compounds have increased dramatically. Today's new breed of shorter, faster, lighter, higher let-off, less noisy, and more trouble-free radical-cam compounds have rating speeds of over 240-fps. Used with light arrows, speeds can exceed 320-fps. The new breed of single-cam bows eliminates tuning problems with some two-cam models.

Advantages	*Energy Storage*—Compounds store more energy per pound of peak weight than other bows. And energy is what ultimately gets the job done.

Energy Storage—Compounds store more energy per pound of peak weight than other bows. And energy is what ultimately gets the job done.

Arrow Speed—With their greater stored energy, compounds will shoot any weight of arrow faster and harder than other bows. This improves trajectory and penetration.

Holding Weight—A compound's lower holding weight at full draw makes it easier to hold back while aiming or waiting for a shooting opportunity.

Shooting Sensitivity—A compound's limbs are dynamically coupled together through its cabling system during the entire the draw-aim-release cycle. This helps to minimize the effects of some types of shooting errors such as inconsistent grip pressure.

Ease of Aiming—A compound's greater mass weight and lower holding weight combine to make aiming easy, with or without sights.

Ease of Learning—Compounds are easy to master due to their forgiving nature and their low holding weight. Compared to recurves and longbows that can take months or years to master, compounds can be mastered in days or weeks.

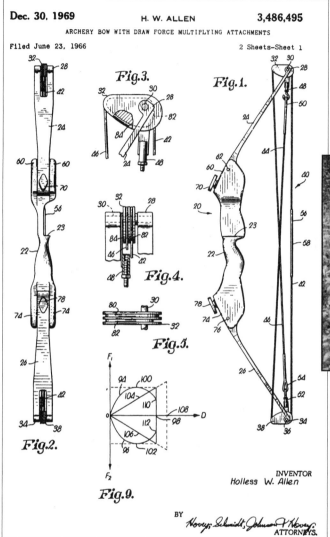

Dec. 30, 1969   H. W. ALLEN   3,486,495

ARCHERY BOW WITH DRAW FORCE MULTIPLYING ATTACHMENTS

Filed June 23, 1966   2 Sheets-Sheet 1

Fig.3.

Fig.1.

Fig.4.

Fig.2.

Fig.5.

Fig.9.

INVENTOR
Holless W. Allen

BY
Novey, Schmidt, Johnson & Novey,
ATTORNEYS.

THE EARLY DAYS. By using a simple physics principal called leverage on his bows, Holless Allen changed the nature of archery forever. Shown at left is his original patent. Although Allen saw the advantages of modern shaped cams, this proved difficult to master so his early production bows (above) had round, eccentric "wheels." This remained the standard for many years.

Tradeoffs

There's no perfect bow. Depending on your shooting style and the type of hunting that you do, they all come with their own set of pros and cons. Here are some important ones to consider:

Bow Length. Although no formal industry definition exists, compounds might be classified into the following general length groups: Short (under 32"), Medium (33" to 38"), Long (over 38"). Most bows sold today fall in the medium category.

Shorter bows are easier to handle in cramped surroundings and usually shoot faster since their shorter limbs weigh less than longer limbs and have a center of mass that lies closer to the handle. This makes them react more quickly during a shot. Shorter bows have more severe string angles at full-draw and are more difficult to shoot accurately using fingers. They work fine with release-aids. Longer bows are a little slower but are more accurate for many shooters.

Handle Shape. Handles may be *reflexed* (the throat of the grip is set behind the limb butts), *deflexed* (the throat is set forward of the limb butts), or *straight* (the throat is even with the limb butts.) Rear-set handles increase a bow's power stroke for a given draw length since they decrease the required brace height. This makes a bow shoot faster and harder, but can also make some more sensitive to errors in shooting form. Forward-set handles are usually more forgiving of shooting errors but are a little slower. Straight-set handles fall in between.

Cam Type. The terminology used to describe different types of cams has changed through the years as cam designs themselves have evolved, and they continue to change today. For our purposes here, they might be classified into three groups: *Eccentric cams* (or "eccentrics"), *intermediate cams*, and *radical cams*.

Eccentric "wheels" are circular with off-center axle holes that give them their let-off leverage. Wheel-bows are generally the most pleasant to shoot for most people due to their slower force buildup and rounded force-draw hump. As a byproduct of these features, they shoot an arrow more slowly than other bows.

Radical cams, as the name implies, are usually large and have complex shapes. They are designed with one purpose in mind: To store maximum energy in a bow for maximum ballistic performance (either speed or launch energy, at the shooter's discretion). These bows usually build up force rapidly when drawn and hold their peak weight for a longer period of time throughout the force-draw cycle before sharply dropping in force at full draw. These same characteristics make the bow less comfortable or less enjoyable to shoot for some people.

Intermediate cams fall at various places between the two extremes above. Most hunters today use one of these bows.

Single vs. Multiple Cams. Early compounds all had two cams. Many were studies in frustration since the cams frequently got out of balance with one another and affected accuracy. Newer two-cam bows are much improved but still require more attention to tuning to keep them in tip-top shooting conditions. The new generation of one-cam (or "solocam") bows have a single active cam on one limb and a round, concentric "idler" wheel on the other end to let the cable harness rotate around it. Once tuned, they generally stay that way.

Let-off Percentage. The "standard" let-off of early compounds was 30%. The standard then moved to 50%, then 65%, and today averages about 80%. Near-100% let-offs are theoretically possible so we can expect these values to keep rising.

Higher let-off bows are easier to hold at full draw but are harder to release cleanly since there's less force trying to pull the string away from a shooter's release hand. Assuming that they're otherwise identical, lower let-off bows store more energy than higher let-off bows, although practical differences in performance are small. They're also more accurate for some people because of their higher initial string force during release which can smooth out ragged releases.

Shooting Noise. Some compounds from just a few years ago sounded like "a plumbing supply truck hitting a telephone pole" when shot, according to one pundit I once overheard at a 3-D shoot. Newer models are quieter but this can vary greatly from model to model. Short, radical-cam bows used with light arrows are usually the worst offenders. A new generation of noise-reducing vibration damping devices are incorporated into many off-the-shelf bows today and are available as add-ons to retrofit older bows.

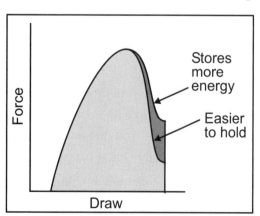

LETOFF PERFORMANCE VS. USABILITY. For identical peak weight and draw length, lower let-off bows store more energy but higher let-off bows are easier to hold while aiming.

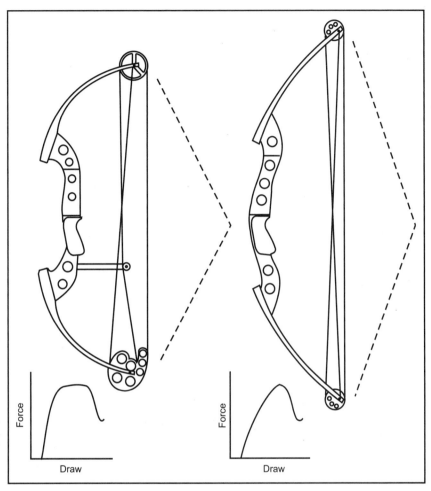

SPEED OR COMFORT? The bow on the left is short and has a radical cam and rear-set handle—features that help to create arrow speed. The bow on the right is longer and has softcams (eccentric "wheels") and a more forward-set handle. These features sacrifice some speed in the interest of more comfortable shooting. It also has a larger string angle which makes it more forgiving to shoot for some people. Most bows fall in between these extremes.

Practical
Decisions

The above factors are guidelines only and may not apply to specific makes and models of bows. Before purchasing any bow, you should shoot and evaluate it for yourself. Consider these additional factors when making your decision:

Technical Performance vs. Usability. Technical performance and usability are two qualities that all product designers wrestle with. These features aren't easy to combine into one product. Race cars and fighter planes have superb speed and maneuverability but aren't comfortable to pilot. SUVs and commercial airliners are workhorses that are a pleasure to travel in but aren't too fast.

Not all bows are equal. Manufacturers struggle to provide both technical performance and easy, rugged usability in their products but are often forced to favor one over the other in a design. This is the reason that they offer so many different models.

Know which one you're choosing. If your primary interest is in maximum ballistic performance, then choose a shorter bow having high energy cams and a rear-set handle. If accuracy and shooting comfort are most important to you, then choose a longer wheel-bow or moderate cam design that will build up force more slowly and doesn't have a pronounced force-draw hump. It will be easier and more pleasant to pull. Also choose one with a more forward-set handle. Most target bows, where accuracy is paramount, all have these features. If you shoot with your fingers, choose a bow in the 38-inch or longer range that will minimize the string's accuracy-robbing finger pinch.

Fitted with a simple, rugged sight and accessories, this equipment combines the performance of modern compounds with the rugged simplicity of old-time equipment.

Accuracy. Over and above other considerations your shooting rig should be accurate. Accuracy comes in two conflicting forms: General shooting and longer range shooting. Fast equipment may give you an edge on longer shots due its flatter arrow trajectory but may be more critical to shoot and cause more errant shots in general. This will not only negate the fast arrow advantage for longer shots, but can cause you to miss shorter shots as well. Choose a bow that you can shoot most accurately for *most* (but not necessarily *all*) of your bowhunting shots.

Let-off and Electronics. Prior to 2003 the Pope & Young Club did not recognize animals for entry into its Record Book of North American Big Game Animals if taken with a bow having greater than 65% let-off. In late 2003, this restriction was removed but animals taken with higher let-off bows were identified with an asterisk next to the entry. At the club's 2005 conference, members voted to remove the asterisk, so that any animal taken with any legal let-off bow may now be entered without distinction.

The club's prohibition against the use of certain electronics still applies.

Let-off and Aiming

It's well known that high let-off bows require the archer to hold less force and therefore increase the time that he can comfortably hold the bow while aiming. What isn't usually appreciated is that high let-off bows can make it harder to hold a sight-pin *still*.

To understand this, imagine holding an undrawn 5¼-pound bow at arm's length. To keep it steady, your shoulder muscles must exert 11 foot-pounds of balancing torque.

Imagine now that the bow pulled 60-pounds and had an 80% let-off so that you were holding 12-pounds of force at full draw. Your shoulder muscles (which act like a fulcrum point) would only have to exert 6 foot-pounds of torque since your stronger drawing arm helped share the burden of holding the bow up. This stabilizing effect is the reason that it's often easier to hold a drawn-bow steadier than an undrawn one. Taking this example one step further: If the bow had a 65% let-off, the contribution of your shoulder muscles would be *eliminated entirely* and you should be able to hold the bow even steadier.

Put simply: The pulling force that you exert helps to balance the bow's mass weight in greater or lesser amounts and this can affect your ability to aim accurately. Experiment to find a bow that lets you aim most accurately—not just aim for a longer period of time.

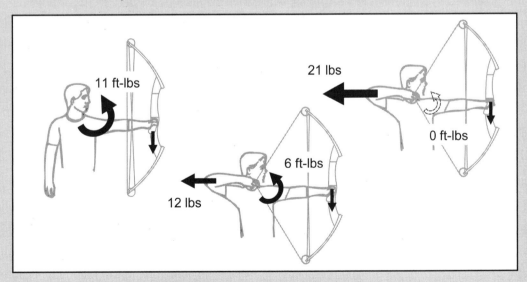

The more muscle groups that you can eliminate when shooting a bow, the more accurately that you'll shoot it. The right amount of pulling force can help you to eliminate the use of your shoulder muscles. Your shooting style and bow will be different from this example. Experiment to find a let-off percentage that you can aim most accurately.

15. Recurves and Longbows

Most anthropologists date the bow and arrow's invention at between ten- and thirty-thousand years ago in the old-world and about six-thousand years ago in the Americas. Contrary to popular belief, a bow's advantage wasn't it's greater energy. Heavy spears or atlatl darts could be launched with more energy than arrows. Rather, its advantage was its extended range. Because or this, bows and arrows were the technological marvels of the time.

These early bows changed little until Fred Bear's patenting of uniaxial fiberglass around 1950. His recurves became the new standard of excellence and until the early-1970s, when compounds came onto the scene, laminated recurves were the near-universal choice of all archers. Since that time, fiberglass laminated longbows have again made a resurgence.

Today's generation of recurves and longbows all have modern performance enhancing features that make them top performers compared to early designs. These include the use of full-cut sight windows, contoured pistol grips, Fast Flight strings, interior carbon limb laminations, synthetic tip overlays, and computer designed limb profiles.

While the popularity of these "stick bows" remains second to compounds, it's growing with each year as archers re-discover their lure.

(Photo courtesy of Washington bowhunter Dale 'Rocky' Holpainen).

EXCELLENT HUNTING TOOLS. Although they require a little more effort to master, recurves and longbows remain the excellent hunting tools that they've been throughout history.

Advantages

If compounds have the edge in technical performance, recurves and long-bows hold the advantage in many other categories.

Noise—Stick bows are usually quieter than compounds. They don't have mechanical parts that can vibrate loose and rattle at inopportune times and they're typically used with heavier arrows that absorb more of the bow's energy. Their low pitched "thut" doesn't disturb a deer as much when you shoot at it.

Shooting Versatility—Where compounds used with sights must be held verti-cally, sightless stick bows can be effectively used from a variety of shooting positions. They can be shot while canted to either side of vertical when shooting through tight brush and even while lying on your back. This can result in fewer lost hunting opportunities.

Field Use—Light weight recurves and longbows are a joy to tote around the woods. They don't have mechanical components that can break or malfunction. With the addition of an inexpensive tip protector, their longer length allows them to be used as walking sticks in uneven terrain or as stable binocular monopods when glassing distant hillsides.

Ease of Use Once Mastered—Although stick bows take more effort to master, many people claim that they are the easiest bows to use once learned. If shot instinctively (as most people do), they can be pointed, drawn, and released in a fraction of the time required using a compound. Rather than having to consciously judge the effects of distance, wind, and slope, the instinctive shooter's mind subconsciously makes these decisions in an instant.

Ease of Transport—Slim recurves and longbows are easy to transport. Take-down models can be easily fitted into a compact airline travel case, a backpack or daypack, or under a truck seat, and quickly reassembled for use.

Tradition—Even with the use of modern materials and design features, stick bows still evoke a strong sense of history. This makes them popular with people who list this among their bowhunting thrills.

Shooting Enjoyment—Recurves and longbows are more fun to shoot than compounds for many people. Most converts can't wait to get home from work and head to a back wood lot to fling a few arrows with them.

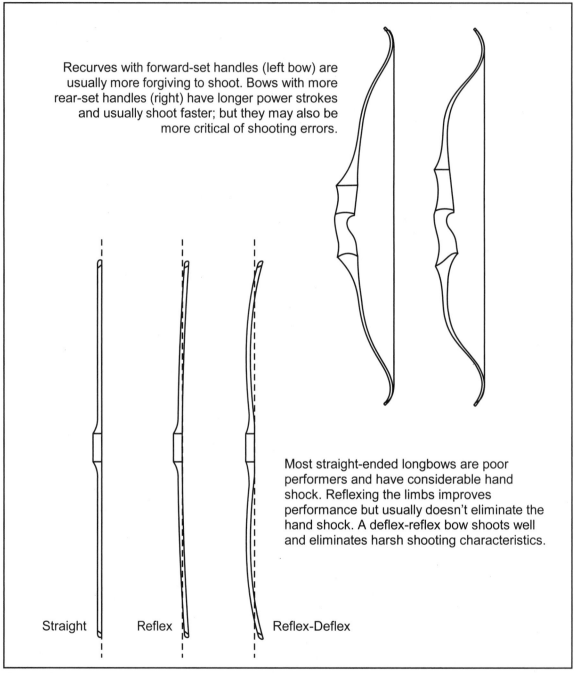

Recurves with forward-set handles (left bow) are usually more forgiving to shoot. Bows with more rear-set handles (right) have longer power strokes and usually shoot faster; but they may also be more critical of shooting errors.

Most straight-ended longbows are poor performers and have considerable hand shock. Reflexing the limbs improves performance but usually doesn't eliminate the hand shock. A deflex-reflex bow shoots well and eliminates harsh shooting characteristics.

Straight   Reflex   Reflex-Deflex

DESIGN OPTIONS. Every bow has a combination of features that makes them better or worse for different archers. The performance tradeoffs here are typical but are not true of every bow. Choose a bow that you can shoot most accurately and don't worry about minor performance differences.

Tradeoffs As in the discussion of compounds, your choice between a recurve and a longbow will involve choosing the right combination of performance and usability for you. Here are a few things to consider when making your decision.

Aesthetics. For their pure sense of history, longbows are unparalleled. Except for the use of modern materials and center-cut sight windows, they've changed little since their invention. Many people like a longbow's long clean lines while others prefer a recurve's more stylized contours and larger handles. The wide variety of exotic woods and custom inlays available on both types of bows is enough to satisfy all but the most demanding purchaser. On the basis of aesthetics alone, any bow that strikes your fancy is a good choice.

Raw Performance. Recurves usually store more energy, pound-for-pound, than longbows. They also have shorter, lighter, faster-acting limbs. These factors let them shoot arrows faster than most longbows. If maximum technical performance is your main goal, then choose a recurve.

Selection Criteria	Recurve	Longbow
Higher Energy Storage (pound-for-pound)	✓	
Ease of Aiming (more mass weight)	✓	
More Versatile Field Handling (generally shorter lengths)	✓	
Accuracy (depends on shooter)	✓ (Heavier mass weight; more center-cut handle)	✓ (Limbs less sensitive to some form variances)
Less Carrying Weight (most models)		✓
Lower Noise (most models)		✓
Tradition		✓

RECURVE OR LONGBOW? Both recurves and longbows have advantages and disadvantages. Make your choice based on your shooting style and the animals that you hunt.

Ease of Handling. For cramped or restricted shooting conditions, recurves usually get the nod since they're shorter than longbows. But this is an overrated concern since longbows can be used equally well in the vast majority of shooting situations, including tree stands. If you like the look and feel of a longbow but also want a shorter bow, many bowyers offer 60- to 62-inch long "bush bows."

Longbows usually weigh less than recurves and this makes them a joy to carry in the woods, especially on western hunts that involve many days of arduous hiking and climbing. With one tip on your boot, the other makes an excellent rest for your binoculars when glassing distant hillsides. Shorter recurves are difficult to use in this way. The final choice here depends on the type of hunting that you do.

Ease of Shooting. This criterion depends a lot on the particulars of your shooting style. Longbows usually have stiffer limbs which makes them more forgiving of many types of shooting errors. Howard Hill frequently expressed this sentiment by saying that he was not good enough to shoot a recurve.

Recurves usually weigh more and this reduces bowhand movement at the moment of release. They also tend to have a little less stacking in their force-draw curve. Most shooters like a low-stack bow; others feel that a little stacking promotes a crisper release. Longbows usually have more hand shock, but on well-designed models this is minimal and easy to get used to. Adding mass weight with a bow quiver can eliminate it entirely.

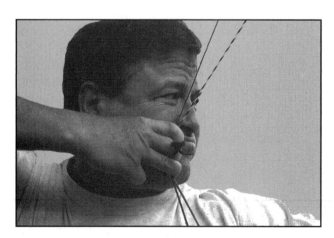

STRING-PINCH. This archer is pulling two recurves at once (hence, his "pleased" expression). The more acute string angle of the shorter bow will make it harder to shoot accurately with fingers. Choose the longer bow even if you have to give up some minor technical performance.

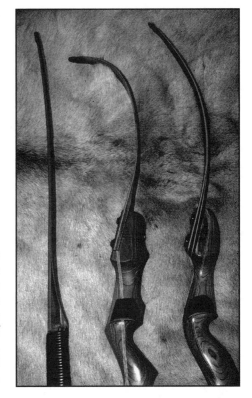

A PERSONAL CHOICE. There's no clear "best" choice among traditional bows. Longbows (left) tend to be quieter and lighter to carry in the woods. Recurves (center) tend to be harder hitting, easier to maneuver in tight cover, and easier to tune. Hybrids (right) combine some features of both recurves and longbows. Any of these bows may be more accurate and effective for you. Consider purchasing one of each for a little variety and use them according to your hunting situation.

Most longbows have straight or slightly dished handles while most recurves have deep contoured pistol grips. Pistol grips promote more consistent hand placement but thin-limbed recurves are also more sensitive to hand placement which offsets some of a pistol grip's advantages. Sight windows on recurves tend to be cut a little deeper than on longbows and this makes them less sensitive to arrow spine or sloppy releases.

The "correct" choice here is a personal one. For some shooters, recurves are more accurate and consistent while the opposite is true for others. Most people start with a recurve when first trying traditional equipment.

Noise. Longbows usually have less shooting and handling noise than recurves. The gap between their string and limbs allows them to be removed more quietly from pegs or branches when hunting from tree stands. Unless

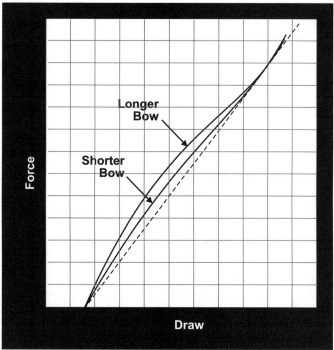

BOW LENGTH VS. PERFORMANCE. Shorter bows—longbow or recurve—have lighter, faster-reacting limbs but they also build up force more slowly due to their sharper string angles. This results in slightly lower stored energy. These offsetting performance features tend to balance out for 60- to 66-inch length bows, which will all shoot an arrow about the same.

recurves are fitted with brush buttons, they're more apt to get caught on twigs and branches when walking and make noise.

Longbows have no string-slap during a shot while the slap on some recurves can be considerable. Adding a moleskin pad between the limb and the string helps but won't cure the problem.

Longbows usually have longer limbs that react more slowly than recurve limbs. Combined with their generally lower energy storage and slower arrow speeds, this usually makes them shoot more quietly than recurves.

Arrow Flight and Tuning. Recurves are usually easier to tune than longbows. This is mainly due to their more center-cut sight windows and the use of elevated, glue-on rests which few longbow shooters use (but might want to try). The greater center-cut makes it easier to adjust arrow flight by moving the rest in or out. Using an elevated rest gives more clearance between the arrow and the arrow shelf. The supporting arm on most glue-on rests also cushions the arrow at release.

Longbows can be tuned very precisely but this usually takes more work since there are fewer things to play with. Tuning is usually done through an exhaustive trial-and-error search of arrow spines, lengths, and balance points.

Hybrids

A new generation of stick bow hybrids, incorporating features of both recurves and longbows, are becoming popular. Often referred to as "longbows," they differ from traditional longbow designs in two ways: They have large recurve-type handles with center-shot or center-cut sight windows and full pistol grips; and they have more heavily deflexed limbs where the string almost (but not quite) touches the limbs below the string-nock groove when the bow is strung. In effect, the limbs act as large recurves.

These recurves-in-longbow-clothing offer some advantages and some disadvantages of both types of bows. They combine some of the user-friendliness of recurves and some of the error-forgiving stability of longbows. Performance-wise, most fall between recurves and longbows.

Shooting Sensitivity

My comment that longbows are more forgiving of shooting errors for many shooters is based on traditional style longbows. This simple experiment will demonstrate what I mean: String a recurve and hold the handle firmly in your left hand and tightly against your body. With your right hand, grip the string at the nockset and move it up and down as far as you can. Now try the same thing with a longbow. Likely, the nockset on the recurve moved up and down an inch or more while on the longbow, it moved only ¼" to ½".

Now torque the limbs sideways on the two bows by gripping them near the tips and see how much the string moves out of alignment with the same force. (Be very careful here not to over-torque the bow and cause the string to come off, which could hurt you or the bow.) Again, the recurve was probably more sensitive.

These same things happen when you shoot an arrow. Recurves are typically faster then longbows but the design features that cause this also make them more sensitive to inconsistencies in form. This general finding won't be true for every bow so experiment to find the one that works best for you.

16. Takedown Bows

In addition to being accurate, hard-hitting, and durable, a hunting bow should be easy to carry and transport. Takedown bows fill this need superbly.

The Chinese had folding, hinged-handled bows three hundred years ago. Takedown bows became common in Europe in the 1700s and 1800s. These were dubbed "Carriage Bows" since they were typically carried under carriage seats for use when traveling. The sleeve-and-socket, hinged, and interlocking latch handle designs, which we think of as modern, were all introduced during this period.

Longbow fever reached its peak in the 1800s in the U.S. and Europe and this spawned many new patented takedown innovations. One interesting design (also thought of as modern) was introduced in 1879. The bow used a metal, shoot-through handle that had sockets where the limbs were inserted. Although it was touted as having both improved accuracy and ease of use, the bow was heavy and unusual looking for the time and never caught on.

Twentieth century bow makers refined many of these earlier ideas. James Duff, a famous Scottish-American bow maker, produced a screw-together bow in the 1920s. "Jointed Bows," as the

AN OLD IDEA. Takedown bows aren't new. This 1930s model not only came apart for storage, but it had a shoot-through handle that was touted for its accuracy.

popular literature called them, were produced by a number of companies in the 1930s. Cliff Zwickey, developer of the popular broadheads that still bear his name, introduced the *Pioneer Bow Hinge* in 1937. A popular design in the 1940s was the *New Moon Latch*. This bow had two interlocking hinged hooks that allowed it to be separated into two parts for storing.

The modern love affair with takedown bows can generally be traced to the commercial success of the *Wing Presentation* and *Presentation II* bows introduced by Bob Lee in the early 1960s. This bow, with bolt-on limbs, was the prototype for most of today's takedown recurves. Fred Bear followed this in 1967 with his now classic *Bear Kodiak Takedown* which used limb sockets, retaining levers, and snaps to secure the limbs.

A later Wing metal-handled design used a slide-lock attachment. Limbs had a dovetailed rail that inserted into mating dovetail grooves in the handle and were held in place with an internal, spring-loaded snap. This may be the finest limb attachment method ever invented for recurves. The bow could be assembled in an instant and it held the limbs secure, without squeaking, and without the need for bolts. Sadly, it's no longer available.

Many of these designs have been adapted or improved upon by today's innovative breed of bowyers. Which of these bows are right for you? Let's explore a few of the options.

Recurves

If you purchase a takedown recurve today, it will probably have bolt-on limbs. On most of them, the limbs will bolt onto the front of the riser. The very popular Black Widow bows, with their rear-bolt arrangements, are notable exceptions. Both front- and rear-bolt designs work well and the choice is personal. A few models have limbs that are mounted in retaining cups or channels. These shoot fine but some lower priced models have a tendency to squeak if the limbs rub against the side plates. Check this out in advance if you're thinking about one.

According to the bowyers who make them, models having two bolts per side hold the limbs more securely and protect the bow better if a string breaks. The down side is that they take more time to put together and take apart. Makers of single-bolt models point out they are quicker to assemble and disassemble. They dismiss the damage issue, saying that it isn't a problem on well-designed bows.

Recurves come in a variety of different styles to match the taste of any consumer. Some bowyers blend the butts of front-mounted limbs into the riser to add streamlining while others leave them square for a more blocky appearance. Again, the choice here is personal. With any bolt-together bow, always carry an extra Allen wrench or two with you. Or invest in a set of knurled thumb bolts that don't require a wrench. Nothing can ruin a remote hunt faster than losing your only wrench in the backcountry. Aside from these considerations, your bow choice should be dictated by personal aesthetics, the feel, and performance factors that you want.

Longbows

From the 1950s to the 1980s, longbows generally followed the age-old one-piece design philosophy. Today, there are a variety of takedown longbow designs to choose from. A few, like Herb Meland's Pronghorn bows, use bolt-on limbs similar to a recurve. Others use through-handle bolts to attach the upper and lower halves of the bow together, thus eliminating one assembly step.

Still others, like Jay St. Charles' Pacific Yew bows, use a classic sleeve and socket arrangement. These bows are easy and quick to use. Simply insert the top half of the bow into the bottom half, string it, and start shooting. The sleeve and socket are hidden behind the handle wrapping which gives these

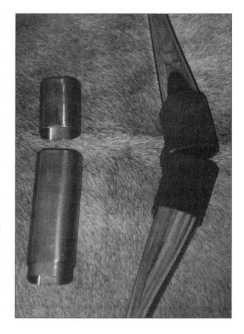

TAKEDOWN LONGBOWS. Longbows generally use three different attachment methods. If they have large handle risers, limbs might attach using bolts like on recurves. If they have traditional slim-handle styling, they might attach using a steel cup-and-sleeve that allows the top half of the bow to be inserted into the lower half; or using a hinged handle that allows the bow to be folded in half when not in use.

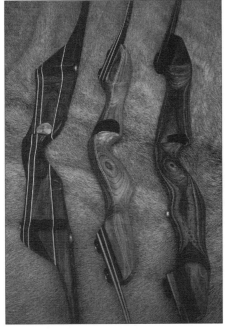 

TAKEDOWN RECURVES. Takedown recurves come in a variety of styles. From left: Rear-bolt limbs, front-bolt limbs, front-bolt limbs in retainer cups, and (far right) snap-on limbs.

bows an elegant one-piece look.

Jerry Brumm and Rick Shepard at Great Northern Bowhunting Company came up with an instant winner a few years ago with their hinged *Jackknife* bows. These bows don't come apart fully; the two halves simply fold together in the center of the handle. Dick Robertson's hinged handle design is similar, except that the two limb halves fully detach so that they can be handled and stored separately. Other bowyers are following these leads.

All of the sleeve-and-socket designs are held securely together by friction and act like a one-piece bow in every way. But some models can squeak as temperature and humidity alter the fit. Spray the mating parts occasionally with silicon to cure this problem. Some hinged designs have the *potential* for damage if a string breaks, causing the limbs to spring forward. This shouldn't happen with proper string care, but it's something to consider if the thought bothers you.

If you're a traditional archer and have never used a takedown bow before, give one a try. Whether you're going on a far-away hunt or just want to store your bow behind a pickup seat, you're almost certain to be pleased with the newfound convenience.

17. Bowstrings for Stick Bows

Bow makers routinely boast of computer designed limbs, carbon laminations, or other "secret" performance enhancing features that will eke another foot-per-second or two out of their products. Aside from arrow weight, though, the thing that affects the performance of recurves and longbows most is your choice of bowstring.

The "Perfect" Bowstring	A perfect bowstring should be durable, strong, light-weight, and not stretch excessively when shot. Until well into the last century, the finest bowstrings were still made of plant fibers such as linen and hemp. The most popular bowstrings over the past thirty years have been made from Brownell's *Dacron B-50* and *B-65* materials. In the late 1980s, Brownell introduced its popular *Fast Flight* fiber. Newer formulations, such as Brownell's *S4* and BCY's *450 Premium* bowstring materials have made inroads into the Fast Flight market and are producing some exciting performance gains. New formulations are sure to come.

For ease of discussion, we'll consider two basic choices here that have stood the test of time—dacron and Fast Flight. Fast Flight is made from a polyurethane fiber known as *Spectra* which effectively combines low stretch characteristics with high strength, low weight, and high abrasion resistance. But, as we'll see in a moment, it's not without its weaknesses and the venerable dacron string still holds some advantages.

Weight & Stretch	Arrow speed is directly affected by bowstring weight. When a bow is drawn and released, its stored energy is used to move the arrow, the limbs, *and* the bowstring. A lighter string leaves more energy to move the arrow. In the 1930s, physicist C. N. Hickman conducted exhaustive research into bowstrings. Using straight-limbed, all-wood bows, he found that every 30-grains of weight removed from a string had the same effect as shooting an arrow

that was 10-grains lighter. Research using modern bows suggests that this relationship varies from design to design, but Hickman's relationship is still a good rule-of-thumb to use when comparing string options.

Fast Flight fibers are half the diameter of dacron fibers and have twice the strength. This means that they can be made into lighter weight, higher strength, higher performing strings. A typical 16-strand Fast Flight string will weight about 100-grains while a typical 16-strand dacron string will weigh a hefty 160-grains or so, and will be weaker to boot.

Bowstring stretch also affects bow performance. Dacron, with over three times the stretch of Fast Flight, saps bow performance by stretching more during a shot.

Test Results

Actual bow performance with different bowstrings depends on a variety of factors. These include bow type, bowstring construction, arrow weight, and shooting style. There are no test results available that fully characterize bowstring performance for all of these factors. Still, some limited testing does show the relative performance differences that you can expect.

In one set of tests, Georgia bow maker, Dan Quillian, reported 10- to 12-fps speed gains for Fast Flight strings using 520- to 608-grain arrows and a 67-pound longbow. Another, slightly more comprehensive test was conducted by traditional archers Dale Dye and Don Welch and reported in a magazine article. Using a 64-pound recurve and 539-grain arrow, they compared arrow speeds for a variety of string materials, constructions, and weights. When compared at equal string weights, the Fast Flight strings or their equivalents were five- to seven-fps faster for a mixture of Flemish and endless-loop constructions. When compared using an equal number of strands, the Fast Flight strings were six- to twelve-fps faster. Although not part of the test, these results suggest that Fast Flight strings would be approximately 15-fps faster than dacron strings when tested at equivalent strengths.

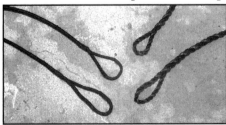

STRING CONSTRUCTION. Endless-loop strings (left) are made by wrapping bowstring material in a continuous loop and then forming the ends with serving material. Flemish strings (right) are made by twisting individual pieces of string material together lengthwise and at the ends.

Similar results are reported by other researchers. Taken together, they indicate that Fast Flight is the undisputed king of bowstrings in terms of pure per-

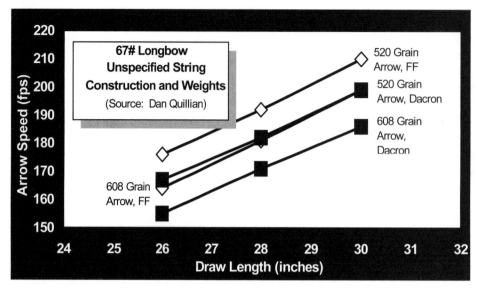

67# Longbow Unspecified String Construction and Weights (Source: Dan Quillian)

520 Grain Arrow, FF

520 Grain Arrow, Dacron

608 Grain Arrow, Dacron

608 Grain Arrow, FF

FAST FLIGHT VS. DACRON. Fast Flight strings will improve the shooting performance of any traditional bow. They're particularly effective on longbows. These test results are typical.

formance. But there's a second factor to consider: Noise. Fast Flight's low stretch, when combined with a recurve's greater limb vibrations and distortion during a shot, often makes it noisier than dacron. In contrast, Fast Flight is usually quieter on longbows since their stiffer limbs don't distort as much during a shot.

Flemish or Endless Loop?

Two types of string construction are popular on today's stickbows: *Flemish Twist* and *Endless-Loop*. Flemish strings are more historical and are also stronger since they have twice as many fibers surrounding the bow tip. But since they are held together by twisting, they require more string material, especially at the tips, which makes them heavier than endless-loop strings. This can cut a bow's performance by several feet-per-second.

On the positive side, heavy twisting distributes tension better among individual string fibers and eliminates high-stress spots that can cause string breakage. Extra-heavy twisting on the ends keeps individual fibers from sticking out and cutting into the bow. This is a minor issue for dacron, which can easily stretch to redistribute forces, but it's critical for Fast Flight which doesn't stretch as much.

Practical Decisions

Bowstring choices will always involve some tradeoffs. Thin strings are lighter and improve shooting performance but break more easily and are harder on a bow. Thicker strings are stronger and more durable but are more sluggish. Endless-loop strings are lighter and perform better but are weaker at the tips where breakage normally occurs.

If you're a longbow shooter, I recommend using Fast Flight. Its higher performance and lower noise with longbows makes it an ideal choice in almost any situation. On any Fast Flight string, stay with Flemish Twist ends to lower the possibility of bow tip damage (especially important for thinner recurve limbs).

Fast Flight may be noisier than dacron on some recurves. If you're hunting very large, slow moving animals, such as moose, you might opt for hard hitting Fast Flight. On spooky whitetails, where penetration isn't a big consideration, you might use dacron to minimize spooking a buck when you shoot. If you're looking for maximum performance at any price, then a light-weight, endless-loop, Fast Flight string is the answer.

Most hunters take a middle-of-the-road approach. For a 60# bow, this means staying with 16- to 20-strand Fast Flight or 14- to 18-strand dacron strings. Choose one that fits your nock properly don't worry about minor performance variations.

Before trying any string that didn't come with a bow, check with the manufacturer to see if using one will invalidate its warranty. Also, replace strings often to avoid breakage.

STRING WEIGHT VS. CONSTRUCTION. Arrow speed is affected by the weight and stretch of your bowstring.

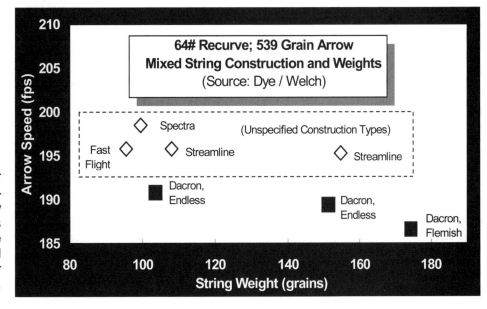

18. A Primitive Bow Primer

Among a small but growing group of bowhunters, primitive gear is "where it's at." Some of these folks are lured by the heightened sense of hunting challenge. Others enjoy the chance to step back in history a few hundred or a few thousand years and experience archery's rich heritage first hand. For most people, it's a bit of both.

Primitive archery isn't likely to take the world by storm, but it can be a fascinating complement to any bowhunter's normal archery pursuits.

What's Primitive?

Many traditional bowhunters like to romantically think of their bows as primitive when they're not. The general form and use of modern recurves and longbows may be reminiscent of earlier bows, but all of them have design features and performance enhancing materials that make them thoroughly modern. Fiberglass laminations, center-shot sight windows, integral arrow rests and some other features have only been in vogue for less than fifty years.

So what is a primitive bow? Among purists, it's a historical replica made using the design, materials, tools, and construction techniques of some bygone era. Others use modern power tools but hold rigidly to the ideal that the bow's materials should be histori-

PRIMITIVE BOWS. Primitive bows will never take the bowhunting world by storm, but they form a fascinating complement to the mainstream bowhunting pursuits of an increasing number of hunter-adventurers.

cally accurate. "Animal or plant products only," they'll say while boiling hide scrapings into a pot of sticky glue or pounding and twisting sinew into a bowstring. Among most primitive practitioners, it simply means using wooden bows and wooden arrows that are roughly comparable to those used by old-time archers. Dacron bowstrings, epoxy glues, and a bit of design latitude are minor and perfectly acceptable substitutions.

Primitive Bow Classification

Modern fiberglass bows are all constructed similarly and are usually classified simply as longbows or recurves. In contrast, primitive bows are referred to by a bewildering and often conflicting set of terms. Construction-wise, they're either *stave bows* or *board bows*. Stave bows are scraped and carved out of tree limbs or trunks that are split longitudinally into one-quarter or one-eighth sections (the "staves"). The back (tension side) of these bows must be carefully reduced to a single growth ring to avoid breakage. Because of this, stave-bow limbs often have undulating or twisting profiles. An exceptionally gnarled or twisted specimen is called a *character bow* or a *snake bow*.

Board bows are made from commercial lumber. Since the growth rings are usually violated in the milling process, following them accurately isn't possible and this increases the chance of breakage. On the positive side, if the growth rings are not followed, the bows can be cut to more even profiles using a band saw. This makes them easier to construct and tiller.

A *laminated bow,* in primitive parlance, is one that's constructed from multiple layers of different woods. This is done for appearance as well as to improve

(Photo courtesy of Mike Schlegel)

DO PRIMITIVE BOWS WORK? Idaho hunter Mike Schlegel certainly thinks so. Mike used a 64# Osage-Orange selfbow and 700-grain ash arrow to down this Shiras Moose. The arrow completely penetrated the bull and stuck in the ground. It went just 40-yards before piling up.

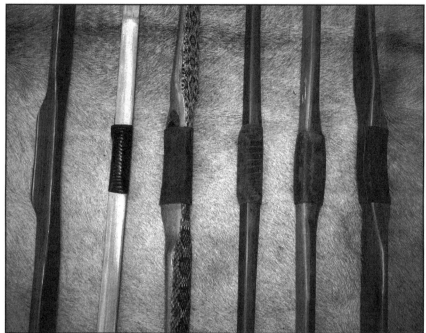

A PRIMITIVE BOW SAMPLER: From left: hickory-backed red cedar (one of Saxton Pope's favorite combinations), bamboo-backed hickory, sinew-backed osage with snakeskin covering, lemonwood, pacific yew, and unbacked osage. The two osage bows and the yew bow are made from tree staves. The others are made from commercial lumber.

shooting performance by using the best wood for the job. One fine example of this is a design sold by Jay St. Charles of Pacific Yew Longbows in Seattle. Jay uses a thin hickory backing for strength in the tension fibers, a lightweight core of yew, and a belly (compression side) lamination of osage-orange. In addition to being a top performer, the bow has a striking beauty. *Composite bows* (sometimes called *compound bows* in the old literature) are typically constructed from diverse materials such as bone, whale baleen, wood, or sinew.

Any of these bows may be backed for additional strength or durability. An all-wood stave bow, without backing, is called a *selfwood bow* or a *selfbow.* Common backings for *backed bows* include sinew, rawhide, hickory, or bamboo. The first two of these are often used to strengthen the uneven contours of stave bows; the last two are very popular for cross-grain board bows. Heavy backings like bamboo add to the structural stiffness and draw weight of the bow while thin ones, like rawhide, are used simply to keep tension fibers from raising up in the wood.

In terms of design, primitive bows are often classified as *D-bows* or *handle bows*. A D-bow bends in the handle and looks like the letter "D" when strung and viewed from the side. The term may also refer to a bow with a flat or slightly concave back and a severely rounded belly (the limb cross-section looks like a "D"). A *handle bow* is one with a pronounced, non-bending wood buildup in the handle region.

Primitive bows are also classified as longbows, flatbows, or recurves, but with slightly different meanings than we're used to. The generic term *longbow* usually refers to any longer than average, generally straight-ended bow with narrow limbs. In Europe, the term refers to an historical Old English-style, all-wood, bend-in-the-handle bow with horn nocks, concave belly and back surfaces, and a limb thickness that's at least three-quarters of its width at any point.

In contrast, *flatbows* have straight or semi-straight ends and a generally rectangular limb cross-section that's significantly wider than its thickness. Some Native American flatbows were up to four-inches wide. Two- to three-inches was typical. Primitive *recurves* usually have semi-rigid, non-working recurves on the ends. Some anthropologists also refer to heavily reflexed flatbows as recurves.

Modern Use

To someone who's never been exposed to primitive bows and arrows, they may seem simplistic and ineffective. Yet, our primitive ancestors made their living with them for over ten-thousand years. If used within their limitations, they're every bit as effective as modern bows. All-wood bows tested using shooting machines can produce nock-splitting accuracy at 30-yards and greater. They do take some getting used to—most notably due to their lack of a center-cut sight window—but they're capable of killing an animal just as effectively as any modern bow.

In terms of raw performance, they can be just as fast and hard-hitting, pound-for-pound, as modern recurves or longbows. But this is a rare specimen made by a highly skilled craftsman from an excellent piece of wood. A good rule of thumb is to expect a ten- to fifteen-percent reduction in speed over fiberglass bows for equivalent bow style and arrow weights.

For a unique bowhunting experience, consider trying a primitive bow sometime.

19. Become a Two-Bow Hunter?

As we've seen in the last few chapters, both compounds and stick bows have their own particular advantages. The choice is usually viewed as an either/or decision when it's not. A growing number of bowhunters use both.

Combo Platter

Industry statistics indicate that traditional archery is the fastest growing segment of the sport. What's fueling this growth? Mostly, it's people who are looking for a little more fun and diversity in their archery activities. An interesting but little known statistic is that about 70% of traditional archers also shoot compounds. Stated in another way: Many modern archers are also traditional archers.

They do their "serious" hunting with compounds but use recurves and longbows for off-season stump shooting, small game hunting, 3-D tournaments, or flinging flu-flus at cow pies.

COMPOUND OR STICK BOW?
Compounds are generally superior in the technical categories while recurves and longbows win in the non-technical categories. Many hunters use both according to the situation, or just for a little shooting fun and diversion.

Selection Criteria	Compounds	Recurves & Longbows
Energy Storage	✓	
Draw Weight	✓	
Shooting Forgiveness	✓	
Ease of Aiming	✓	
Ease of Learning	✓	
Ease of Use Once Mastered		✓
Mass Weight		✓
Ease of Transport		✓
Noise		✓
Shooting Versatility		✓
Field Handling		✓
Mechanical Reliability		✓
Archery Tradition		✓

Or, they hunt seriously with both by choosing the right tool for the occasion. If they're stalking whitetails in close cover, they might use a quick-pointing recurve. For longer range shooting on open-country animals such as caribou or antelope, they might use a compound.

Join the Crowd

There's no law saying that you can't become an equal opportunity archer. If all you've ever shot is a compound, try a recurve or longbow to learn a little about old time archery and your ancestors who practiced it. Most people who've done it say that it has expanded their overall understanding and enjoyment of the sport.

A Better Hunting Machine?

If most people like longbows and recurves for their sense of history, or just because they're fun, others actually consider them to be superior hunting implements. Mike Palmer is one example. Palmer has spent a lifetime in bowhunting. He's a former national champion archer and compound bow sales rep who, by some estimates, has taken more Pope & Young sized whitetails than any hunter in his home state of Texas. In his words:

"You have to understand that I don't shoot recurves for their aesthetics. I shoot them because they're better hunting machines for me. I can shoot three-inch groups at 70-yards on the target range with a compound. I can't do that with a recurve, but I can take a recurve and kill a deer much easier with it.

"I like to explain it this way: If I'm trying to shoot an apple off your head, I'll want a compound. I'll know you aren't going to move, I'll know the exact distance, I'll have all the time I need to make the shot.

"But if I'm trying to *kill* you, I'll want my recurve. You're going to be moving around trying to avoid me, I won't know how far you are, and I'll probably to have to shoot quickly when I get the chance. I'll have a much better chance with the recurve."

Trophy whitetail gurus Gene Wensel, Barry Wensel, Roger Rothaar, and elk/mule deer expert Larry Jones, are other examples of hunters who favor stickbows for their quick in-the-field effectiveness.

(Photo courtesy of Mike Palmer.)

Mike Palmer and a trophy Texas buck that gave him just a fleeting instant for a shot. He credits this success to his recurve's accurate, quick shooting capability.

20. Choosing a Bow Weight

The argument over bow weight is a common one. Depending on who you talk to, you need a 35-pound or a 45-pound or a 55-pound bow for deer; and a 55-pound, 65-pound, or a 75-pound bow for elk or moose. There are both heavy-bow and light-bow proponents who believe passionately in their positions.

And each may be right based on their own experiences. Any reasonable weight of hunting bow will do the job if used skillfully and within its limitations. Most Native Americans used bows that pulled 40- to 50-pounds and they did very well with them. Every year, there are elk taken with 45-pound recurves.

Yet, the simple fact remains that you'll rarely get into trouble by being over-bowed, while being under-bowed can cause problems.

Accuracy Is Paramount

Problems with light bows arise from less than perfect hits. An arrow shot from a 40-pound bow may stop cold on a deer's rib where a 60-pound bow will likely drive the arrow through it and into the vitals. The accepted rule is to shoot the heaviest bow that you can *handle accurately*. Implicit in this, but not always stated, is that the bow and arrow must be properly tuned to insure maximum accuracy and penetration. The lighter the bow, the more important tuning becomes. These two requirements are the first considerations for any bowhunter.

Most people can't accurately shoot the heaviest bow they can pull. A good rule-of-thumb is to pick one that's a bit lighter—one that you can pull without consciously thinking about it. Maximum-pull bows are also harder to bring to full draw in cold weather or when buck fever rears its ugly head. "My muscles turned to Jello," one guy told me recently. "Try as I might, I just couldn't pull the bow to full draw. I finally had to just let [the deer] walk

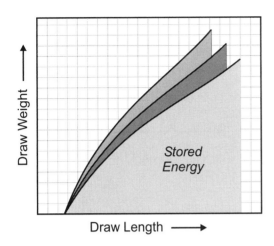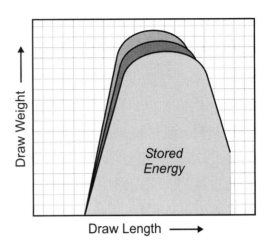

THINK "ENERGY." Draw weight doesn't determine how effective a bow is. The combination of bow weight *and* draw length does. In this figure, the three recurves on the left all have the same energy and the three compounds on the right all have the same energy, even though they each have different peak weights. Choose a bow based on its ability to store and deliver energy, not on its draw weight alone.

away." If you fall into this category, then choose a lighter bow.

At the other extreme are those folks who are so full of adrenaline that they can easily pull heavier bows when hunting. If you can handle a heavier than normal bow in the heat of battle, then don't handicap yourself with a light one.

Think Energy, Not Weight

Beyond these considerations, the argument over bow weight is often a silly one. Bow weight doesn't determine its effectiveness. The combination of bow weight *and* draw length does. Draw a 50-pound bow 30-inches and it may store the same energy as a 60-pound bow pulled 27-inches.

Find your *maximum, comfortable* draw length and then choose a bow weight that gives you the launch energy that you need for different game animals.

Compound Shooters

I see more and more compound shooters these days using bows that they can't pull without pointing them at the sky to gain muscle leverage. Not only is this an extremely dangerous method on the practice range or at 3-D shoots (many tournaments outlaw the practice), but the added movement can easily spoil a hunting opportunity.

Draw Length (inches)	Weight at Indicated Draw Length (pounds)			
	50	55	60	65
25	39	43	46	50
26	41	45	49	53
27	44	48	52	57
28	46	51	55	60
29	48	53	58	63
30	51	56	61	66

STORED ENERGY VS. BOW WEIGHT. The values in this table represent stored energy (in foot-pounds) for a typical recurve. Note the near-identical energy (shaded cells) for different combinations of bow weight and draw length. The numbers would be different for compounds but the general trend would be the same.

Use a bow that you can draw comfortably while pointing the arrow at the target.

Traditional Shooters

Compound shooters will probably have a consistent draw length with any weight bow. Traditional shooters may find that their comfortable draw length changes with different bow weights. You may be able to comfortably pull a 55-pound bow to 30-inches, a 60-pound bow to 29-inches, and a 65-pound bow to 27-inches. This is because your shoulder muscles compress more with heavier weights and your mind tells you to get rid of the string sooner due to the discomfort. In your quest to shoot the heaviest possible weight, you may actually end up with a lower performing setup.

Find the best performing combination of draw weight and draw length by measuring launch energies for each one. You may be able to choose a lower weight bow, shoot it more accurately, and still have a top performer.

Compound shooters who move to traditional equipment frequently make the mistake of over-bowing themselves. They assume that if they were shooting a 70-pound compound, they should be able to shoot a 70-recurve. They overlook the fact that they were only holding 15- or 25-pounds at full draw with the compound but are holding the full 70-pounds back with the recurve. They may shoot accurately for awhile but could develop a bad case of target panic over time due to the added strain and discomfort.

A better approach would be to start with a bow that's 15- or 20-pounds less than the compound bow weight that you're used to and build up to heavier weights slowly over time.

Arrow Weight Revisited

Factor arrow weight into your bow weight decision. For equal downrange penetration, choose a little heavier bow if you shoot light arrows. If you shoot heavy arrows, you can choose a lower bow weight that you can pull easier and shoot more accurately.

Determining Bow Performance

Measure your arrow's weight on an archery grain scale and then shoot several shots through a chronograph to get an average arrow speed (most pro shops will have both items). Calculate energy as follows:

Launch Energy (foot-pounds) = Arrow Weight (grains) x Arrow Speed (fps) x Arrow Speed (fps) / 450,240

Example: 500-grains x 225-fps x 225-fps / 450,240 = 56 foot-pounds of launch energy.

At 40-yards, figure about 16% of lost energy for a typical 400-grain arrow, about 13% for a 500-grain arrow, and about 11% for a 600-grain arrow.

Momentum is also an important arrow performance factor. Calculate momentum as follows:

Launch Momentum (grain- seconds) = Arrow Weight (grains) x Arrow Speed (fps) / 32.2

Example: 500-grains x 225-fps / 32.2 = 3,494 grain-seconds of launch momentum.

At 40-yards, figure about 9% of lost momentum for a typical 400-grain arrow, about 7% for a 500-grain arrow, and about 6% for a 600-grain arrow.

21. Static Design Efficiency

Most people naturally equate a bow's performance to its dynamic properties—how hard or fast it shoots an arrow. This is only part of the picture. Other than arrow weight, the thing that affects a bow's dynamic performance more than anything else is its static design efficiency. This is determined by the energy that it stores.

Energy Explained

Pull a bowstring with one-pound of force and it will move some distance. Since energy is measured in units of force and distance (most commonly in foot-pounds in the U.S.), this will describe how much energy it took to move the string. Add another pound and the string will move some more. Add the energy that it took to the first number and you'll know how much total energy it took to move the string to this second position.

Keep doing this and when you reach full draw, you will have created a force-draw curve. The area under the curve will be the total energy that the bow stores.

What It Tells You

The more energy that a bow stores, the harder and faster it will shoot an arrow. Traditional bows store the least amount of energy for a particular peak-weight and draw length. Eccentric-wheel compounds store more than stick bows; soft cam bows store more than wheel-bows; and radical cam bows store the most.

A good measure of a bow's static design efficiency is to take the total energy that it stores and divide by the bow's peak weight. Using industry averages for a 60-pound bow pulled 30-inches, traditionally-styled longbows will store about 0.9 foot-pounds of energy per pound of weight, recurves will store about 1.0 foot-pounds per pound; and compounds (all types combined) will store about 1.25 foot-pounds per pound.

Compounds

When choosing a new bow for performance alone, get a good technical report on it (Norb Mullaney's are the best that I've seen) and look first at its energy storage efficiency. This will be its most telling performance factor. Next, look at its *hysteresis* losses. As used in archery, this term refers to the amount of energy that is lost due to friction between the bow's moving parts (cams and axles, cable guide and slider, etc.) as the bow is drawn and let down without shooting.

The greater the hysteresis losses, the more lost performance since this energy isn't available to more the arrow down range. All compounds will have some hysteresis losses. On well designed models, these will be a few percent of the stored energy. On poorly designed bows, hysteresis losses can be 15% or greater.

Recurves & Longbows

Recurves and longbows have negligible hysteresis since they don't have any moving parts that rub against each another. Using a published test report again, choose one that builds up force fairly rapidly as you draw it and then levels off near your draw length.

Do this by drawing a line from the start of the force-draw curve (zero force) to the point where it's tangent to the force-draw curve. The curve should be flattest at this point and adjacent to either side of it. This is called the *sweet-spot* and a bow with a generous sweet-spot is said to be "smooth pulling."

A bow with a relatively steep force-draw slope at your

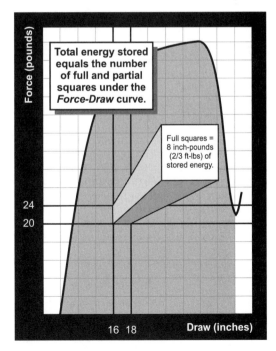

Total energy stored equals the number of full and partial squares under the *Force-Draw* curve.

Full squares = 8 inch-pounds (2/3 ft-lbs) of stored energy.

Force (pounds)

24

20

16 18

Draw (inches)

DETERMINING STORED ENERGY. The energy that a bow stores is equal to the area under its force-draw curve. In this example, each full square represents 8 inch-pounds (2/3 foot-pounds) of energy. Add up the full and partial squares to determine the bow's total stored energy.

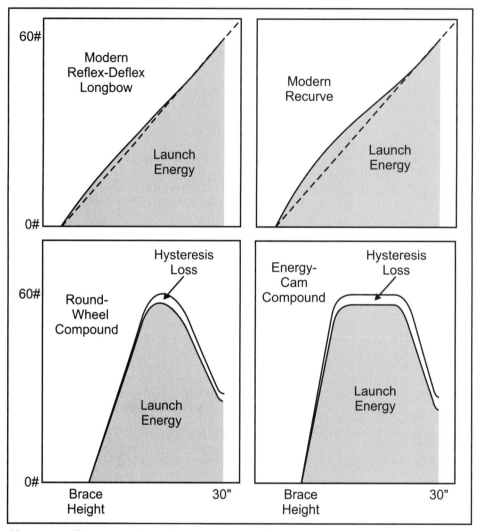

HYSTERESIS EXPLAINED. A bow's static design efficiency is determined by the amount of energy that it stores, minus the energy that it loses due to friction between moving parts when it's released—its hysteresis losses. All compounds have some hysteresis losses while recurves and longbows have almost none (there's a small amount of internal material friction) since they have no moving parts.

draw length is said to *stack*. If you pull 28-inches, you should choose a bow that shows little stacking from about 27- to 29-inches. While some people prefer a bow that stacks slightly, most will find non-stacking bows easier, more accurate, and more enjoyable to shoot. There are several reasons for this. First, the draw weight on a smooth pulling bow feels lighter, even if it's

For a Typical …	Stored Energy (foot-pounds, 60# @ 30")	Stored Energy Per Pound of Peak Weight (foot-pounds)
Longbow	54	0.90
Recurve	60	1.00
Compound (all types combined)	75	1.25

STATIC DESIGN EFFICIENCIES. Static design efficiency varies by bow type. These values are typical.

the same as on a bow that stacks, and this will keep you from tensing up on the release. Second, a bow that stacks adds or subtracts slightly more energy to the arrow than a non-stacking bow if you miss your normal draw length slightly. This will affect vertical accuracy at longer distances. Third, most bows will shoot best at their sweet-spot.

Also look for a bow that stores high energy per pound of weight at your draw length. If you're comparing two bows that were measured with different brace heights, then you'll have to account for this when comparing the areas under their force-draw curves.

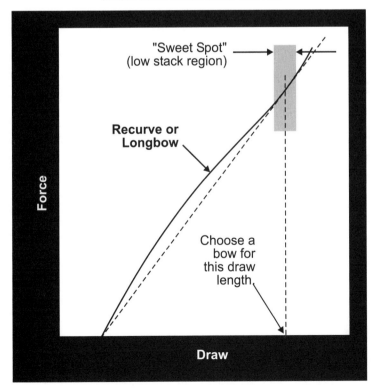

SWEET SPOT. Recurves and longbows generally have the highest static design efficiency (and are the most enjoyable to shoot) when pulled to their "sweet spot." This point is determined by the bow's limb profile and length.

22. Dynamic Shooting Efficiency

A bow's dynamic shooting efficiency is affected by a variety of factors. Here are a few to consider when choosing a new bow or deciding on the best setup for one that you already have.

Rating Speed

Two bows that store the same amount of energy and have identical hysteresis losses may not shoot an arrow the same way. The reason is that it takes energy to move the bow's limbs, cams, cable harness, string, *and* the arrow. Heavier components use more energy during a shot and this leaves less energy to propel the arrow.

If the components on two compounds weigh the same, but are located at different distances from the handle, more or less energy is also needed to move them. If a longbow has heavier tips than another, more energy will be needed to move them. Strings that have silencers, brush buttons, or peep-sights will shoot slower than bows without them. The principle is similar to swinging a hammer when holding it by its handle versus swinging it while holding the head.

When choosing a bow for its performance properties, start by looking at its *rating speeds*. This is an industry-adopted number that's used to compare two bows on an apples-to-apples basis. It's the speed at which a 60-pound bow will shoot 540-grain arrow (nine-grains per pound of peak weight) and a 360-grain arrow (six-grains per pound) when drawn 30-inches.

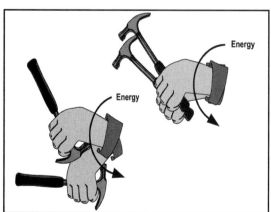

WEIGHT PLACEMENT. Just as it's easier to swing a hammer by its head than by its handle, fixed energy bows that have more weight located farther from their handles will have a lower dynamic shooting efficiency. Mount your accessories as near to the handle as possible.

Arrow
Weight
Important

Rating speed is a good value to look at for average conditions; but if you favor different arrow weights than those used for testing, it doesn't tell the whole story. Some bows will shoot lighter arrows better than other bows; and some bows will shoot heavier arrows better. Factor this into your decision.

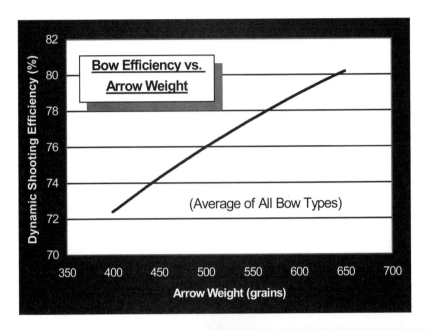

EFFECTS OF ARROW WEIGHT. Dynamic shooting efficiency goes up with heavier arrows (above) while launch speed goes up with lighter arrows (right). This is true for all types of bows.

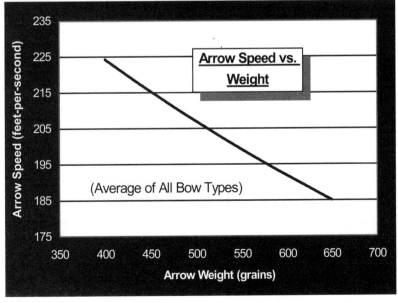

23. Maximizing Bow Performance

Before moving on to non-bow topics, let's summarize some of the key points presented in this and the previous section. Too many times, a bow and arrow's shooting performance is viewed as something that you purchase with it, or something that you're stuck with. Actually, the choices that you make can greatly affect your equipment's performance.

A Balancing Act

Rather than raw speed alone, a good hunting bow should have several important characteristics. Foremost among them, it should be stable and accurate under field conditions. This means that it shouldn't be sensitive to sloppy form that we can all have in high stress situations, or when shooting from awkward positions. It doesn't make any difference how fast or hard hitting a bow if you miss that once in a lifetime shot. The first task, then, is to find the bow that you shoot best—under *field conditions*.

Second, the arrow should have enough punch to do the job when it finds the mark. This means that it should have enough energy to handle problem hits such as spine and shoulder blade hits. On chest hits, it should have enough penetration to drive the arrow all the way through the body and out the other side in the majority of cases. This will give you the best possible blood trail to follow. To ensure this, choose the heaviest weight bow that you can handle *accurately*.

Third, a good hunting bow should be quiet so that it doesn't overly disturb an animal when you shoot at it. Often, that split second in a deer's delayed reaction time between a noisy bow and a quiet bow will spell the difference between success and failure.

A Few Tricks

Once you've picked a bow that meets these needs, there are a few simple things that you can do to maximize its hunting performance. Always re-tune

Improving Penetration (Recurve Example)

Change Made	Launch Speed (fps)	Launch Energy (foot-pounds)	Energy Increase	Launch Momentum (grain-seconds)	Momentum Increase
Recurve with an 8-inch brace height, 18-strand dacron string, shot with a 500-grain arrow	176	34	---	2,733	---
Replace dacron string with 14-strand Fast Flight string	182	37	+7%	2,826	+3%
Change from a 500-grain to a 600-grain arrow	169	38	+11%	3,149	+15%
Lower brace height from 8-inches to 7-inches	172	39	+15%	3,205	+17%
Increase draw length from 28-inches to 29-inches	181	44	+27%	3,373	+23%

Improving Trajectory (Compound Example)

Change Made	Launch Speed (fps)	Launch Energy (foot-pounds)	Max. Arrow Rise Above Line-of-Sight (anchor 3" below eye)		
			20-yards	30-yards	40-yards
Compound with a 10-inch brace height, shot with a 540-grain arrow	216	56	2.5	7.5	14.8
Change from a 540-grain to a 400-grain arrow	240	51	1.8	5.8	11.7
Reduce let-off weight from 80% to 65%	244	53	1.8	5.6	11.3
Increase draw length from 30-inches to 31-inches	249	55	1.6	5.3	10.8
Lower brace height from 10-inches to 9-inches	252	56	1.5	5.1	10.5

REAL WORLD EXAMPLES. These tables show examples of how two archers were able to increase the performance of their bows by using the tricks in this chapter. The numbers in both tables would change for different bows but the general improvements shown would be the same.

your equipment for optimum arrow flight and accuracy after making any change.

Increase Your Draw Length. This will increase the energy that a bow stores by lengthening its power stroke. Some compounds have cam adjustments that will let you do this.

Change Arrow Weights. If you want more speed and a flatter trajectory, shoot lighter arrows. If you want more penetration, shoot heavier arrows.

Reduce Let-off Weight (compounds). Reducing let-off weight will allow the bow to store more energy.

Lower Your Brace Height (traditional bows). Many bows will shoot as well (or better) with lower brace heights than the manufacturer's recommendations. Lowering the brace height will increase the bow's power stroke and the energy that it stores.

Change Strings (traditional bows). If your bow has a dacron string, replace it with a Fast Flight or other new-generation high performance string. Check with the manufacturer first if you're worried about invalidating the bow's warranty.

Change Fletching. Switch to large, helical (and/or four-fletch) feathers. This will slow the arrow down by a very small amount—a foot-per-second or two at 60-yards—but will straighten out the archer's paradox more quickly and ensure that the arrow hits with its full punch behind its point at close distances. It will have minimal effect on trajectory at longer distances.

Change Balance-Point. Avoid doing anything to an arrow that will move its balance point too far to the rear. Always use a balance-point that's *at least* 10% forward-of-center. If necessary, switch from vanes to feathers, or use a heavier broadhead to move the balance point forward. For a small cost in trajectory, the arrow will be more accurate.

Change Broadheads. If maximum penetration or broadhead reliability is your goal, use a sturdy, cut-on-impact head. If these considerations aren't important, any well made head will do.

Use Silencers. Adding silencers—to the bow or to the string—will slow most bows down by a few feet per second but this is a small price to pay for quieter shots. This simple addition will often pay rich dividends when shooting at high strung animals like whitetails.

Part 3. The Technique

Over and above their hunting skills, most top bowhunters are excellent shots. They don't miss very often. This demands sound shooting technique.

Glance down the practice line at a 3-D shoot sometime and you'll see all manner of shooting styles. Some individuals with very unorthodox styles drop their shots into the bull's-eye with unerring accuracy. Others with seeming textbook form spray their arrows all over the target. What causes these differences?

In this section, we'll look at a few key form elements that are crucial to good shooting. We'll also take a look at the many ways to aim an arrow, from sights to out-of-mind, Zen-like subliminal shooting.

These are complex subjects that many entire books have been devoted to. For this reason, I've only addressed a few key points that you may want to consider. In all examples, I'm assuming that you're a right-handed shooter.

24. An Age-Old Subject

For as long as men have pulled a bent stick and set a feathered shaft into the wind, shooting technique has been a hot topic of discussion—and the source of a few good laughs. Before getting down to the nitty-gritty of improving your own shooting, consider some of Roger Ascram's comments regarding his fellow 16th century archers:

Some shooteth [with] head forward, as if to bite the mark; another winketh with one eye and looketh with the other; another bleareth out his tongue; another biteth his lips.

Another maketh a wrenching with his back, as though a man pinched him behind. Another cowerth down and lay out his buttocks. Another setteth forward his left leg, and draweth back as though he pulled at a rope.

Some men draw too far, some too short, some too slowly, some too quickly; some hold over-long, some let go over-soon. Some [point] their shaft [at] the ground, and fetcheth him upward; another pointeth up toward the sky, and so bringeth him downwards.

Another I saw which, at every shot, after the loose, lifted up his right leg so far that he was ever in jeopardy of falling. Some stamp forward, and some leap backward.

Now afterward, when the shaft is gone, some men [cry] after the shaft, and speaking words scarce honest for such an honest pastime. Some will take their bow and writhe and wrench it...when [the arrow] flyeth wide... Some will give two or three strides forward, dancing and hopping after his shaft, as long as it flyeth... Another runneth forward, when he feareth to be short, heaving after his arms, as though he would help his shaft to fly. One lifteth up his heal, and so holdeth his foot still, as long as his shaft flyeth.

Now imagine an archer that is clean without all these faults, and I am sure every man would be delighted to see him shoot.

As this narrative shows, things have changed little in the ensuing 450-years. Now, let's see what you can do to avoid some of these time-worn pitfalls.

25. Sights or No-Sights?

Whether you use sights or not right now is probably determined by whether you shoot modern or traditional equipment. Part of this is due to practicality. Sights are easier to use on fast, high let-off compounds than on recurves and longbows. But part of your decision is probably also due to arbitrary convention. Most compound shooters use them and most traditional shooters avoid them—simply because that's the way most people do it.

It's important to recognize that compounds can be shot well without sights and that stick bows can be shot well with them. In the pre-compound era, many archers used sights; and in the early days following the compound's introduction, many archers shot without them. Some people from both camps continue to do the same thing today. Choose the aiming style that best fits *your* needs.

Conscious or Instinctive?

It's common to call any archer who shoots without sights an "instinctive archer." This isn't necessarily true. While the use of mechanical sight-pins requires conscious aiming, there are a number of conscious ways to aim without a sight.

True instinctive archers don't aim consciously. They just look at the spot they want

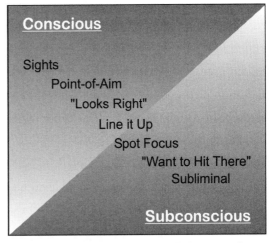

Conscious

Sights
    Point-of-Aim
        "Looks Right"
            Line it Up
                Spot Focus
                    "Want to Hit There"
                        Subliminal

Subconscious

CONSCIOUS OR SUBCONSCIOUS? A bow can be aimed effectively using conscious, mechanically precise means, subconsciously based on "feel," or with a combination of the two. The conscious methods are easiest to learn. The subconscious methods can be more effective under fast-paced field conditions but take more time to master.

to hit, pull back and release, and the arrow goes there. It's more appropriate, then, to divide the various aiming methods into *conscious* or *instinctive* categories. For ease of discussion below, I'll refer to all conscious aiming methods as sight-shooting.

Making the Choice

The main advantage that sights have is that they provide a physical reminder to *aim* at a precise point. This is particularly advantageous during the stress of a hunting shot. A sight is also a comforting old friend for people who have transitioned directly from firearms to archery and have no previous experience shooting without one.

There are also several disadvantages to using sights. They require you to measure or guess shooting distance fairly closely, they require you to shoot with the bow held vertically, they demand very precise shooting mechanics, and they may be slow to use in a field situation. Yet, they can be extremely accurate when all of the right conditions are present.

Instinctive shooting has two main advantages over sights. First, an instinctive shooter's mind judges shooting range and other shooting variables without conscious thought. Although good shooting mechanics are still important, his mind can also recognize minor variances in shooting form and automatically compensate for them when he releases.

The second advantage is that instinctive shooting is usually faster than sight shooting. Most instinctive archers can draw and release an arrow in a fraction of the time that sights shooters can.

The main disadvantages of instinctive shooting are that it's not as precise as sight shooting at known distances and it's more difficult to master.

Accuracy Compared

The net result of the above factors is that a good sight shooter will usually outperform a good instinctive shooter under favorable conditions—known distance, flat ground, no wind, perfect setup, ample shooting time, and so forth—while a good instinctive shooter often has the edge in less than perfect situations. The sight shooter is consciously overriding subliminal corrections that his mind may want to make for extraneous factors while the instinctive shooter is relying on them to help.

Data from studies bear this out. They show that few traditional shooters

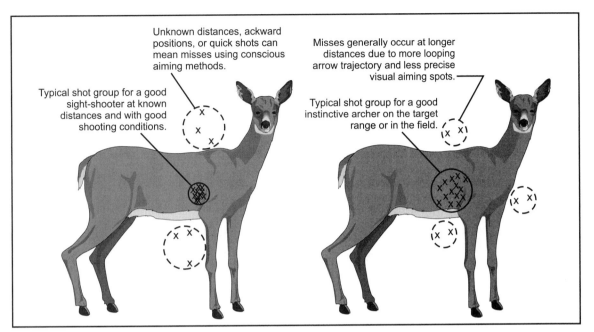

Unknown distances, ackward positions, or quick shots can mean misses using conscious aiming methods.

Typical shot group for a good sight-shooter at known distances and with good shooting conditions.

Misses generally occur at longer distances due to more looping arrow trajectory and less precise visual aiming spots.

Typical shot group for a good instinctive archer on the target range or in the field.

ACCURACY COMPARED. Sights or other conscious aiming methods are designed to produce pin-point accuracy under favorable shooting conditions. Quick point-and-shoot instinctive aiming is designed to produce kill-zone sized groups at close range under imperfect conditions. Although both are highly effective once mastered, each has its own good and bad points.

can match a sight-shooter's precision on the target range. But in many fast paced hunting situations, or at unknown shooting distances, instinctive shooters often perform better. We'll look at some of these data later in the book. The key word here is "good" instinctive shooter. Since sight-shooting is easier to learn, a mediocre sight shooter may greatly outperform a mediocre instinctive shooter under any condition.

In short: Instinctive shooting isn't designed to produce nock-splitting accuracy on the practice range. It's designed to produce *kill-zone sized groups* on animals. It's an effective method of aiming but takes a lot of practice effort to master.

In the next three chapters, we'll look at some ways to aim both with and without sights. Then, in *Part 5, The Tricks*, we'll look at some ways to elimination the main disadvantage of sight-shooting—having to know the precise range.

26. Aiming With Sights

Most of today's compound shooters use sights. Some traditional shooters also use them. Here are a few things to consider.

Compounds

Compound shooters who have no trouble holding a sight steady should choose small sight pins and mount them well in front of the bow to increase their sighting resolution. Choose a model with an ample pin-guard that protects fragile pins from damage or interfering brush and branches as you walk. Other than this, just pick a model that you like.

Recurves & Longbows

Mechanical sights can be highly effective on stick bows. In the 1950s and 1960s many hunters used and touted them. Jack Howard, a well known California bowyer and trophy-elk expert from this period, is one notable example. Jack says that the first time he tried one his accuracy immediately improved. He made the change and never looked back.

Sights used on stick bows are more difficult to master than with compounds so don't expect instant success. There are several reasons for this. First, a stick bow's lower mass weight, coupled with its higher holding weight, makes it more difficult to hold steady for extended aiming. Second, form is more difficult to master with a stick bow and the bow itself is more sensitive to variations in form.

Still, traditional shooters who are having trouble mastering any of the non-sight aiming methods might want to try sights. For best results, choose a model having large sight beads and mount the sight-bar on the side of the bow closest to you to make them appear even larger. This will lower your sighting resolution slightly but will make it easier to hold the pins steady by reducing pin "dancing" that often comes with holding heavy stick bows at full draw.

Aiming Technique

Aiming with sights is pretty straight forward. Just put the pin on the spot you want to hit and release. Most experts allow the pin to settle down on the spot and release while it's not moving. This insures that all of their muscles are correctly aligned at release and that they help to push the bow toward the target when the arrow is launched.

Poor sight shooters often "pass-shoot" as the pin swings briefly across the target. This makes it hard to release at the right time since there's a momentary lag between the visual image and the mental instruction to release. This may cause the bow to move off line during that critical instant between release and launch.

One helpful technique to get a sight-pin to settle down is to put it as near the aiming spot as possible and then *consciously* alter the muscle tension in your bow arm and release arm by flexing your muscles back and forth slightly. Find the tension where the sight settles down and then release smoothly while the pin stays there.

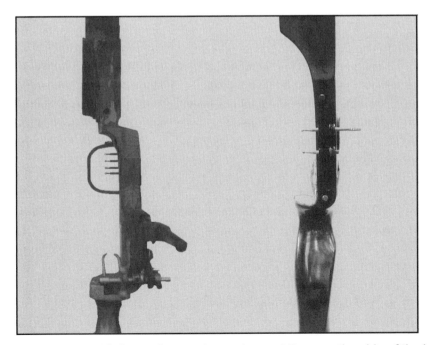

SIGHT OPTIONS. Compound shooters who have no trouble holding a sight steady should choose smaller sight pins and mount them on the far side of the bow for maximum sighting resolution. Recurve and longbow shooters should choose larger pins and mount them on the side of the bow closest to you to help eliminate pin "dancing" (shown here is an old Merrill *Heart Shot* sight with the bottom pin cut off to prevent snagging on brush).

27. Aiming Without Sights

There are a number of ways to aim without sights and they can be used with any type of bow. Some are as conscious and mechanically precise as sight-shooting while others are as "out-of-mind" as simply pulling the bowstring back and releasing it. Here are a few methods to consider.

Point-of-Aim

Prior to the advent of mechanical sights, one of the most popular aiming methods was *point-of-aim*. This is a sight-shooting technique without the aid of sight-pins.

Instead of visually aligning a sight-pin on the spot you want to hit, visually align the point of your arrow on some appropriate spot above or below the target. The distance between the arrow point and the impact point is called a *gap*. The range where you can put the point on a spot and hit it is called the *point-on* range (or *point-blank* range in some of the older literature).

For most close-range bowhunting shots, this technique works best when using a high anchor point and a three-fingers-under, *Apache* style release. Just sight down the arrow shaft like it's the barrel of a shotgun. One friend of mine shoots this way and is able to put the tip of his broadhead on the bottom line of a deer's chest at 20-yards. At 30-yards, he moves the point to the top of the deer's lungs. He hasn't missed a shot in years.

Marks & Blemishes

If your bow has distinctive marks, blemishes, scratches, dings, or other features on the riser, they might make effective sighing aids, either as primary aiming devices or as a reality-check when aiming instinctively.

"Looks Right"

With the point-of-aim method, you consciously picked a gap for a known range. With the *looks-right* method, you still look at the gap between your arrow point and the target, but you don't consciously adjust it. You just hold

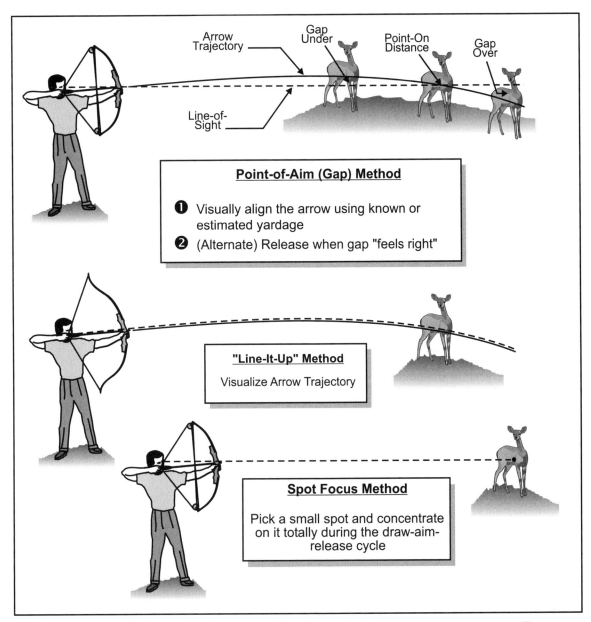

"NON-SIGHT" AIMING METHODS. There are a variety of ways to aim an arrow without sights. These are some of the most popular. All have their place depending on the situation and the shooter's experience.

Gap Method
(Put the point over
or under according
to distance)

"Line It Up"
(Visualize the
trajectory)

**High Anchor
"Apache-Style"**
(Like looking down
the barrel of a
shotgun)

Spot-Focus
(Let everything but
the spot blur into the
background)

A BIRD'S-EYE VIEW. Shown here are a shooter's viewpoint of several common non-sight aiming techniques.

the bow at full draw until the gap looks right based on your previous experience. A variation to this technique is to consciously line up the arrow point vertically with the aiming spot (for example, a deer's foreleg) but set the gap through feel. The vertical alignment will give you the security of sight or point-of-aim shooting and the instinctively set gap will eliminate the need for range estimation.

"Line It Up"

In 1957, Texan Bill Negley became the first modern hunter to take an elephant with a recurve. In his film recounting the event, Negley explained that "a line seemed to form in front of me…" What he was doing was visualizing the trajectory of the arrow. Like Fred Bear, who also used this technique, Bill visualized the arrow's arc and then pulled it back along the perceived trajectory line.

Spot Focus

This is the most popular instinctive aiming technique used today. Lying roughly midway between the conscious and subconscious shooting methods, it requires concentration but uses your subconscious mind to do most of the difficult work. Once mastered, it's highly effective. Experts at this technique can shoot aspirin or coins out of the air with uncanny ease.

With this method, your mind is programmed to recognize the different subconscious sight pictures required for bull's-eye shots at different distances, wind speeds and directions, terrain, lighting and other factors. Simply pick a small, distinctive spot on the target and focus all of your concentration on it throughout the entire draw-and-release process. Let everything else fade from conscious view.

A good aiming spot on whitetails is the 90-degree angle formed by the

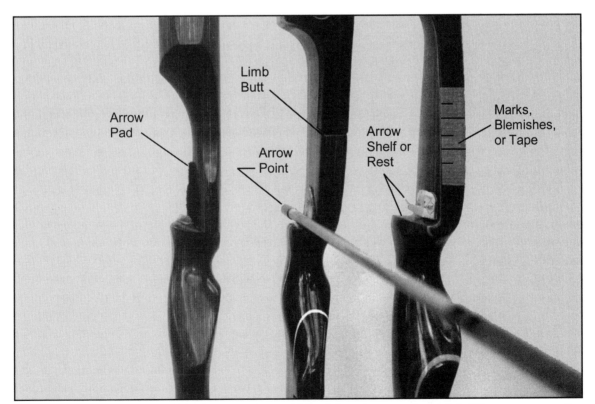

NON-SIGHT "SIGHTS." Parts of the bow, marks and blemishes, tape, or the point of the arrow can all be used as effective, makeshift sighting aids.

bottom of an animal's chest and the back of its foreleg. Since whitetails tend to drop when they hear the string, this should put your arrow solidly in the heart-lung region at 20-yards and under. If you don't expect an animal to move, concentrate on the shadow formed by the fold of skin behind its front shoulder muscle. Some folks like to imagine a silver dollar or other object covering the spot they want to hit and then try to center it with their arrow. Experiment a bit with different mental cues that work for you.

The Howard Hill Method

Howard Hill used a hybrid aiming method where he shot his first arrow instinctively, but noted the position of his arrow point in his secondary vision. He called this *split-vision aiming*. If his first shot missed, he just moved the arrow point up or down by the appropriate amount and was usually deadly on his next arrow.

"Want to Hit There"

This is a slight variation on the spot-focusing technique above. It starts, as before, by consciously picking the specific spot where you want the arrow to hit. Once that's done, however, your concentration should shift from the spot to the key shooting thought: "I want the arrow to hit there." Your mind will remember where your intended aiming point is so long as you "programmed" it properly first.

To understand this distinction, it's important to recognize that your mind is capable of producing precise results if given precise instructions. When you concentrate on a spot while aiming, you're programming it to perform an *action* ("look at the spot"). It's possible to do this and still have the arrow pointed off-line at release.

When you train yourself to hold until everything necessary for the arrow to hit in a certain spot is right, you're programming your mind to achieve a *result* ("hit there"). This distinction is difficult to describe in words. Try it yourself to see what I'm talking about. One word of caution: You must really *believe* that the arrow will hit the bull's-eye or it won't happen.

Subliminal Shooting

Finally, we come to the highest form of instinctive shooting—subliminal. The following chapter gives this rich subject the space it deserves.

28. Subliminal Shooting

"The eleven-pointer was calmly browsing below me and would have made an easy target except for three does that were all nervously looking around. Suddenly, all four deer turned and looked away from me. But before I could consciously do anything, I saw a sudden flash of color and then bright orange fletching buried tightly behind the buck's shoulder as he vaulted over a low bush. My first thought was that some other hunter had slipped in unseen and shot my buck. But when I looked down, there was no arrow on my string. I'd made a perfect shot on the buck but didn't even remember it."

This story, related to me by an excited bowhunting friend a few years ago, illustrates what is perhaps the ultimate way to "aim" a hunting arrow. There's no distance to estimate, no pin to choose, no spot to pick, and no mental cues or checklists to remember. You don't see the bow or the arrow and you might be only vaguely aware of your physical surroundings. You just pull the string back and release it and the arrow hits the bull's-eye.

Like Throwing a Baseball

Consider this situation: You're playing third base on your weekend softball team and the batter hits a slow dribbling ball at you. You charge forward, grab it with your free hand as you run, pivot, and throw without straightening up. The first baseman stretches and catches the ball an instant before the runner tags first. Cheers erupt from the small gallery of spectators.

Now lets analyze what happened. Your every action during this brief moment was purely reflexive. You didn't say to yourself: "Let's see, the first baseman is standing twenty-two yards away and I can throw a softball at seventy-eight feet-per-second, so I should loft it at the guy in the stands with the blue shirt." You didn't pick an aiming spot on the first baseman's glove. You just did it. Your subconscious mind took-in and analyzed all of the necessary information in an instant and knew precisely what to do on its own.

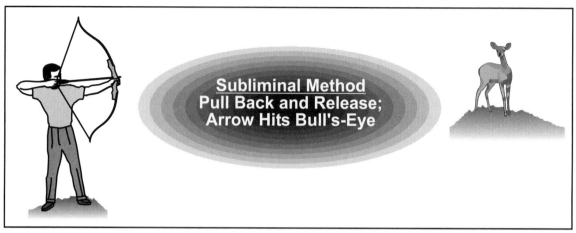

SUB*LIM*I*NAL: *1: inadequate to produce a sensation or a perception; 2: existing or functioning outside the area of conscious awareness.*

The "Solution"

A buddy of mine is a former Vietnam fighter pilot and a superb instinctive bow shot. He explains subliminal shooting with this flying analogy: "The control stick in a modern fighter has to be an extension of your arm and respond instantly to your thoughts. You don't steer the plane, you wish for it to move and it does! If you think, you're dead. When you're shooting at a target with today's sophisticated electronic weaponry, you acquire the target and lock-in on it. When the weapon system reaches a *solution*, it fires the missile itself. In bowhunting, I know where I want to hit before I pull the bow. When my mind reaches a subconscious solution, the bow shoots itself."

An Ancient Method

In his book, *Zen In the Art of Archery*, author Eugen Herrigel is told by his Zen Master to draw the bow and then wait for the shot to happen. After a poor effort, the Master cautions him to "Stop thinking about the shot. That way it is bound to fail. The string must fall from your fingers at the right time as naturally as a plum falls from a tree when it is ready."

"How can the shot be loosed if I do not do it?" Herrigel asks. "It shoots," the Master's replies. "The proper way to aim is not to aim at all. *It* knows nothing of a target that is set up at a definite distance from the archer. It only knows of the goal which cannot be aimed at technically."

Finally, after many months of effort, Herrigel starts to get the hang of it. "Do you now understand what I mean by *It Shoots, It Hits*?" the Master asks. "I'm afraid," Harrigel responds, "that I don't understand anything more at all. Is it I who draws the bow or the bow that draws me into the highest state of tension? Do I hit the goal or is it the goal that hits me? Bow, arrow, goal, ego all melt into one another so that I can no longer separate them. And even the need to separate has gone. For as soon as I take the bow and shoot, everything is so clear and straightforward and so ridiculously simple..."

"Now at last," the Master broke in, "the bowstring has cut right through you!"

Modern Explanations

All of this may sound overly mystical, but it has a rational basis in modern science. According to Maurie Pressman, of the Association for the Advancement of Sports Potential, the dominant side of the brain is given to the details of language and thinking, to building up pieces of a puzzle into a larger picture. The non-dominant side of the brain is given more to feelings, to the perception of whole movements, to whole pictures rather than component parts.

Therefore, when we inhibit or suspend the functions of the dominant side of the brain, the non-dominant side is freed and takes over. This reduces tension, unbinds the muscles, and allows performance to flow more easily. "We believe," says Pressman, "that insofar as we suspend the functions of the left side of the brain, we release the personality to flow into its activity, unselfconsciously, and with smoother coordination."

In other words, when the conscious side of your brain is overly engaged, the unconscious side loses its influence and the result is frustration, anxiety, or inadequate physical movement.

Practical Decisions

Whatever analogies you choose, subliminal shooting clearly works. Don't immediately abandon conscious, mechanical aiming if this works for you. But *do* spend some time trying to purge all conscious thoughts from your mind while shooting. You'll know when you've arrived at true, unconscious subliminal shooting when the shot just "happens."

29. Instinctive Shooting Made Easy

Most people who have never shot a bow instinctively are intrigued with the idea but are reluctant to try it, thinking that it's too difficult. This concern is usually unfounded. Let's look at a few ways to make the journey easier.

Trust It

In order to shoot well instinctively, you have to first trust that it works. This is a difficult step for people who have used rifles and bows with sights all of their lives. The first thing to realize is that, as humans, we have evolved though millions of years with an extraordinary, innate hand-eye coordination. Early cave men who were able to feed themselves with spears, atlatls, and bows survived and passed these skills along to their descendents. Those who lacked them quickly died out.

You have within you all of the requisite talent for shooting a bow instinctively. Prove this to yourself with a simple experiment. Clasp your palms together so that there's a small gap between them and hold your hands at your waist. Now, look at a doorknob and—without consciously "aiming"—quickly bring your hands up and center the knob in the hole. Repeat the experiment on a cabinet hinge, faucet, and other objects around you.

You did this naturally and without thought, and each "target" centered itself nicely within your aiming window. This is all of the skill that you need for instinctive shooting—if you'll trust yourself to make it happen.

Point Your Finger

Try a second experiment. Instead of clasping your hands together, just stand with your arms at your side and then bring your left arm up and point at the doorknob, hinge, or faucet. Same result. You were able to point at them without conscious thought.

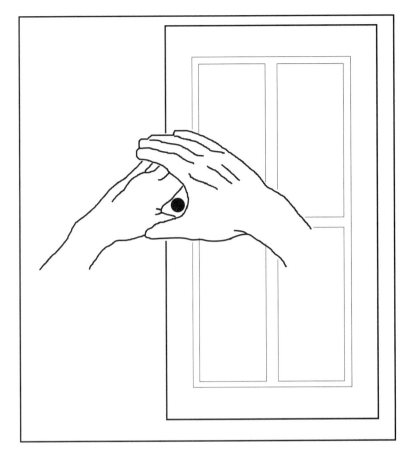

ALL THE INSTINCTIVE SHOOTING SKILL THAT YOU NEED. Place your hands together and hang them in front of you. Now bring them up quickly and center them on some object as shown here.

This is all of the hand-eye coordination that you need to shoot a bow instinctively—and you were born with it.

Now grab a bow and extend your left finger while you grip it. Bring it up while drawing it back and point your finger at the bull's-eye on a target. Release the arrow and it will probably land very close to it. After a time, you can stop pointing your finger and just look at the spot you want to hit; or think of your arrow as a finger and point it where you want it to go.

Takes Practice

Don't expect perfect results the first few tries. Because your arrow lies above your hand when shooting, it isn't exactly like pointing your finger. But with a little practice, your shot groups should start to move to the center of the target.

Start by shooting from very close to the target—five-yards is about right—and practice until you can place all of your arrows in a small circle.

Then move back to eight-yards and practice until you can shoot well there. Continue moving back a little at a time, and over a few weeks time, you'll be shooting well from normal bowhunting distances. In the process, your mind will memorize the different subconscious sight pictures necessary at different distances and will replicate them without conscious thought.

Starting from close range is vitally important in building your confidence and belief in this aiming system. Most beginners make the mistake of shooting from too far too soon and develop a lack of confidence that may follow them for years.

Ease the Transition

If all of this is too radical a change for you, then consider using one of the conscious, intermediate aiming methods mentioned in the chapter on *Aiming Without Sights*. Learn to use your arrow as a sight first. Then transition from the more conscious methods to the less conscious methods, but keep true instinctive shooting as your ultimate goal.

Trouble Shooting

Instinctive shooting isn't for experts only. I've had the pleasure of teaching two Native American Inuits to shoot this way, and each of them was able to hit ptarmigan-sized dirt clots at 30-yards within an hour. (The extraordinary hand-eye coordination of these race of people probably had a lot to do with this, so don't expect the same results.)

In contrast to most beginners, who don't pressure themselves for immediate results, many experienced shooters often develop problems by trying to force things to happen too soon. They might also develop target panic over time. If you start off shooting well, but develop problems over time, these are the likely causes.

"Aim" Doesn't Exist

According to one instinctive-shooting guru: "*Aim* is not in the vocabulary of an instinctive archer. You don't aim the arrow. You pick a spot, pull the string to a comfortable spot, and release."

This is one of the simplest and most satisfying experiences that you can have as a archer, whether you shoot a compound or a stick bow. It works. Give it a try.

30. "Release-Aids"

Tab, glove, strap, rope, ledge, thumb ring, mechanical. Unless you pull back and release an arrow with your bare fingers (ouch!), you're using a release-aid of some type. For most people, the choice isn't whether or not to use one—it's choosing the best one for them. Before exploring this question, let's take a look at the venerable history of release-aids.

The Early Years

It probably didn't take early archers very long to realize that if they protected their fingers with a piece of hide, it kept them from getting sore and also improved their shooting. By the middle ages, archers in Europe were routinely using *finger stalls,* made by sewing leather into tapered cylinders.

During this same period, Asian archers were using thumb rings made of metal, bone, or stone for their unique locking-thumb release style. Some anthropologists even point to early Roman bronze artifacts that strongly resemble 1970 vintage ledge-type releases and suggest their use for this purpose.

Tabs & Gloves

Medieval archers who didn't like finger stalls often used tabs that were remarkably similar to the ones we use today. The first modern shooting glove was patented by Fred Bear six decades ago. Frustrated by fin-

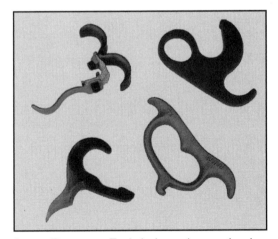

LEDGE RELEASES. Early ledge releases (and many bloody noses and split lips from pre-fires) were the norm in the early 1970s. The flexible-strap release in the upper left was the forerunner to all movable trigger releases used today.

ger stalls that were easily lost and easily pulled off during a shot, Fred came up with a simple solution. Simply sew the stalls to a piece of leather and wrap the upper end around your wrist to keep everything in place. Until the early 1970s, the vast majority of all archers in this country used either a tab or a glove of some type.

Ledges, Ropes, & Straps

A small number of archers were using rigid, one-piece ledge releases in the early to mid-1900s. These differed from later ledge releases in that the archer triggered the shot by rapidly and consciously twisting or rotating the release to disengage it from the string. This created a crisper release than possible with fingers and reduced the accuracy-robbing "S-curve" oscillation as the string slipped sideways from a shooter's fingers and then recovered while pushing the arrow.

Other people used braided rope or straps of leather. They attached them to their wrists, wrapped the two protruding ends around the bowstring in opposing directions, and clamped them tightly together with their thumb and forefinger. Like ledges, they took conscious effort to release but did send the string off more in-line with the arrow. Complex manufactured variations of both rope and strap designs were popular thirty-years ago.

Then, about 1970, some innovative individual had an idea that would alter archery forever. Rather than rapidly twisting a ledge release at the last moment, what if he just applied slow, increasing pressure until the ledge rotated enough to suddenly release the string as a surprise? This is what you do with a rifle, after all. You don't jerk the trigger which ruins accuracy. You slowly squeeze it until the shot takes you by surprise. A very simple design modification was all that was needed. Dozens of variations soon followed.

Ledge releases of all types posed one significant problem: the dreaded pre-fire. In order to be effective, the ledge had to lightly hold the string while drawing so that only minor force was needed to rotate and release it. All too often, the things went off while pulling the bow. This sent the arrow wildly downrange and the shooter's hand into his face with sizable force. Bloody noses and split lips became common tournament sights.

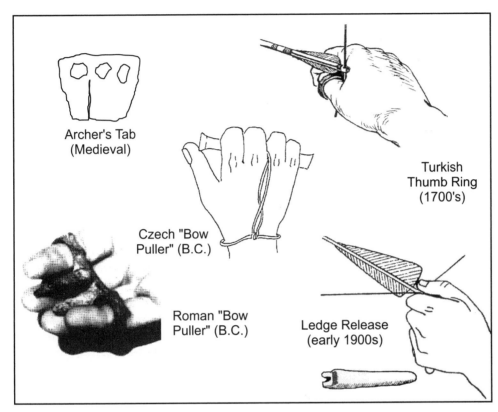

Archer's Tab
(Medieval)

Czech "Bow
Puller" (B.C.)

Roman "Bow
Puller" (B.C.)

Turkish
Thumb Ring
(1700's)

Ledge Release
(early 1900s)

EARLY RELEASE AIDS. Release aids, even mechanical ones, have have a long history.

Trigger Releases

Mechanical trigger-releases are usually thought of as thoroughly modern, but they date back to at least the late 1800s. One patent application from this period shows a very modern looking release with a spring loaded movable trigger. There is little evidence that people actually used it, however.

A forerunner to modern trigger releases appeared around 1973. This innovative hybrid had three pieces. The forward part consisted of a rigid ledge and trigger tab. The rear part was a two-finger holding grip. These were connected with a short piece of canvas strap. This allowed the ledge and trigger to rotate independently of the handle and virtually eliminated pre-fires.

Once the idea of the movable triggers gained acceptance (this took several years of debate), the door was opened to the many designs that we have today. We'll look at these in the next chapter.

31. Mechanical Releases

Modern mechanical release-aids (or *releases*) are an extremely accurate way to release an arrow and the majority of today's compound shooters use them. Though more rare, some recurve and longbow shooters also use them due to disability, incurable target panic, or other reasons.

Advantages

Efficiency and Repeatability—Releases set the string on its course more crisply and impart a few extra feet per second of speed to the arrow. They also release the string more consistently without the pronounced S-curve string oscillation present with finger shooting. With fingers, it's common to see five- or ten-fps differences in arrow speed between crisp and poor releases. With releases, differences are insignificant.

Surprise Shot—Used correctly, releases create surprise shots that don't give a shooter the chance to ruin a shot by anticipating it.

MODERN RELEASES. Modern releases fall into three categories: Handheld, wrist, and palm models. They may attach to the string using a caliper, a movable pin or ledge, or a rope. They may be actuated using a trigger, button, or the archer's back tension. All will work, though each style has its own set of advantages and disadvantages.

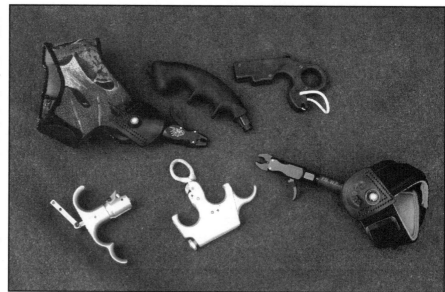

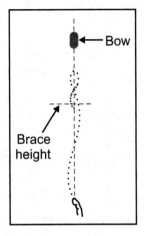

Bow

Brace
height

S-Curve Oscillation. Mechanical releases eliminate the S-curve string oscillation caused by finger-shooting. This puts more of the bow's energy behind the arrow

Target Panic—Releases can eliminate or significantly reduce the symptoms of target panic for people who are cursed with this ailment. There's little chance of a premature release with one since they take conscious effort to trigger. Finger shooters with target panic may be unable to get the arrow to full draw before releasing. Releases that are triggered using back tension rather then a release button or trigger will help eliminate the accuracy robbing fault of punching the trigger for people with target panic.

Choosing a Release

Releases fall into three basic categories. Handheld models can be carried in a side pocket, allowing full use of your hands, and then quickly retrieved for a shot. Wrist-strap models are usually kept on for most hunting activities but can be quickly rotated to the back of your hand when not in use, and quickly repositioned for a shot. Models that strap into place around your hand and into your palm reduce the free use of your release hand but allow you to hold the bow's weight with both your wrist and fingers. Many heavy bow shooters like this additional feature.

Releases also attach to the string in different ways. Some grip the string using a caliper, some have a rotating ledge or round bar that slides in front of the string, and some use a rope that wraps around the string. Some are released using your pinky finger, some with your thumb, and some using back tension.

All will work well and the choice is personal. Try several and choose the one that appeals to you. Avoid cheap models that can break and injure you or malfunction and cost you a shot.

Release Shooting Technique

Like expert rifle shooters, expert release shooters line up the sight with the target and slowly apply trigger pressure until the shot "happens." Poor shooters, or those with target panic, often punch the trigger when the sight suddenly lines up on the target. Avoid this bad habit for peak shooting performance.

32. Finger Shooting

As in the comparison between compounds and stick bows, finger shooting doesn't have the technical advantages of mechanical releases, but it has several non-technical advantages.

Quick Use—Fingers are generally quicker to use in the field than releases. It takes time to set a release on the string, draw, aim, and slowly squeeze a trigger before it goes off. During this time, the animal may have turned or your shot opportunity may have disappeared. Fingers can be quickly placed on a string (without looking), pulled, and released as the situation demands. Quick shots at deer that are passing between trees, or delayed shots when a deer looks at you at full draw, are both accomplished with equal ease.

Versatility—When shooting with fingers, there's no release to get in the way when you're doing other things with your hands. It's a snap to peer through your binoculars or get a call out of your pocket with a glove or tab on, and then quickly draw the string when you put them down. Your fingers are always there for instant use.

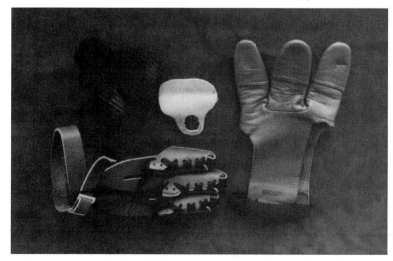

MODERN TABS AND GLOVES. Both tabs and gloves have pros that make the choice between them personal. The tab in the center is homemade from a single thickness of leather and lacks a center cut for shooting three-fingers-under.

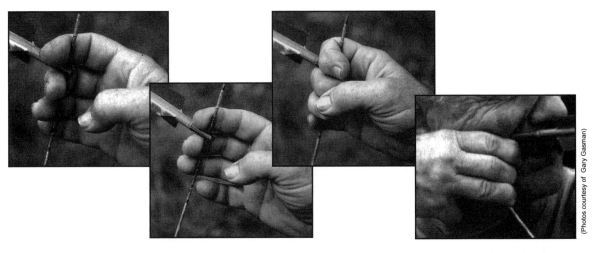

(Photos courtesy of Gary Gasman)

STRING GRIPPING METHODS. The most common way of gripping a bowstring is to place the string in your first finger joint (left). A *light-hook* (left-center) can give some archers a cleaner release while a *deep-hook* (right-center) can give archers with target panic a greater feeling of control over their release. Placing all three of your fingers under the nock (right) can eliminate accuracy-robbing finger pinch and aid in aiming for non-sight shooters. All will work but each may send the arrow to a different place so practicing with the method selected is essential.

You may have to put a release down or reposition on your wrist to do these things, then pick it up or re-reposition it before you can shoot.

Loss or Malfunction—Today's releases are more reliable than early designs but they can still break or malfunction occasionally. They can also be lost. Your fingers are always there with you, and aside from occasional stiffness on a cold day they'll always work properly. Lose or damage your tab or glove and you can still shoot your bow without them.

Tradition—Even though some archers used crude ledge or strap releases centuries ago, most did not. Fingers are clearly a more traditional way of shooting. Archers who include this as an important part of their bowhunting satisfaction usually shoot using their fingers.

Tab or Glove?

Tabs can be easily rotated to the back of your hand when not in use and quickly moved back into position for a shot. Gloves can get in the way of some activities but are always there for instant use.

Some gloves can form a permanent string groove across the fingertips through use. Some shooters like this feature and some don't. The string grooves on tabs are usually not as pronounced but the tab can twist on your finger and may require minor re-positioning before a shot. Some tab designs come with an insert that helps prevent compressing the nock between your trigger and index fingers while shooting. This is a handy feature for use with shorter bows that have severe string angles at full draw.

As with release-aid styles, a finger-shooter's choice between a glove and a tab is mostly personal. Try several makes and models of each before making a decision.

Finger Shooting Technique

The most common way of shooting with a glove or tab is to place the bowstring in the groove between the first and second digits of your fingers, draw and aim the bow, and then release. Good shooters release smoothly using minimal, or relaxed, finger tension. Poor ones often grip the string too tightly and jerk the string when they release.

If you have this problem, consider this mental trick: Rather than "releasing" the string, try just "relaxing" your fingers and letting the bow's weight pull the string from them naturally when it's ready. Or try a *light hook* by placing the string more forward on your fingers, nearer to your thumbnail. This will prevent you from "hanging up" on the string.

People who have target panic and tend to release the string prematurely might try the opposite. Grip the string using a *deep hook* by placing it in your second finger groove, nearer to your wrist. This will give you a greater feeling of control over the bow.

Light hook, *normal hook*, and *deep hook* string gripping styles will all work but each may send the arrow to a different place, so practice them before taking them to the field.

Releases and Fingers

If you're a compound shooter, there's one final reason to learn to shoot with your fingers. I see too many compound shooters these days who have never released an arrow with their fingers. Then they lose or damage their releases on a hunt, don't have a backup, and are dead in the water. If you use a release, spend some time learning to shoot your bow without one. That way, you'll always have a backup method with you.

33. Shooting Flaws

There's a saying among professional tour golfers: Your score isn't determined by the quality of your good shots—it's determined by the quality of your *bad* shots. All of them hit plenty of extraordinary shots. But they also hit some really bad ones that can quickly sabotage things. Eventual winners are able to control the damage through four-days of play. Losers can quickly kill their chances with a few errant efforts.

In contrast to amateurs, who like to spend their time practicing how to make good shots, pro golfers spend a lot of time developing swings that produce the least destructive results when they start "leaking oil." They want solid mechanics that keep them in the hunt when they get nervous or their swings start breaking down under pressure.

ELIMINATE SHOOTING FLAWS. Most shooting styles produce a combination of good and bad shots (above). Your first goal should not be to improve the quality of your good shots, but to improve the quality of your bad shots so that they are as close as possible to your good shots (right).

Think about this for a moment, for the same thing is true in archery. As bowhunters, we don't often have to shoot perfect bull's-eyes on animals. The kill zone is eight- to twelve-inches in diameter and any shot within this area is just as effective as the next.

We don't have to consistently hit in the center, but we *do* have to hit the kill zone.

Anything Will Work

What determines our ability to do this? For most people, it's the *number* and *severity* of shooting flaws in their form. Think of these as statistical probabilities. Flaws won't always produce poor shots and any shooting style will work some of the time. But the more flaws in your form, the greater your *chance* for a bad outcome on any particular try. Good bowhunters are usually able to place a killing shot with the occasional ragged release or short draw. Mediocre ones are not.

Shooting a bow is a complex athletic feat and everyone has their own particular shooting demons. Based on my association with many bowhunters over the years, though, I believe that a few key shooting flaws cause more missed shots than others.

The Goal

The next few chapters cover these key form elements. Keep one thought in mind when reading them. You goal isn't to improve your good shots. No matter what shooting style you now use, you likely get plenty of bull's-eyes. All shooting styles work sometimes.

Your goal is to improve the quality of your *bad shots* so that they are as close as possible to the quality of your good shots. This will demand a different way of thinking about things, and a different way of practicing.

34. Shot Setup

Competitive rifle shooters are taught to eliminate all unnecessary muscle tension that can throw off a well aimed shot between ignition and the instant that it takes for the bullet to leave the barrel. Archers don't have this luxury. It takes muscle tension to draw a bow and hold it steady prior to release. And when we release the string, our arms move due to the suddenly released tension. This recoil can dramatically affect the arrow during the roughly one-hundredth of a second that it remains on the string.

Shoulder Angle

A primary accuracy-robbing culprit for many folks is inconsistent shoulder angle. The graphic here shows the reason.

When we draw a bow, we pull the string to the side of our bow arm and chest. This requires two separate forces: one to hold the string back and one to hold our bow hand on line laterally. Inconsistent

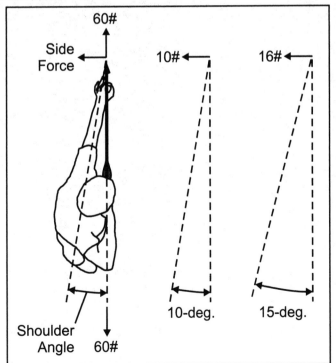

SHOULDER ANGLE AFFECTS ACCURACY. Wider shoulder angles require more side force to hold a bow on the target-line before release. This will cause the bow to recoil more to the side when released. Any shoulder angle is fine as long as it's consistent.

shoulder angle affects the resultant recoil of your bow arm when you release the string. The archer in the center has an angle of 10-degrees between his arrow and bow arm. To hold the handle on-line at full draw, he has to apply 10-pounds of side force. The archer on the right has a bow arm angle of 15-degrees and needs to apply 16-pounds of side force to hold the bow steady. It isn't hard to see why the second archer's arm will move more at release.

There's no magic formula here. The only criteria is that the angle formed by your shoulder and your arrow must be *consistent*. Find one that's natural (this will make it more easy to repeat over time), that let's you draw to the same length each time, and that let's the string consistently clear your arm and chest with hunting clothes. Beyond that, just work to ensure that you carefully repeat this angle each time you shoot.

Stance

Theoretically, any stance will work as long as it allows you to setup with a consistent shoulder angle. Most archers find this easiest to do by matching the angle of their feet with their shoulders. Get into this habit. Set your feet, check to see that your shoulder angle matches your feet, and then draw.

First and foremost, your stance should provide a stable *shooting platform*. Target archers, who shoot under carefully controlled conditions, often place their feet and shoulders in line with their arrow to minimize lateral holding force that can cause errant right and left shots. This requires the bowstring to pass close their arms.

Most bowhunters prefer a more open stance where one foot is placed outside the arrow's trajectory line. This rotates the bowstring away from their bow arm and any heavy clothing that might snag it. It also provides more shooting stability in uneven terrain or when they brace their body against cross winds.

Again, any stance will do. Just work on consistency. Practice shooting from awkward, twisted positions where you can't do this to see what effect it has on your shots.

Elbow Angle

Different elbow angles require different muscle tension and can cause the bow to recoil differently from shot to shot. Many people eliminate this variable by locking the elbow of their left arm throughout their draw. This pretty much restricts them to pointing the arrow at the target and holding it there while drawing and aiming. Others favor a slightly bent elbow at release. This absorbs some of the bow's jar and also lets them push-pull the bow to full draw from cramped shooting positions. Either is fine as long as it's repeated from shot to shot.

Shooting Medicine

If you shoot well with your present setup, then don't fool with it. If not, then consider making these changes:

❖ Heavy bow are harder to hold back and may require a more closed stance to bring the string closer to your arm. If you're having a hard time holding your bow hand steady, close your stance a little.

❖ If your bowstring occasionally slaps your arm guard or catches against your hunting clothing, open up your stance a bit. Just one muffed shot on a deer due to catching the string against a fat fold in your favorite hunting jacket is too many.

❖ If you have a right-left accuracy problem, or if the nock of your arrow occasionally hits your rest or handle riser and causes erratic arrow flight, close your stance to decrease the amount of lateral bow recoil and allow the arrow more time to clear it.

35. Drawing the Bow

There are two basic ways to draw a bow. One is to point the arrow toward the target and pull it back. The second is to start with the arrow point above or below the target and bring it on line while drawing.

The major advantage of the in-line draw method is that it requires minimal movement when drawing the string back. In addition, this movement is better hidden from a deer since it's camouflaged against your body.

When you start by pointing your arrow at the target, you are basically using two major muscle groups to draw the bow—one to push it towards the target and one to react its sideways pull (the effort to hold up the bow is negligible here). When you start your draw from a high or low position, a *third* group of muscles comes into play that can help stabilize the first two muscle groups.

To understand this, think of these different muscle groups as the legs of a stool. With some effort, you can make a two-legged stand up on the floor, but only for a moment. Since it's inherently unstable, it will soon topple over. Setting the three-legged stool requires no skill and it will stand up forever due to its inherently stable design.

The off-line drawing method requires more movement but has a compensating benefit. Rather than having to hold your un-drawn bow up for long periods of time while waiting for an animal to walk into position for a shot, you can leave it hanging comfortably at your side.

Both shooting methods will work well. But each may cause your arrows to hit in different spots due to different muscle tension, and the way they cause your bow to recoil when you release the string. Once you choose one, just be consistent.

(Photos courtesy of Gary Gassman/Gassman's Archery)

DRAWING STYLES. The in-line draw (top) requires less movement. The off-line draw (bottom) is easier on your muscles while waiting for an animal to move into position for a shot, and also helps to stabilize shooting muscles better for many shooters.

Having said that, it's important to mention that a surprising number of the best shooters throughout history have favored the off-line draw method. Howard Hill started with the arrow pointed at the ground, drew while bringing it up, and released when it lined up on the target. Fred Asbell, in his excellent video, also suggests this as the best method for instinctive archers. Japanese archers pointed their arrows horizontally down range during setup but held them well above their heads before bringing them down and releasing. Plains Indian buffalo hunters pointed their arrows toward the sky and then brought them down to shoot (probably to avoid interfering with their galloping ponies in this case).

I've used both methods extensively over the years. And both have worked well for me. But looking back, my most consistent results have come when I started with the bow at my side and brought it to full draw while raising it. Using a straight-armed, in-line method, I would shoot well for a time but my shots definitely wandered more from day-to-day or week-to-week.

Experiment with these two methods and see which one works best for you over time.

36. Dynamic Tension

Inconsistent muscle tension and shot follow-through have probably caused more missed shots than any other reason. This is more prevalent among traditional shooters who hold more weight back and have lighter mass-weight bows, but it can affect any archer. It's especially true for anyone fighting target panic.

Don't Fight Mother Nature

When you release an arrow, your bow should naturally recoil to the *left* (due to suddenly unleashed force) and *downward* (due to the mass-weight of the bow). Your release hand should naturally recoil rearward. Simple physics dictate these movements.

Poor shooters often fight these natural forces. They push their bows to the right of the arrow's flight line or have fly-away releases that leaves their hand to the right of their faces. Finger shooters might completely collapse at release and end with their hands nearer to the target than when they released.

A Simple Test

Just how important is proper dynamic tension during a shot? I've performed the following test several times over the years with the same results each time. I'll shoot a dozen shots while totally concentrating on aiming. Then I'll shoot another dozen shots while putting my *main* concentration into coming to a full and complete draw, pushing and pulling the bow and string with all of my might until it feels like I can't eke another millimeter of draw length out of it; and then releasing.

In every instance, I get crisper releases, more natural bow arm and release hand recoil, and tighter groups by concentrating on my dynamic tension. Good shooting mechanics will naturally send the arrow where it should go. But all of the aiming angst in the world won't produce a good shot if you don't release the arrow crisply and consistently using proper back tension.

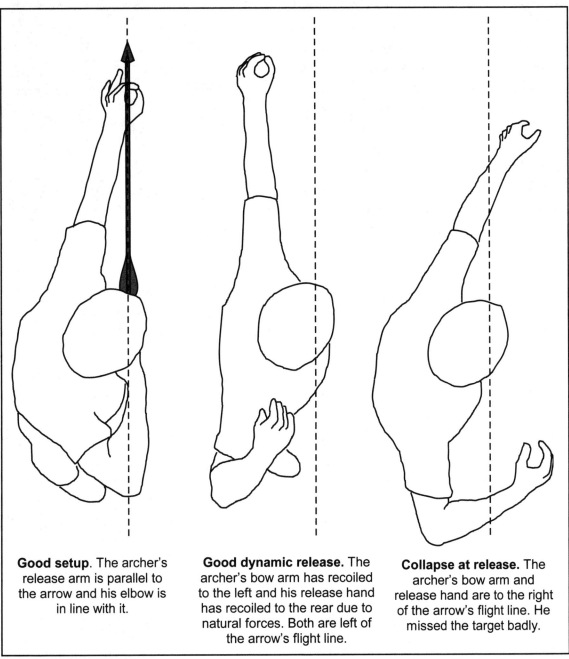

Good setup. The archer's release arm is parallel to the arrow and his elbow is in line with it.

Good dynamic release. The archer's bow arm has recoiled to the left and his release hand has recoiled to the rear due to natural forces. Both are left of the arrow's flight line.

Collapse at release. The archer's bow arm and release hand are to the right of the arrow's flight line. He missed the target badly.

LET NATURE TAKE ITS COURSE. Good dynamic form is largely a matter of physics. Fighting these physical forces can cause poor shots. These sketches were compiled from actual photographs of an archer shooting a heavy poundage, low let-off bow. Light poundage or high let-off bows won't react as much as shown here, but the natural movements at release should be the same.

Try this little test yourself and see what results you get. Then work to cultivate a crisp, dynamic release with a full, natural, follow-through.

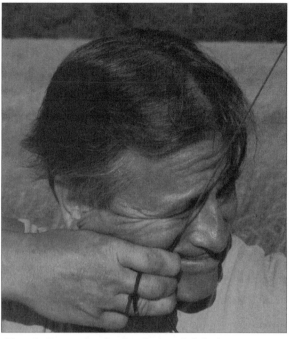

KEEP IT LIGHT. Anchoring in too tightly to your face—using either your fingers *or* a release—can cause you to reduce some of your holding force on the string and result in poor releases.

Finger Shooters

Many instinctive archers use a *pull-through* release. This works well with both compounds and stick bows. They draw back, touch their anchor point momentarily, and then release in one motion as they continue to pull back with their hand. Done correctly, their release hand never pauses until the arrow is gone.

Finger shooters who use sights should guard against anchoring in too tightly to their faces while aiming since this can cause them to reduce holding force and create release problems. Touch your anchor point lightly and concentrate on holding back the full weight of the bow until release, without pushing your hand into your face.

Release Shooters

Compound shooters who use sights and releases should use a peep-sight rather than relying on a precise anchor point as a "rear sight." It might help to anchor low, off of your face, to avoid the temptation of supporting some of the bow's weight by pushing your release hand tightly into your face. In addition to increasing your arrow's depth-of-kill (see Chapter 46), this will force you to hold the bow's entire weight with your arm and should improve your shooting consistency.

37. Pressure Point Control

There are many ways to grip a bow and pull the string back, each with their own pros and cons and their own devotees. The way in which you do this can dramatically affect your accuracy.

Gripping the Bow

The sketch on the next page was compiled from photos of a 3-pound recurve and illustrates three common gripping styles. Note the radically different limb distortions caused by different handle pressures. These effects won't be as severe for a compound or for any hunting-weight recurve or longbow, but grip pressure will still play a part in shooting accuracy.

Varying grip pressure from shot to shot can create two problems. It can change the dynamic limb tiller of a bow and cause the arrow to fly differently from it; and it can cause the bow to recoil from your hand differently when you release the string.

Choose a grip that's comfortable and then work to groove it. Strive to find one where the bow naturally and repeatedly settles into your hand without any hand tension (up-and-down or sideways) to hold it there. It's helpful here to let the bow recoil from your palm at release and catch it with your lightly encircled fingers.

This will provide instant feedback that you're not affecting the shot with faulty hand tension. Or, use an inexpensive bow-sling or finger-sling. After you get the hang of it, you can dispense with the sling for hunting.

Gripping the String

In you release the string with your fingers, inconsistent tension in each finger can also affect your accuracy. Find a way to grip the string precisely the same way each time you draw, without applying upward or downward string torque due to unbalanced finger pressures.

Some shooters find that a three-fingers-under release let's them place

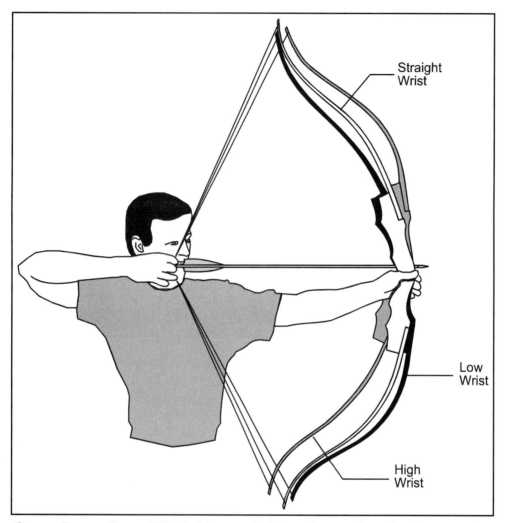

GRIP VS. DYNAMIC TILLER. This sketch, compiled from photos taken of a three-pound recurve, dramatically illustrates the effect that different grip pressures can have on a bow. Compounds and longbows (which have stiffer limbs) and any normal weight bow won't react as much as this, but varying grip pressure can still affect accuracy for any archer.

their fingers on the string more consistently and keeps them from pinching the arrow. Try this if you continue to have problems. Or, keep your split-fingered release but eliminate your ring or index fingers for a crisper release. Surprisingly heavy bows can be shot with two fingers.

38. Shooting Tempo

This last tip is strictly for shooters who aim instinctively. In contrast to the deliberate *draw-aim-hold-release* style of sight-shooters, the more dynamic *draw-release* style of most instinctive shooters demands more precise coordination and timing of movements.

Prove It

Try this test. First, draw and shoot an arrow normally. Next, draw your bow back and hold it for thirty seconds. Note how secondary muscles come into play as primary ones fatigue and start to give out. You might also find yourself gripping the string tighter and tighter in your effort to hold it back. Now release the arrow. Finally, after resting a few moments, snatch the string back to full draw as quickly as possible and release it. Note again how the muscles used, and the overall feel of the shot, just isn't the same as when drawing normally.

Now look at your shot pattern. Your three shots likely hit in very different spots. Normal everyday variances in tempo may not produce such dramatic results as these, but they can still affect shot placement.

This problem often rears its ugly head while hunting. When you practice on a stationary target, you tend to draw and release in a relaxed manner using a comfortable tempo. A live deer, though, often forces you to change your shot routine—speeding it up or slowing it down depending on the situation.

I believe that many misses which instinctive shooters blame on hunting nerves are really caused by tempo problems. The nerves cause a change in shooting tempo but the tempo change causes the actual miss.

A Two Step Solution

The solution is twofold: First, practice using a tempo that you'd find comfortable on a real deer; then, shoot at real deer using the same tempo that you've practiced.

If you normally draw on a real deer in a more deliberate manner than you do on an artificial one, then practice this. If you normally shoot a little quicker in the field, then practice *this*. Imagine that you're always shooting at a live deer, and find a tempo that's comfortable for you for most situations that you're likely to encounter.

Then, shoot at a real deer as if it was the McKenzie target you've been practicing on. Don't worry about the deer looking up and catching you in mid draw—he probably won't—or he'll just stand and look in your direction after you've already finished your draw.

When the shot presents itself, just use your normal tempo and take it. You'll be pleasantly surprised.

Part 4. The Tricks

Shooting at a deer on the target range is one thing. Shooting at a live animal in the woods is quite another.

Skilled bowhunters have a keen sense of how their arrow rises and falls as it moves downrange. They are able to shoot over or under intervening obstacles or through holes in the brush with unerring accuracy. They know how to compensate for imperfect range estimates so that they will still hit solidly in the boiler room. And they know how to gauge the effects of upward and downward shots, errant winds and breezes, deer movement, and other common field variables.

There's no substitute for experience here, but learning a few tricks of the trade can short circuit this learning process.

We'll look at a few of these tricks in this section.

39. Shoot Low for High Success

Most bowhunting misses are on the high side. Prove this to yourself by sitting down sometime and listing all the animals that you've shot at and missed over the years, or the ones that you hit higher or lower than intended. You'll probably find that most of your errors have been on the high side. There are many reasons for this. The top contenders are listed below.

Vitals are Low

A frequent reason for shooting high is aiming in the wrong place. In contrast to many 3-D deer targets which have "kill zones" horizontally centered on the body, the vital organs of a real deer lie in the lower part of its chest cavity. This means that you have to aim below the horizontal mid-line on a deer's body to get a center-lung hit. Shooting for the center of an animal's chest, rather than the *center of it's vitals*, causes a bias for high hits.

Low Light

Most hunters do their practicing under well lit conditions. Hunting shots are often taken early or late in the day, under poor light, or in the woods under a dark canopy of vegetation. Low light can cause a deer to appear farther away than it really is. The result can be a high shot.

Vegetation & Topography

If you practice guessing range on flat, relatively uncluttered terrain, intervening obstacles can alter these visual images. Deer that are standing behind vegetation can appear farther than they really are. Gullies and depressions have the same effect. A deer that's standing 30-yards away across an intervening chasm may look like its 40-yards away. Add in low light from the overhanging trees and he'll appear to be even farther.

Then there's the normal human tendency to add a little elevation to help clear obstructions. Instinctive shooters are particularly prone to this fault. One guy I know is a crack instinctive shot but managed to shoot over three deer one season because their legs were hidden by low brush.

Deer Movement	The most common reason for shooting high on nervous whitetails is movement after the animal hears the bowstring. The deer hears the shot, has time to drop down before the arrow gets there, and the shot flies high.

Shot Angle	High shots are the rule when shooting uphill, downhill, or from tree stands. The following two chapters will cover this special problem in more detail.

Range Estimation	In studies conducted under simulated hunting conditions, experienced bowhunters guessed ranges under 25-yards, where most deer are killed, to be five- to eight-percent farther than they really were. This can cause high shots.

Excitement	Finally, there's the unexplained human tendency to shoot high when excited or under stress. Ulysses Grant was noted for riding among his troops urging them to, "Shoot low boys, shoot for the knees..." Many modern infantry officers do the same thing today.

MOST SHOTS ARE HIGH. For a variety of reasons, most bowhunting shots are on the high side. One common tendency is to over-estimate distance under low light conditions (right).

Another is the unexplained human tendency to shoot high when excited, like when a big bull elk answers your bugle and suddenly appears from nowhere (left). There are others.

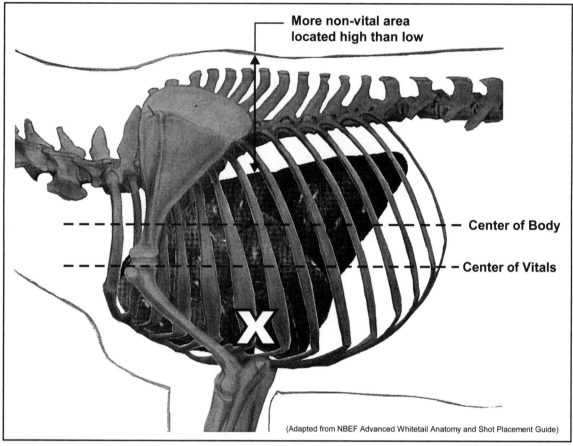

More non-vital area located high than low

Center of Body

Center of Vitals

X

(Adapted from NBEF Advanced Whitetail Anatomy and Shot Placement Guide)

SHOOT LOW. Aim at the X to avoid the pitfalls mentioned in this chapter. (Note that what appears to be heavy bone on the shoulder of a live animal is just muscle. The scapula actually lies well forward on the rib cage and won't deflect a well placed chest shot.)

Bowhunting guides routinely tell stories of excellent archers, both with and without sights, who overshoot elk by two- or three-feet at 20-yards when a bull comes in bugling and busting brush.

The Cure
It helps to always be aware of the many reasons why we shoot high when hunting and to practice under those conditions as much as possible. Beyond that, always remember this simple rule while in the field:

In more cases than not, the natural tendency for most people is to shoot high on game. So just aim a little bit lower next time to increase your odds.

40. Shooting From Tree Stands

When I was a teenager cutting my bowhunting teeth, a grizzled old-timer once told me to always aim low when shooting down because "the arrow will rise." He had the right idea but the wrong reason. Arrows don't rise when traveling downward; they just don't fall as much.

Here's what happens: When you shoot an arrow over level ground, it's launched at a slight upward angle relative your line-of-sight. Its arching flight path is caused by gravity pulling it back down to earth. When you shoot downward from a tree stand, the ground distance to the target is shorter than the arrow's flight distance and gravity acts on it for a shorter period of time so it doesn't pull it down as much. The result is that downward shots will always fly higher than equivalent-length shots over level ground.

Minimize Shooting Angle

The higher you place your stand, the more acute the shooting angle and the lower you have to aim. The worst case is when shooting from a high stand at close range. As you lower your stand, you can aim closer to the spot you want to hit since your arrow's trajectory is closer to what it would be at level ground.

Measure Distance Along The Ground

Measuring distance with a rangefinder can produce some whopping misses from high stands. A much better approach is to measure shot distances to different landmarks from ground level before climbing into your stand. Then shoot using these figures. Even if a deer walks between landmarks, and you have to guess-timate the actual distance, you'll still be better off than using the range finder.

An example: Suppose that a deer is standing 15-yards from your tree. If you measured its distance from a stand height of forty-feet, you'd get a reading of 20-yards and shoot a foot high with a mid-speed arrow. If you had

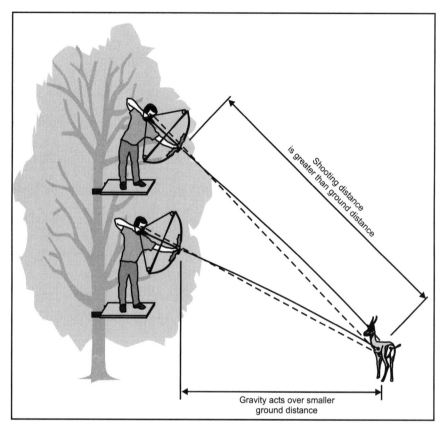

Shooting distance is greater than ground distance

Gravity acts over smaller ground distance

AIM LOWER THAN NORMAL WHEN SHOOTING FROM TREE STANDS. Whenever we shoot downward, the horizontal distance to the target is shortened and gravity has less time to act on the arrow. If your bow was sighted-in over level ground, this will cause the arrow to shoot high.

paced the distance to the bush he's standing next to, you'd shoot about three-inches high.

This is an extreme example, but you get the idea. Ground-paced distances are always better.

Arrow Speed Not Critical

If you pace off your shooting distances, arrow speed has little effect on trajectory for most close range tree stand shots. If you took a shot from a twenty-foot high stand at a deer standing 20-yards away (a common situation), a 260-fps arrow would strike just one-tenth of an inch higher than a 180-fps arrow.

Check Your Form

All of this assumes that you execute a shot perfectly. Many bowhunters find that they shoot much higher than the numbers shown in the accompanying table. The likely reason is faulty form. Always bend from the waist when shooting downward. The common mistake of just lowering your shooting arm, and not bending at the waist, changes your whole shot setup and can cause some very high misses.

Practical Decisions	

High shots are caused by acute shooting angles. Remember the 20-Rule: A 20-yard shot from a 20-foot high tree stand has a shooting angle of just under 20-degrees. Trajectory problems in this situation will be minimal. Just aim in the heart area. I usually set my stands ten- to twelve-feet high for shots of 10- to 20-yards and have had very few problems being seen or scented.

Always pace off your shooting distances if you've sighted-in your bow over level ground. Better yet, sight-in your bow from your tree stands so that you don't have to adjust your aim at all. (If you do all of your shooting out of tree stands, why would you ever want to use ground level sight settings?)

Finally, practice shooting from tree stands to perfect your form and see what effect this has for your equipment. This is particularly important for instinctive shooters who can't sight-in their bows and must rely on a catalog of subconscious visual images when "aiming."

Shot Distance (yards)	Tree Stand Height (feet)	Distance Measured Along Ground*			Distance Measured Along Line-Of-Sight*		
		Arrow Speed (fps)					
		180	220	260	180	220	260
10	10	0	0	0	1	0	0
	20	1	1	1	3	2	2
	30	3	3	3	Very Large		
	40	6	5	5			
20	10	0	0	0	0	0	0
	20	1	0	0	2	1	1
	30	1	1	1	4	3	2
	40	2	2	2	9	6	5
30	10	0	0	0	1	0	0
	20	1	0	0	2	1	1
	30	1	1	1	4	2	2
	40	2	1	1	7	5	3

IMPACT POINT ABOVE YOUR LINE-OF-SIGHT (TO THE NEAREST INCH). The more acute the shooting angle, the higher the shot. Measuring distance from tree stand height over your line-of-sight makes matters worse. Take shots at moderate angles using ground-paced distances to minimize trajectory problems.

* Low-drag 220-fps arrow anchored 3" below shooter's eye; sighted-in over level ground.

41. Shooting Uphill & Downhill

Some years ago I was on an Alaskan mountain goat hunt with a good friend. Bob is a flat-lander who has done a lot of tree stand hunting but not much western hunting. On the first morning out, we put a superb six-hour stalk on a big billy that had bedded down for the day. We were left with a thirty-yard opportunity and I gave Bob the honor.

There was just one problem. The goat was below us down a sixty-degree slope. Bob aimed a few inches low and turned loose. The arrow cleared the animal, slammed into the rock it was laying on, and ricocheted off into the chasm below. In his confusion, the billy made a wide swing around us and stopped again thirty-yards uphill. Bob held a few inches high and cleared him by three-feet this time.

This was Bob's only opportunity for a mountain goat in a lifetime of hunting—and he blew it by not understanding the severe effect that steep slopes can have on arrow trajectory.

Harder Than Tree Stands

As we saw in the last chapter, shooting from tree stands isn't

HARDER THAN TREE STANDS. Though not a common situation, every hunter should learn how to shoot in severe terrain and know which shots to take or pass up.

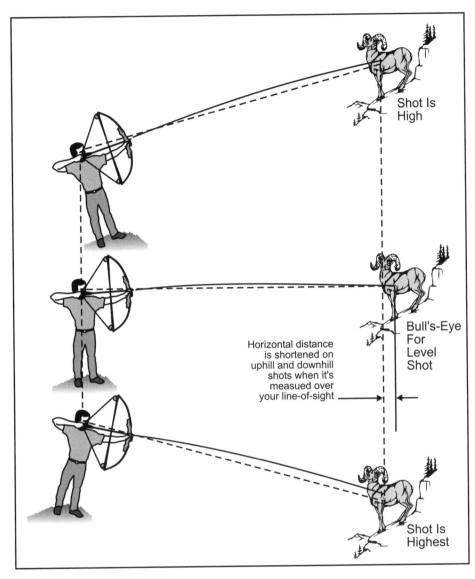

Shot Is High

Bull's-Eye For Level Shot

Horizontal distance is shortened on uphill and downhill shots when it's measued over your line-of-sight

ALWAYS AIM LOW. The effect of gravity is less when shooting either downhill or downhill so always aim lower than normal. The greatest effect is for downhill shots.

Shot Is Highest

hard. If you place your stand at a reasonable height and pace off ground distances, all you have to do is hold a few inches low. In contrast, shooting in mountainous terrain can be a real challenge. Unlike tree stands, you have to measure or guess the range along the sloping terrain and this affects your accuracy more. Longer shots compound the problem. The table on the next page shows some examples.

Always Aim Low

Most hunters who have spent some time hunting from tree stands know to hold low when shooting downhill. But, like my friend Bob, many make a common mistake when shooting uphill: They hold high when they should hold low. They figure that since gravity is fighting an arrow as it travels uphill, that it will fall lower than normal.

Though it seems counter-intuitive, the opposite is true. Like the tree stand example in the last chapter, the horizontal distance to the target is shortened when we shoot uphill. Gravity has less distance to act on the arrow and doesn't pull it down as much. Since gravity pulls against an arrow when we shoot upward, and helps it when we shoot downward, it *will* fall more than a downward shot at the same angle. But it still won't fall as much as over level ground.

Always remember one important shooting rule: *Whenever you shoot at targets that are above or below you, always aim lower than normal for that distance.*

The Good News

Don't be scared by Bob's frustrating experience. The good news is that slopes severe enough to radically affect arrow flight are rare. Brake-burning mountain highways only have slopes of fifteen-degrees or so—not enough to cause large misses. Unless you're hunting goats or other severe terrain animals, the slopes you encounter are easy to compensate for.

Practical Decisions

When shooting uphill or downhill, make an extra effort to get close to an animal. An arrow can fly three times higher

Shot Direction	Shot Angle (degrees)	Impact Point Above Aiming Spot (to nearest inch)*		
		20-yards	40-yards	60-yards
Uphill	50	10	32	69
	40	5	17	36
	30	3	8	17
	20	1	3	6
	10	0	1	1
Level	0	0	0	0
Downhill	10	0	1	3
	20	1	5	11
	30	3	10	24
	40	6	20	44
	50	10	25	77

EFFECT OF SLOPE ON ARROW TRAJECTORY. The shaded values in the table are shots that are not recommended due to their high chance for a poor outcome.

* Low-drag 220-fps arrow anchored 3" below eye; sighted-in over level ground; distance measured along line-of-sight.

at 40-yards than at 20-yards; and six times higher at 60-yards. Practice shooting in the hills and valleys where you hunt. Learn what your arrow will do under the conditions that you're likely to encounter.

When still hunting in severe terrain, avoid shots up or down slopes that are difficult to walk on, or where the angle makes footing feel unsafe. Finally, form is important here too. Practice bending at the waist when shooting over any uneven terrain.

Judging Slope Severity

Many archers figure range by learning to recognize 10- or 20-yard distances and then estimating how many of these increments there are between them and the target. You can learn to judge shooting angle in the same way. Learn what a 10- or 20-degree slope looks like and then mentally add or subtract them for the shot at hand. Or, try these tricks:

❖ When you come across highway signs that say *Caution, xx% Grade*, make a mental note of what they look like. Get off the roadway and imagine what a deer or elk might look like at different distances.

❖ Use a compass having a clinometer to measure slope angles from a distance. Then walk across the slope and see what it looks like up close.

❖ If you can stand sideways on a hillside and touch the ground with your outstretched hand, the slope is about 60-degrees. If you have about eighteen-inches between your outstretched hand and the ground, the slope is about 45-degrees.

❖ Most architect-designed stairways have slopes of about 30-degrees. In the field, slopes of 30-degrees or greater are difficult to climb without resting frequently.

❖ On 45-degree slopes, footing is slippery and unsafe. Sixty-degree slopes normally occur only on cliffs.

❖ Some range finders come equipped with slope indicators. Use one to make a table of aiming corrections that you can carry with you in the field. Measure the slope and distance, consult your aiming table, and make the shot.

42. Shooting Angle

Deer and other critters are hard to sneak up on. They also have a nasty habit of looking our way when we're trying to shoot or catching our movement in their peripheral vision. We solve these problems by hiding above them in trees or letting them walk past us so that they're looking downrange when we make our move. These tricks solve one set of problems but create others.

Target Size

Any time that an animal isn't standing directly broadside from you, the target area that you need to hit is smaller. This is true of both quartering shots and elevated shots. The worst case is when these situations are combined.

The reason is that a deer's vitals are three-dimensional. Its lungs lie side-by-side in its chest. A direct broadside shot that hits one lung will also hit the second lung. As the animal turns, though, it's possible to hit a single lung and miss the second one. As a result, you have to make a much more accurate shot on angled deer.

Penetration

The shortest distance through a deer's vitals is from a direct broadside position. If it's below you or turned at an angle to you on the ground, the arrow has to penetrate more tissue to do the same damage. It has to penetrate more before it gets to the vitals, penetrate more to go through them, and penetrate more to create an exit wound.

Since arrows have a fixed amount of impact energy, the usual result is that angled shots don't penetrate as much as broadside shots.

Think in 3-D

My experience in teaching bowhunting education classes is that hunters don't always appreciate these facts, or don't realize just how much their aiming

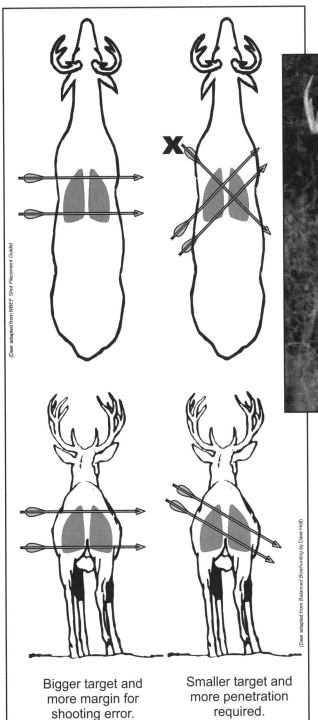

(Deer adapted from NBEF *Shot Placement Guide*)

(Deer adapted from *Balanced Bowhunting* by Dave Holt)

Bigger target and more margin for shooting error.

Smaller target and more penetration required.

PASS UP THIS SHOT. There's just too much heavy bone and muscle to penetrate.

ANGLED SHOTS REDUCE YOUR CHANCE OF SUCCESS. Broadside shots over level ground give you the largest target area and the largest margin for shooting error. They also result in more penetration than angled shots so that you have a greater chance for a pass-through hit.

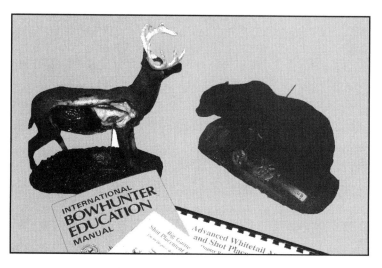

THINK IN 3-D. The *National Bowhunter Education Foundation* (*NBEF*) makes a number of training aids to help bowhunters. Tops among these are its series of 3-D animals that show vitals exposed on one side (deer and bear models shown here). Simply stick a pin in one side at your shot angle and see what happened on the other. Attend a local NBEF course to play with one yourself.

point has to change to compensate for shooting angle. The *National Bowhunter Education Foundation's (NBEF)* 3-D animal series provide excellent tools for learning to think in three-dimensions. One side shows a normal animal, but the opposite side is cut away to expose the vitals. By sticking pins in the first side, you can flip the model over and see what the arrow will hit.

Purchase one of these models from the NBEF or attend one of their classes to play with one yourself. At the minimum, get into the habit of visualizing the three-dimensional location of an animal's vitals and use this to alter your aiming point appropriately.

Practical Decisions

Since few of us ever shoot perfect bull's-eyes on live animals, try for broadside shots whenever practical. This will give you more margin for shooting error. Conversely, whenever a deer is below you or angled away from you, try to shoot from a little closer distance than normal so that you can place your shot more precisely.

Whenever shooting at a large, tough animal, strive for broadside shots. This will help ensure pass-through penetration and a good blood trail. Elk are one excellent example. On a quartering-away shot at an elk, the arrow has to pass through its grass-filled stomach before reaching the vitals. This can stop an arrow as effectively as a grass target mat.

Finally, pass up shots were an animal is angled toward you. There's just too much bone in the way, and the target that you have to hit is too small.

43. Shooting Through Brush

Imagine that you're still hunting through heavy cover and a magnum buck suddenly steps into an opening 30-yards away and stops. Halfway between you is a six-inch tree branch that shields his lung area. Do you take the shot, knowing that the arrow will safely loop over the branch and drop down in time to nail him? Or do you pass the shot and hope for another opportunity as he continues his trek?

Know Your Equipment

Most hunters have a pretty good feel for the trajectory of their arrows near the target, but few know what their trajectory is away from the target. In order to accurately shoot over, under, or through obstructions in the field, you need to know how much your arrow rises and falls during its flight path.

TAKE OR PASS THIS SHOT? Assuming that you knew you were good enough to hit this small shooting hole, your decision could only be made by knowing your arrow's trajectory.

Aiming Distance (yards)	Arrow Launch Speed				
	175-fps	200-fps	225-fps	250-fps	275-fps
20	5	3	2	2	1
30	12	9	7	5	4
40	23	17	13	11	8
50	37	28	22	18	14

*Typical mid-weight arrow anchored 3" below the eye.

MAXIMUM TRAJECTORY HEIGHTS (NEAREST INCH) FOR DIFFERENT ARROW SPEEDS AND DISTANCES. Faster arrows allow you to shoot under obstructions while slower arrows allow you to shoot over them. Determine your own arrow's trajectory on the practice range.

Measuring Trajectory

While measuring your arrow's depths-of-kill at different distances (see Chapter 6), measure its mid-range trajectory as well. Aim at 10-, 20-, and 30-yard targets using your 40-yard pin; or 7-, 15-, and 23-yard targets using your 30-yard pin, and so forth. See how high the arrow hits in each case.

The distance where the arrow reaches its maximum arc is the most important number in this exercise since it will fly lower at every other distance along its flight path. Commit these values to memory. Knowing these numbers, you can determine what obstructions you can safely shoot over and under.

Practical Decisions

Back to our dilemma: If you're shooting a 200-fps arrow, take the shot. It will safely clear the obstruction. If you are using a 250-fps arrow, pass the shot. It will nail the tree limb.

Keep in mind that there's no advantage to one arrow speed over another here. Both will work in some cases and not in others. If the limb shielded the deer's spine, you could safely take the shot with the faster arrow but not the slower one.

If you don't know how your arrow shoots, pass any shot where intervening brush might deflect a shot. No matter how big a buck is, he doesn't deserve to pay for our mistakes.

44. How We Judge Range

Forget your bow. Forget your arrow. Forget your precision aiming and your flawless release. If you're a sight-shooter, the single most important factor in hitting a deer at unknown distances is your ability to judge shooting range accurately. I've mentioned this in earlier chapters, and will do so again in more detail later.

For now, let's see what's involved in this difficult process.

Both Eyes

We use two basic types of vision to judge range. Since our eyes are set in the front of our heads a few inches apart, each can see a different part of a distant object. This *binocular vision* helps us to tell what the object looks like in three dimensions and approximately how far it is. A number of *monocular vision* (one-eye) cues then add other important distance information that helps us to refine our binocular vision estimate.

Binocular Vision

When we look at an object that's in front of us, a principle called *retinal disparity* allows our left eye to see the front of the object plus a portion of its left side, and our right eye to see the front plus a portion of its right side. Light from the front part of the object also reaches our eyes a few milliseconds before light from the parts in back. Our mind then combines all of this information into one image and tells us what the object's actual shape is.

To determine how far the object is, our mind calculates the *convergence* angle between the two paths of light that strike each eye. This is similar to the vanishing lines in a painting that are used to give it an illusion of depth. The lenses of our eyes also change shape when viewing objects that are at different distances. This change, called *accommodation*, is added to the other distance information.

(Photo Courtesy of Robert R. Wooding)

ILLUSIONS. Judging shooting distance is a difficult feat. Although these two deer appear to be at different distances, they are actually the same distance from the camera. Different lighting, shadows, and side hill elevations combine to create this optical illusion.

Monocular Cues

A variety of monocular cues help us to refine basic binocular vision estimates. The most important cues for hunting purposes are:

Elevation—Animals that are on different planes appear to be at different distances. If two deer are standing on a hillside that slopes from left to right, the one standing on the uphill side will usually appear to be farther away.

Viewing Angle—Animals that are above or below you appear to be closer or farther than they do over level ground. A deer viewed from a tree stand may look closer than it is and a mountain goat on a ledge above you may appear to be farther than it is.

Size—We know how big the animals that we hunt are from past experience. When we suddenly see a larger animal, we may perceive it as being closer than it is. If you're a whitetail hunter on his first elk hunt, you may perceive that a bull is closer than it is because you're not familiar with its enormous size.

Texture—Animals with more visible surface detail are perceived to be closer than those with lower detail. If a dark bear and a cinnamon bear appear at the same distance from two different directions, the light colored one will usually appear to be closer since you can see more detail in its coat.

Brightness and shadows—Bright, sun-lit animals have more visual texture and are usually perceived as being closer than those appearing at dusk. Well defined shadow lines help to define an animal's surface contours and make them appear closer than they are. A black feral hog may appear to be farther away than a deer at the same distance because its dark coat obscures shadows.

Weather—Haze, fog, rain, mist, and wind blown particles can hide surface details and make animals appear farther than they are. A deer viewed in crisp, clean, desert air usually appears to be closer than the same animal seen in a damp eastern forest.

Reference objects—Animals in the open don't have things around them to provide size references and may appear to be farther or closer than woodland animals standing next to trees and bushes. Animals standing on the other side of creeks and gullies don't have as many reference objects in front of them and may appear to be farther or closer than they are.

Illusions

As we can see from these complexities, judging shooting distance is not always easy in the field. When we have experience in a particular situation, we usually make better distance estimates than when factors that we're not familiar with come into play. These "illusions of reality" can often sabotage our performance.

An example: At one 3-D tournament, eighty-one shooters shot at targets placed in wooded terrain at distances of 20- to 55-yards. They scored 44% more kills on targets that stood next to trees than they did on targets set at the same distances in clearings. They also scored 26% more kills on level-terrain targets than they did on uphill or downhill targets.

Closer is Better

Beyond 30-yards or so, depth perception cues become so weak that it's difficult for anyone to estimate shooting distance accurately enough to place *consistent* killing shots. At the 3-D tournament above, the ability of shooters to judge range accurately went down sharply as distance increased. This was due to the smaller convergence angles of their eyes and the greater difficulty in seeing important visual estimating cues as distance increased.

45. Learning To Judge Range

Y ou were born with the innate ability to judge range. This is what an instinctive shooter relies on. When he "learns" to shoot instinctively, he's just programming his internal computer to recognize different subliminal sight pictures needed to hit targets at different distances. Ask him if a target is 26- or 34-yards away and he probably can't tell you, but the arrow will hit there if he's practiced enough.

Shooting with sights at unknown distances is a bit more difficult. While your mind may know "how far" a target is, it won't know that it's "33-yards" since distance units are an arbitrary human concoction. It takes conscious practice to estimate yardage in a manner that let's you choose the correct sight pin.

Bowhunters estimate range in many ways. The following three methods are the most common.

Fixed Increments

This is probably the most widely used method. Learn what 20-yards looks like and then visualize 20-yard increments on the ground in front of you. If there are one-and-a-half 20-yard increments, then the target is 30-yards away. Some people use 10-yard or other increments sizes. Smaller increments can add accuracy but take more time to use. Find one that works best for you.

Split and Double

Other hunters look at the target, visualize the half-way point, estimate its distance, and then double it to find the full distance. As with the previous method, the advantage here is that it's easier to recognize small distance increments were visual cues are more abundant, and then use them to figure the full shooting distance.

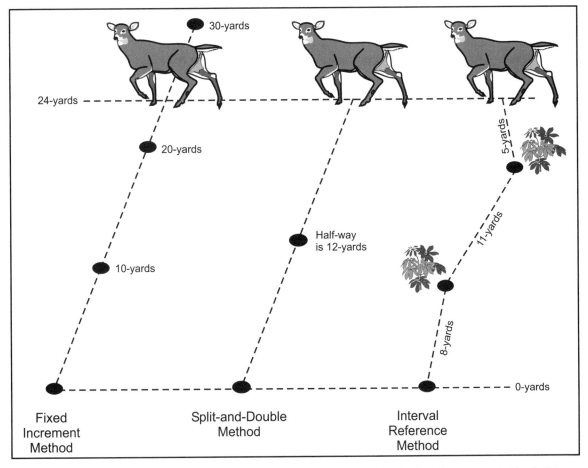

COMMON RANGE ESTIMATING METHODS. There are many ways to estimate shooting range in the field. These three are the most common. Find one that works best for you. Better yet, use more than one method as an accuracy check.

| Interval References | A third method is to estimate the distance to a visually prominent object such as a bush, tree, or rock; then estimate the distance to a second visually prominent object and add it to the first estimate; and continue adding estimates until you get to the target. The advantage of this method is that by using objects having size, shape, and texture, each estimate is likely to be more accurate than estimates made to nondescript flat ground as in the first two methods. The disadvantages are that it's a slower method since there are more estimates involved; and the different distances that are added together don't always lie in a straight line. |

Use Them All

If you've got the time, estimate the range to an animal using more than one method to see if they agree. If they do, the distance is probably accurate. If not, be wary of taking the shot.

Practice Makes Perfect

Studies show that people can judge range more accurately in familiar situations than they can in unfamiliar situations. You may be able to flawlessly judge passing distance in a car since you drive a car everyday, but have trouble guessing shooting distance since you only bowhunt a few months out of the year.

Practice your range estimating skills all year round. Practice in open and wooded areas, in bright sunlight and at dusk, on targets above and below you and on side hill planes, in all types of weather conditions, and on large, small, light colored, and dark colored targets.

Spend most of your time practicing in conditions that you're more likely to encounter, but don't short-change less frequently encountered conditions. If you hunt from tree stands, spend some extra time practicing while sitting in them. Or, if you normally hunt from ground level and shoot from kneeling or other uncommon positions, practice estimating range from these positions. The different perspective may affect your results.

Get into the habit of practicing guessing range in your everyday life. If you're walking to the corner deli for lunch, guess the distance to a corner mail box and then pace it off as you walk. On your weekend walks in the woods with your dog, visualize a deer standing behind a bush on the trail in front of you and pace it off.

In the spring, shoot 3-D tournaments. As the hunting season draws near, take to the woods and spend some time stump shooting. Learn how far you can accurately shoot from before the season opens.

Author's Note: Much of the information in this and the preceding chapter is adapted from Robert R. Wooding's excellent pamphlet, *Estimating Distance for Bowhunters*, published by Dry Ridge Company, P.O. Box 18814, Erlanger, KY 41018. Thanks are given to the author for permission to use this and for supplying the photo on optical illusions.

46. Eliminate Ranging Errors

Even with lots of practice, most people will never become expert range estimators. It's just too hard.

What if you had a way of shooting an arrow that would eliminate the need to guess range for most of your bowhunting shots? As it turns out, there's an easy but little known way to do this.

Depth-of-Kill Revisited

Recall from *Part 1* that the term *depth-of-kill* refers to the distance in front of and behind an animal where an arrow will hit the kill zone if you miss-guess the true distance. If you anchor at the corner of your mouth (typically about three-inches under your eye), and aim at the center of a deer's chest using your 30-yard pin, a 225-fps arrow will hit high in a six-inch kill zone at 26½-yards. It will hit the center of the kill zone at 30-yards, and will hit low in the kill zone at 32½-yards. At distances less than 26½-yards or farther than 32½-yards, the arrow will miss the vitals.

There are two easy ways to increase this six-yard depth-of-kill—aim lower and anchor lower.

Aim Lower

Because an arrow constantly loses speed as it travels downrange, it will always drop more at the tail end of its arc than in its earlier flight. This means that the greatest margin of error when guessing range always lies in front of an animal where trajectory is flatter. In the above example, you would kill the deer if you miss-guessed the range by 3½-yards in front of him but only 2½-yards behind him.

You can increase your depth-of-kill simply by aiming lower. Instead of aiming at the center of a deer's chest, imagine that you aimed at the bottom of its heart-lung area, just above its lower chest line. You'd make the kill anywhere between 22- and 30-yards. You'd have a depth of kill of eight-yards

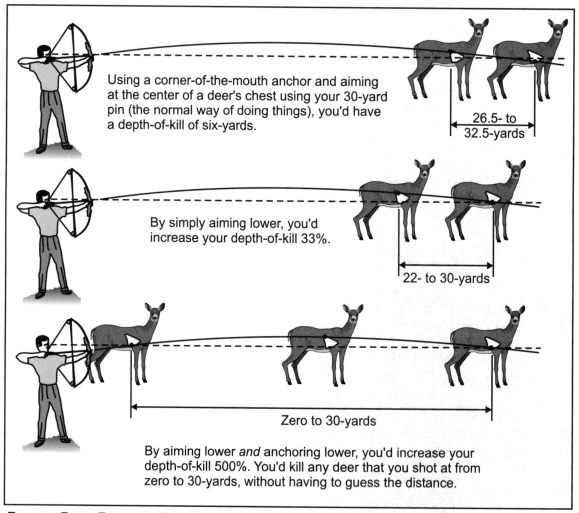

Using a corner-of-the-mouth anchor and aiming at the center of a deer's chest using your 30-yard pin (the normal way of doing things), you'd have a depth-of-kill of six-yards.

26.5- to 32.5-yards

By simply aiming lower, you'd increase your depth-of-kill 33%.

22- to 30-yards

Zero to 30-yards

By aiming lower *and* anchoring lower, you'd increase your depth-of-kill 500%. You'd kill any deer that you shot at from zero to 30-yards, without having to guess the distance.

ELIMINATE RANGE ESTIMATING ERROR USING THESE TWO EASY STEPS. This example (shown for a 225-fps arrow) illustrates how by simply aiming lower and anchoring lower, you can eliminate the need to judge shooting distance for most of your bowhunting shots.

instead of six-yards—a thirty-three percent increase—by just lowering your aiming point a few inches.

Anchor Lower

When you anchor below your eye, the arrow starts off below your line-of-sight. It then passes your line-of-sight several yards in front you, rises to its maximum height about mid-range, and crosses the line-of-sight a second time at the target. Anchoring lower causes the arrow to cross your line-of-sight the first time farther in front of the bow. This will increase your depth-of-kill.

For the 30-yard shot in our example, moving your anchor point from three-inches to 4½-inches below your eye—and still aiming at the bottom of the kill zone—would increase your depth-of-kill from eight-yards (22- to 30-yards) to eleven-yards (19- to 30-yards). You would have increased your depth-of-kill almost forty-percent.

Moving your anchor point six-inches under your eye would give you a depth-of-kill of from *zero to 30-yards!* If you shot at any deer that you knew was under 30-yards (by pre-pacing the distance across an opening from your stand, for example), you'd never have to worry about estimating range. You could just shoot at its heart and know that you'd hit it in the heart or lungs.

Another Advantage

Note in the above examples that all of your margin for error occurs in front of the animal. Far from being a disadvantage, this situation creates a nice side benefit—you're more likely to either kill an animal or miss it cleanly. If it was under 30-yards, you'd kill it. If it was farther than the 30-yards you guessed, you'd shoot low where there's little non-vital area to hit.

The Secret

Your arrow speed, style of shooting, and the size of the animal you're hunting will determine your particular depth-of-kill. The secret to eliminating range estimation problems is to aim low on the animal, find the distance where your arrow never rises above the kill zone, and then stay within this distance for all of your shots. Extend this range by anchoring as low as possible while still being able to shoot accurately.

Range Finders

Range finders eliminate the need to estimate shooting distance or to employ shooting tricks like the one in this chapter. Some bowhunters welcome them as the next logical step in the technological evolution of bowhunting. Others feel that they remove a core element of what bowhunting has always been—the need to get close to a quarry due to looping arrow trajectory. The choice is a personal one.

If you use a range finder, purchase one of the new laser models rather than the old split-image optical models. It will be smaller, more reliable, easier to use, and more accurate.

Sighting Tips. Sight-in your bow using laser-indicated distances rather than ground-paced distances. Your stride may not be exactly one-yard or you may be walking over broken terrain.

When tree stand hunting, sight-in in your bow from your tree stand. These settings will only work from *that stand*, or one set at an identical height. And they won't work once you're back on the ground. An option here is to shoot at laser-indicated distances from your stand using your ground-level sight settings and see how high you shoot at 20-, 30-, 40-yards, etc. Commit these corrections to memory and then adjust accordingly for your shots at deer.

When pre-measuring likely shooting distances from your stand, avoid measuring to poorly-defined points, or at least use the scan mode to pan above and below the shooting spot and convince yourself that the reading is reasonably accurate. A better approach is to measure the distances to trees lying on two sides of a trail and then guess-timate the actual trail-distance using your laser readings.

Use your range finder to help you learn how to judge range so that you don't become totally dependent on it. On your walks through the woods, practice guessing distances and checking them.

Range Finders and Arrow Weight. Archers who use range finders might also re-evaluate their choice of arrows. Recall from *Chapter 7, Arrow Weight* that there's just one compelling reason to use light, fast arrows—to eliminate range estimation errors at unknown distances. With this can come a host of problems.

All of these problems vanish if you know your shooting range precisely. The slowest equipment in the world will be more accurate at known distances than the fastest equipment at unknown distances. A better approach might be to use heavier arrows and just shoot at known distances. Pace off your shots when hunting from blinds or tree stand or use a range finder to pinpoint distances precisely.

Chuck Adams, the first bowhunter to take all Pope & Young Club recognized species of North American big game, has long followed this philosophy and he's done pretty well.

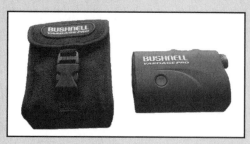

Although they're a bit more expensive than older optical, split-image rangefinders, the new generation of laser range finders are easier to use and also more accurate.

47. Single-Pin Success

In the early days of sight-shooting, single-pins were the norm. This provided some of the quickness and simplicity of instinctive shooting with the precision of sights. In the intervening years most sighting systems have become very complex.

Multiple-pin sights have advantages but also have several problems associated with them. First, they're difficult to use quickly. Any time you have to stop and figure out which pin to use, the optimum moment for taking a shot can be lost. This is a frequent problem in fast paced hunting situations.

A second problem for animals standing at distances that are between pin settings is moving the pin in the wrong direction—holding high when you

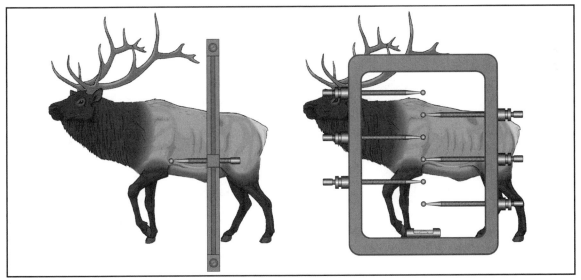

WHICH IS QUICKER? Anytime that you have to stop and figure out which sight-pin to use, you can lose a shooting opportunity. In many hunting situations, nothing beats the simplicity of a single, fixed-pin sight. Used correctly, a single pin will handle the majority of your bowhunting shots without the need to judge shooting distance.

should hold low and holding low when you should hold high. Again, this is frequently a result of making quick aiming decisions.

Third, some multiple-pin systems sold today are fragile and subject to problems during rough field use. Even on the sturdier models, you have more pins to worry about and maintain. With single-pin sights, problems or mis-adjustments are easy to spot and correct; with multiple pins, problems can go unnoticed and cost you a shot.

These things don't occur very often, thank goodness, but most hunters can recall at least one instance of missing a deer or elk for one of these reasons.

To solve these problems, some bowhunters today are returning to the simplicity of a single, rigid, fixed-pin sight. Coupled with the aiming method described in the previous chapter, a single, rugged, quick-pointing sight-pin is all that you should ever need.

You'll never choose the wrong pin, never move the pin in the wrong direction (just always hold low) and your bow sight problems will be reduced.

Works for Most Shots

Hunting statistics show that most whitetails are killed at distances under 20-yards. Most western game is taken under 30-yards. As the table below shows, a single pin is all that you need for these cases.

Depths-of-kill with your equipment will be different than these typical examples. Experiment to find your own maximum shooting range. Then learn what that distance looks like in the field under different conditions and stay within it.

MAXIMUM "ONE-PIN" SHOOTING DISTANCES FOR DIFFERENT SIZED KILL ZONES. This table shows the distances (in yards) where an arrow will never rise above different sized kill zones when aiming at the bottom of the kill zone. Sight-in your bow at these distances, learn what they look like in the field, always aim low, and then shoot with confidence at any shorter distance.

Arrow Speed (fps)	6-inch (Whitetail)	8-inch (Mule Deer)	10-inch (Elk)
\multicolumn{4}{c}{(Side of Face Anchor, 3" Below Eye)}
175	22	25	28
200	26	29	32
225	28	32	35
250	31	35	39
275	34	38	42
\multicolumn{4}{c}{(Under the Chin Anchor, 6" Below Eye)}
175	24	27	29
200	28	31	33
225	31	34	37
250	34	38	41
275	37	40	44

20xx aluminum arrows with 4"-5" feathers

48. "No-Pin" Success

The same simplified sighting method described in the last two chapters—with a couple of twists—also works for archers who forego mechanical sights and use the point of their arrow to aim with.

Gap-Shooting Problems

Many of the top archers throughout history have used the point-of-aim, or *gap-shooting*, method. Many traditional shooters (and a few compound shooters) continue to do this today.

Rather then putting a sight-pin on the spot they what to hit, these archers look at their arrow point and move it up or down relative to the target. This works well at longer distances where the point is in the vicinity of an animal (fifty- to seventy-yards is common), but notoriously poor at closer distances where the point must be visually lined up with a leaf or twig on the ground well in front of the animal. Gap-shooting also requires accurate range estimates and all of the attendant chances for failure that comes with this.

Luckily, these problems are easily solved for most hunting shots.

Shoot Point-On

In the old archery lexicon, *point-on distance* is the distance where you can put your arrow point on the spot you want to hit, and then hit there. For short range shots, this is easily done by moving your arrow nock closer to your eye.

Grip the string with three fingers under the nock, *Apache-style*, and anchor as high as you can so that you're looking down the arrow as if it were the barrel of a shotgun[*]. Find the distance where you can hit the *bottom* of a deer's kill zone when you the put the point of the arrow there. This distance will probably be under 25-yards. Aim at this spot and your arrow should hit

---

[*]Some archers like to grip the string at different distances below the arrow nock so that they can shoot point-on at different ranges. This technique, called *string walking*, is similar to using different sight pins. It's an effective target technique but difficult to use with broadhead-tipped arrows that demand precise tuning to a consistent shooting style.

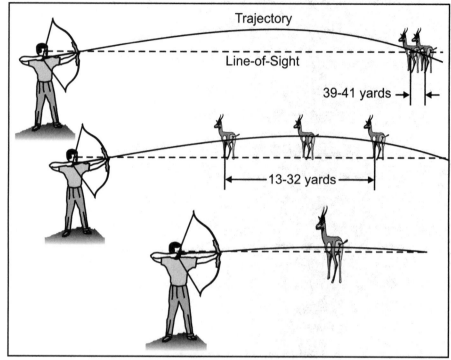

GAP-SHOOTING MADE EASY. The archer in the top sketch is aiming "point-on" at the deer's lungs which gives him a very narrow depth-of-kill. In the middle sketch, he has extended his depth-of-kill considerably by aiming at the animal's foot. In the bottom sketch, he is using a three-fingers-under anchor for close range shooting. This gives him a consistent aiming point at the bottom of the deer's kill zone.

somewhere in the kill zone at any closer distance. Check this out and make any adjustments necessary.

Longer Distances

For intermediate length shots, keep your one-finger-over, Mediterranean-style, release. Find an anchor point that gives you a point-on distance of about 40-yards. Now, aim *at the foot* of a 3-D deer so that you use the flattest part of your arrow's trajectory. For a normal-speed recurve or longbow, this should give you a depth-of-kill of about 13- to 32- yards without having to judge range. Check this out for your own equipment.

Repeat the exercise for other anchor points. Find the distances where your arrow hits solidly in the kill zone when aiming at a deer's or an elk's foot. The advantage of this method, in addition to eliminating most of your range estimation problems, is that you will always be aiming at some point *on the animal* and can easily maintain your aiming spot while it moves.

For longer shots, simply move your arrow point up and estimate range in the conventional manner.

49. String Jumping

The preceding chapters on depth-of-kill—and the aiming tricks that are based on it—assume that the animal you're shooting at stands perfectly still and takes the shot calmly. This isn't always the case.

Some animals can react extraordinarily fast when they hear you shoot and this can foil the best aimed arrow in the world. For most hunters, high-voltage whitetails are the main source of concern, and they demand special treatment.

Squat and Go

Everyone who has hunted whitetails for very long can conjure up an image of a shot sailing high while the deer bounds away. It all happens very fast which leaves the impression that the shot missed before the deer reacted.

Gene and Barry Wensel's excellent video, *Hunting October Whitetails*, gives one of the best illustrations that I've seen of what really happens. In it, an alert whitetail doe is shot at from about 20-yards. At normal frame speed, the arrow looks like it's cleanly over the deer's back. But in slow motion, the camera shows that she drops a full chest-height at the sound while the arrow passes where she was a moment before.

Some hunters claim they've had deer *consciously* duck an arrow, but this is impossible at short range. When a deer "jumps the string," it's just reacting instinctively to the sudden noise. It must first drop down and coil up its leg muscles before it can push off for parts unknown. Prove this to yourself by standing upright with your back to a friend. When he claps his hands, try to jump out of the way as quickly as you can. You'll have to drop down before you can move laterally.

A Sack of Potatoes

The table on the next page shows my calculation of how much a deer can move if it drops down like a sack of potatoes when it hears a bowstring (since it can't push itself down, it can only drop using its weight). The numbers are based on one-third the reaction time of a human and agree with most slow motion video clips that I've seen (and my own considerable experience with flaky central Texas whitetails).

Fast Arrow or Slow Arrow?

A common misconception is that fast arrows eliminate bad hits due to string jumping. While they do reduce the time a deer has to react to the shot, they don't eliminate the problem. A rifle bullet travels faster than the speed of sound so that it has already passed through a deer before the animal hears the shot. In contrast, the fastest bow available today only shoots an arrow at about one-quarter the speed of sound (1120-fps at sea level). The sound still gets there well before the arrow and this gives a deer ample time to react.

Rather than reducing string jumping, fast arrows may actually increase it because of they make a bow noisier. Many hunters find that they have fewer string jumping problems using a well silenced bow with heavy arrows. Not only is bow noise minimized, but it tends to have a lower frequency which doesn't disturb a deer as much. Perhaps the low-pitched *Thut* of this rig sounds more natural, like an apple or branch falling from a tree. It may cause a deer to look up and investigate, but not bolt immediately. In contrast, the high-pitched *Twaannggg* of some speed rigs is totally foreign to the woods and may cause an immediate, violent reaction.

Even if this hasn't been your experience, keep in mind that fast arrows provide few real benefits in the string jumping department. Choose your arrows based on other considerations.

Arrow Speed (fps)	Shot Distance (yards)			
	10	**15**	**20**	**25**
175	3	8	*	*
200	2	6	*	*
225	1	4	9	*
250	1	3	7	*
275	1	2	5	10

* Deer has time to drop, spin, and go

DISTANCE THAT A DEER CAN DROP (IN INCHES) AFTER IT HEARS THE SHOT. Distances are calculated based on high speed video sequences. The un-shaded shots are situations where you could aim at the bottom of a deer's lungs and make the kill whether it moved or not. The shaded numbers represent situations where the deer's reaction, more than shooting skill, will determine the outcome.

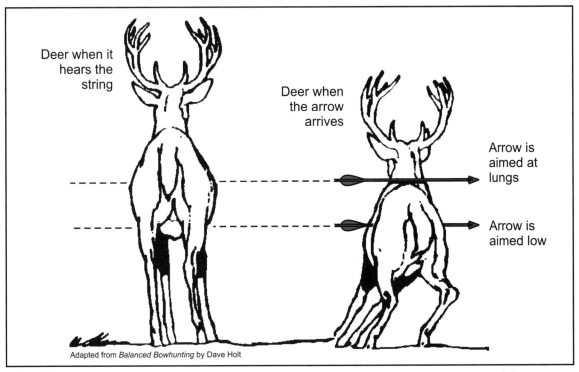

Deer when it hears the string

Deer when the arrow arrives

Arrow is aimed at lungs

Arrow is aimed low

Adapted from *Balanced Bowhunting* by Dave Holt

SQUAT AND GO. High-strung animals (whitetails are among the worst) have an uncanny ability to react to the sudden noise of a bow shot. Before they can run, they have to drop down and coil up their legs to push off. Aim low and shoot from close range to compensate for this tendency.

Practical Decisions

Deer movement is minor up to about 10-yards and little aiming compensation is required. At this distance, just aim at the spot you want to hit. At 15-yards, a deer has time to hear and react to the noise and start dropping. Aim low in the chest for these shots. You'll make the kill whether it moves or doesn't move.

Somewhere between 20- and 25-yards, depending on arrow speed, a deer has time to hear the noise, drop down, spin, and push off for parts unknown. Avoid these shots. If you manage to hit the kill zone, this will be due to the deer's reaction—which you have no control over—rather than any skill on your part. Save him for another day.

The bottom line: When hunting high-string animals, get close and shoot low. It's hard to go wrong with this time-proven strategy.

50. Shooting in the Wind

Wind is something that all bowhunters have to contend with from time to time. In fact, some of your best hunting is probably on breezy days when the sounds of swaying limbs and rustling leaves cover your footfalls—or your heartbeats when that *muy grande* steps into your shooting lane. Steady breezes also let you manage your scent better.

In most hunting situations, wind speed is minor and its effect can be ignored. But in higher winds, accurate shooting can be extremely difficult. I once spent seven days hunting caribou on Alaska's North Slope with sixty-mph gales whipping off the Arctic Ocean. This forced us into hours of arduous belly-crawling across mosquito infested tundra to get 15-yard shots, the only ones we felt we could make.

When you're faced with a similar situations, consider these tips.

Wind Effects

Wind does two things to an arrow. Headwinds or tailwinds cause it to shoot high or low, and side winds cause it to drift away from your aiming line. In ballistics jargon, direct headwinds and tailwinds are known as *low-value* winds since they have the smallest effect on a projectile's trajectory. Direct side winds are called *full-value* winds since they produce the greatest change in impact point. Quartering winds are called *partial-value* winds. They produce a combination of these two effects. Excessive side winds can also push the fletching end of the arrow off line in flight and reduce penetration.

Aiming in the Wind

It's rarely possible to estimate wind speeds and directions accurately in the field. It's also impossible to know what the wind is like between you and the target, or if it will pick-up or die while the arrow is in the air. The secret to accurate shooting in the wind, then, is to never shoot beyond the distance where potential wind effects are greater than the size of the animal's kill zone.

The unshaded values in the table on the next page represent combinations of wind speed and distance where you could aim at a whitetail's kill zone with a mid-speed arrow and make the kill whether the wind was blowing or not. The shaded values are for situations where you'd have to aim outside the kill zone. Do this and the chances of a bad hit go up dramatically.

Heavy or Light Arrow?

A frequently asked question is whether heavy or light arrows are better in the wind. Light arrows fly downrange more quickly and give the wind less time to affect them. But they also have less mass to resist the wind forces that they do encounter.

Without getting into the complex technical reasons, the short answer is that heavier arrows always perform better. In one test, a 300-grain arrow drifted 35-inches at 60-yards in a stiff crosswind. A 700-grain arrow (shot from an identical bow at the same time) only drifted 24-inches.

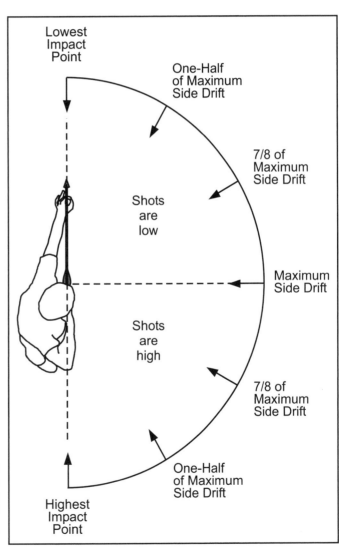

Wind Clock. It doesn't take much of an angling wind to affect an arrow's impact point. Even winds that are quartering at you from 1:00 o-clock can produce half of the drift of direct side winds.

When two different arrow weights were both launched at 220-fps (it was necessary to use two different weight bows to do this), the effects were more dramatic. A 600-grain arrow drifted 18-inches at 60-yards while a 400-grain arrow drifted almost 50-inches.

The same relative results were obtained for other arrow weights and speeds, and for all wind directions and speeds. The heavier the arrow, the better it performed in the wind.

Practical Decisions

Since you can never know exactly what effects wind will have on your arrow, adopt a windy weather rule of shooting from much closer distances than normal. Some bowhunters will not shoot over one-half or one-quarter of the distance where they can place a killing shot on a still day.

Use a heavy mass weight bow or add a heavy stabilizer which will lower wind buffeting and improve your aim. Remove your bow quiver and keep other wind catching attachments to a minimum. Given the option, shoot heavier arrows, smaller diameter shafts, and low profile vented broadheads to minimize side drift.

Wind Speed and Direction	Shooting Distance		
	20-yards	40-yards	60-yards
10-mph			
12:00	0	1	2
1:00	1	2	5
2:00	1	3	8
3:00	1	4	9
20-mph			
12:00	0	1	4
1:00	1	4	10
2:00	2	7	16
3:00	2	8	18
30-mph			
12:00	0	2	7
1:00	1	6	15
2:00	2	10	24
3:00	3	12	27

60# compound, 500-grain arrow, and making a perfect shot

REALITY CHECK—AIMING CORRECTIONS FOR WINDY DAYS (IN INCHES). Since we rarely know wind speed or direction at the target exactly, the best course is to never take a shot where the arrow might drift out of the kill zone. Shown here are the distances in inches that a mid-weight arrow will move (combination of lateral and vertical directions) for various wind speeds and directions.

Assuming that you made a perfect shot, you could safely aim near the edge of a whitetail's kill zone and make a killing shot in any situation that's unshaded. The shaded values show situations to avoid. Note that it's best to avoid longer shots in all but the mildest breezes.

Try to maneuver to get the wind directly in your face since direct upwind and downwind shots are least affected. Pass up shots where the wind is blowing so hard that you can't hold your bow steady enough to aim, or where you have to aim outside of the kill zone. In other words, pass up all shots that you don't *know* you can make.

Finally, consider retiring to the hunting cabin on really bad days and using your time stump shooting to determine how to aim in windy conditions the next time you have to.

Estimating Wind Speed

Small, handheld wind speed indicators are used by competitive rifle shooters and make excellent training aids. If you live in windy country, consider getting one and practice estimating wind speeds to see how accurate you are.

The U.S. Marine Corps suggests the following quick ways to estimate wind speed:

- ❖ *Light Breezes* (5-mph) can be felt on your face and cause leaves to rustle;
- ❖ *Gentle Breezes* (10-mph) keep leaves and small twigs on trees in constant motion;
- ❖ *Moderate Breezes* (15-mph) raise dust and loose paper and cause branches to move;
- ❖ *Fresh Breezes* (20-mph) cause small trees to sway and raise small crests on water;
- ❖ *Strong Breezes* (30-mph) cause wires to whistle and large branches to sway;
- ❖ *High Winds* (35-mph) keep entire trees in motion and cause some difficulty in walking;
- ❖ *Gale Force* Winds (40-mph) cause twigs to break off trees and make walking difficult.

The Flag Method. If you can see a flag (or any cloth-like piece of material similar to a flag), estimate the angle in degrees formed by the juncture of the flag and the pole. Divide this angle by four to get wind speed in miles per hour. If the angle is 60-degrees, the wind speed is about 15-mph. When stand-hunting, hang strips of cloth to trees at expected shooting spots and use them to determine wind severity.

The Pointing Method. Drop a cloth from shoulder height and then point at it on the ground. Divide the angle between your arm and body by four to get wind speed in miles per hour. This is a handy trick when stalking an animal.

51. Draw-Checks

[Arrows should] keep a good length, for a man pulleth them no farther one time than at another; for in feeling the plump end always equally, he may loose them.

Roger Ascham, 1544

Draw with your right, and push firmly with your left hand until your arrow's head rests on the lowest joint of your left forefinger, [then] let go the string.

Maurice Thompson, 1878

Draw the arrow...so that when the full draw is obtained, the arrow [point] touches the left hand...

Saxton Pope, 1923

Draw-checks have been used for at least 450-years and probably thousands of years before that. This simple technique—which can cure a variety of shooting woes for both release and finger shooters—is so effective that I'm surprised so few people use it.

A Simple Concept

The draw-check concept is a simple one. Use something to alert you when you reach full draw. Then condition yourself to make a surprise, break-away release at precisely the same moment. A properly used draw-check also makes it difficult to release an arrow without good dynamic back tension. A third benefit is that drawing and releasing at exactly the same point every time promotes consistent muscle alignment while drawing and anchoring.

These elements of form are all important to accurate shooting. But there's a fourth reason for using a draw check—the dreaded dragon, *target panic!* Draw checks are the quickest and easiest way to slay this dragon. It does this by mentally triggering the shot with a surprise stimulus before target panic symptoms can occur.

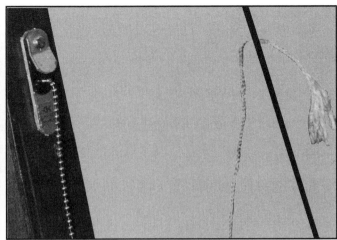

DRAW-CHECK OPTIONS. The simplest draw-check for traditional shooters who use bows with low-crowned arrow shelves is to pull the arrow back until you feel the broadhead (left), and then release. An O-ring or duct tape wrapped around the shaft will serve the same purpose on target arrows.

A mechanical "clicker" (above) works by producing a clicking sound when a metal tab is bent at full draw using a cord attached to the bowstring. It attaches easily to a compound or a stick bow.

A Universal Problem

Look down the practice line at almost any traditional shoot and you'll see all manner of problems: Short-draws, false releases, collapsing, and general target panic are common sights. All of these maladies can be cured with a draw-check.

The use of compounds usually reduces short-draws and target panic, but they still allow for variable draw lengths if the shooter doesn't pull tightly against the bow's "stop" at the end of its force-draw curve. Using a draw-check will help compound shooters to insure that each arrow is released with precisely the same energy. This is important to vertical accuracy.

Traditional Methods

The simplest draw-check for traditional shooters is the one described by Roger Ascham and other famous archers of old. For longbows or recurves with low crowned arrow shelves, simply draw your arrow back until you can feel the back of the point or broadhead against the upper finger of your bow hand. Then release in a continuous motion while maintaining back tension.

For hunting arrows, this works best with broadheads having nearly vertical rear blade angles. Snuffers, Woodsmen, Grizzlies, Black Diamond Deltas, Magnus heads with bleeder blades, and other similar designs will all work well.

You can do the same thing with your Judo points. Just rotate one of the small springs down so you can feel it at full draw. For your target arrows, try fitting the shaft with a small rubber o-ring (duct tape wrapped around the arrow will also work). The ring will roll back when it hits a 3-D target and can easily be put back into position for the next shot. This trick also works well with hunting arrows.

Modern Methods

People with serious shooting problems or who are fighting a bad case of target panic may need some stronger medicine. A mechanical draw-check may be just what the doctor ordered. They're also the cure of choice for traditionalists who use elevated arrow rests.

Mechanical draw-checks tend to work better than the traditional methods since they give a more dramatic draw indication and can therefore eliminate shooting faults in a shorter time period. There have been a host of innovative models over the years but the most popular models all work by producing a clicking sound (hence, their common name, *clickers*).

One popular add-on model is the CRICK-IT. It mounts on the inside of the bow and attaches to the bowstring with a thin string. When the bow is pulled to full draw, the string pulls taut and bends a small metal tab which clicks. This and similar devices are easy to attach, easy to adjust, and don't require any arrow modifications. They work on compounds or stick bows. Compound shooters might try models that attach to the bow's cams or cable guards.

Draw-Check Tips

The first time you use a draw check, you may have trouble pulling to the point of the arrow or getting the clicker to click. The first culprit to look for is an unrealistic idea of what your true draw length is. Many people judge their draw length by practice drawing an arrow. When they actually shoot—especially during the excitement of a hunting shot—they don't draw quite as far. Forget about what you *think* your draw length should be—use the one that's most comfortable for you *in the field when shooting at game.*

If you're a traditional shooter who is still having trouble, this may indicate that you're not pulling hard enough. Consciously try to push and pull the bow to full draw, or concentrate on forcing your shoulder blades together. Compound shooters should get into the habit of always pulling the string back hard until it stops at the end of the bow's natural force-draw valley at the end of its power stroke. These acts by themselves may noticeably improve your shooting.

Traditional Clicker Politics

To many traditionalists, clickers are viewed as high-tech wizardry. To others, they're just another modern tool like a fiberglass bow, cushioned arrow rest, or bolt-on bow quiver. Archery writers Larry Jones and Dan Bertallan, or Predator recurve maker Ron Pittsley, all use them in the field and swear by them.

This is an individual choice. Even if you don't like them for hunting, don't overlook them as a valuable training aid. Use them periodically to work on your form or to nip a bout of target panic before it becomes uncontrollable. In many cases, a clicker can solve your problems in a fraction of the time that it would take without one.

Don't swayed by peer pressure. Neither decision is right or wrong. Do what allows you to enjoy the sport more! If the legion of shooters who have dropped out of archery due to "incurable" target panic had tried one, they'd probably still be with us.

Bowhunting writer and video maker, Dan Bertalan (right), is one traditional shooter who likes clickers. He has one mounted on the lower limb of his bow on this Quebec caribou hunt.

52. Magnum Arrows

People who travel the globe in search of its largest and toughest animals generally favor heavy bows. They also favor magnum-weight arrows. Even if you don't aspire to shoot an elephant or a half-ton bear, heavier than normal arrows can still provide advantages. They are the solution of choice whenever maximum penetration is the goal. Many people favor them for elk and moose due to their hard hitting ability.

Boosts Bow Efficiency

Why do heavy arrows perform so well? Because they absorb more of a bow's stored energy and shoot more efficiently. Yet, few commercially available shafts have enough mass weight to eke the efficiency out of heavy bows that they're capable of.

For fifty- or sixty-pound bows, there's an assortment of 400- to 600-grain arrows available to do the job. These arrows, weighing 8- to 12-grains per pound of bow weight, provide the tradeoff between penetration and trajectory that most folks want. The low end of the range provides better trajectory; the higher end provides better penetration.

Problems arise, however, as we move to heavier bows. The heaviest arrow listed for a 95-pound bow in one aluminum arrow chart that I checked weighed just 579-grains, or just over six-grains per pound. It stands to reason this arrow will not shoot as hard as one weighting 10- or 12-grains per pound.

Easy Solutions

If you favor heavier than ordinary arrows, plan on assembling them yourself. A quick, inexpensive trick for doing this is to fill an aluminum or carbon shaft with salt, sugar, sand, expanding foam, another arrow shaft, or lengths of solder or wire, to get the weight that you want. Or cut a small piece of all-thread steel rod and bond it in place behind the broadhead adapter using heat cement. Be sure to use enough cement or the plug could come loose

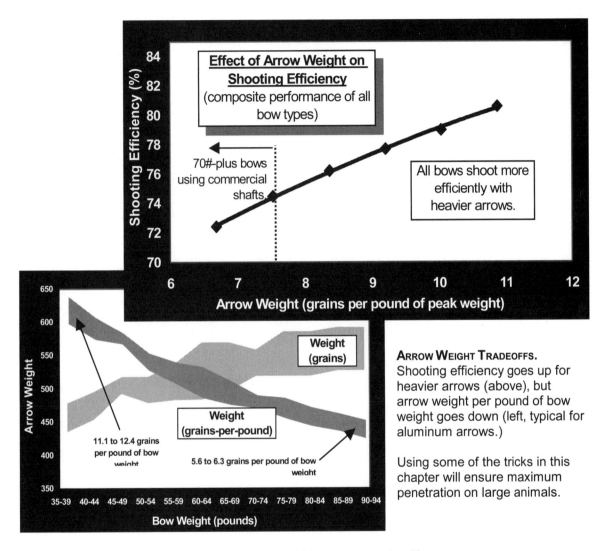

ARROW WEIGHT TRADEOFFS. Shooting efficiency goes up for heavier arrows (above), but arrow weight per pound of bow weight goes down (left, typical for aluminum arrows.)

Using some of the tricks in this chapter will ensure maximum penetration on large animals.

during a shot, slide back, and blow your nock off.

Filling a thin carbon shaft with pepper will boost its weight to over 600-grains. Filling a full diameter carbon or aluminum shaft will boost its weight to 700- or 800-grains. Also check out the internal weighting systems that some carbon arrow manufacturers offer.

Traditional wood arrow aficionados are a little more limited. Choose the heaviest species of wood that you can find or use compressed shafts. You can also cut off the tip of the broadhead taper and wedge a .22-caliber bullet in the forward part of the broadhead ferrule.

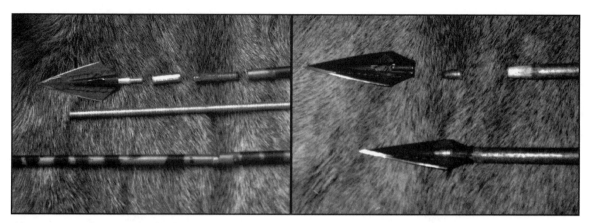

HEAVYWEIGHT OPTIONS. (Left): The top arrow has a 125-grain piece of all-thread rod (available at hardware stores) glued into the shaft behind the point to boost arrow weight. The bottom arrow has a smaller aluminum shaft inserted into a larger one. (Right): Wood arrow users should choose a heavy wood species and a heavy point to boost weight. Adding a .22-caliber bullet behind the point will add another 50-grains. Every little bit helps.

Tuning Tips

Any of these modifications will alter an arrow's dynamic spine so be sure to tune your new arrows to your bow. Adding a filler material of any kind will increase its spine. If the filler has structural rigidity, such as an internal wood dowel or another arrow shaft, it will add stiffness directly. If the filler adds weight but no rigidity, such as salt and pepper, the greater weight will cause the shaft to bend more slowly when shot and will have the same effect.

Adding tip weight alone (a heavier broadhead or internal steel rod behind the point) will have the opposite effect. It will lighten the spine by moving the arrow's balance-point forward. Choose an arrow that's both over-spined and physically heavier, and bring it back to the correct spine by adding tip weight.

Heavier shafts are more sluggish as they bend around a bow and this makes them harder to stabilize. Solve this problem by using larger then normal feathers to grab the air and straighten it out quickly.

Experiment

Other ideas and possibilities are as limitless as your imagination, so experiment a little. And remember, heavy arrows aren't just for heavy bows. As long as you're shooting an arrow that is heavy enough, any bow is capable of shooting an arrow with high efficiency and hard hitting ability.

53. Keep It Simple

It was late December and I was on a New Mexico mule deer hunt with a group of friends. Mark's troubles started on the first day when he missed an easy shot at a record book buck. Evidently, his sight bar had been jarred loose when he slipped and fell on an icy patch while heading up the mountain in the dark, and he hadn't realized it. A little quick re-sighting-in had cured the problem but not before he lost a wonderful hunting opportunity.

Two days later, he missed the same buck again when the spring mechanism on his rest froze up and sent the arrow in a fish-tailing loop past the animal. A third opportunity at a lesser buck on the fourth day was foiled when the dry, frigid air caused his cams to creak at the wrong time and spooked the deer to parts unknown. He had left his can of lubricant in camp.

Finally, to add insult to injury, he misplaced his release and couldn't find his spare which he was "sure" that he'd packed. This reduced him to shooting with his fingers which neither he or his bow were used to.

His nightly complaints turned nearly to tears by the end of his fruitless hunt. Driving home, I'd finally had enough: "You know, Mark, every one of your problems was equipment related. It doesn't matter if you have the fastest, most accurate whiz-bang bow in the world on the target range if you can't kill a deer with it. If you'd simplify things a bit, you wouldn't have most of these kinds of problems."

A Common Problem Mark isn't alone here—I've seen similar, though less dramatic, instances in many hunting camps—but his story does illustrate a dilemma that many hunters face. Manufacturers are quick to provide a plethora of accuracy aiding devices and accessories, some useful and some questionable. And many hunters are quick to buy them in their quest for success. These items may provide quick and easy advantages, but they come at a cost. The more equipment items that you use, the more time you have to spend adjusting and tuning them; the more you become dependent on them; and the more problems they cause when they are lost or malfunction while hunting.

Using technology isn't the problem. When we use even the simplest bow, we're employing technology. The real question is: How much technology is helpful—over the long run, not just in some cases—and how much of it hurts us? I'm not talking philosophy here. I'm talking pure practicality.

Practical Decisions

Every archer will have to answer this question for himself. The important point is to give it some serious thought before making a decision to buy or continue using some equipment item. Look back over the years and consider all of the tradeoffs for each equipment item that you use. How often has each added to your success, and how often has it caused a problem? How often has it allowed you to get off a quick, accurate shot, and how often has it cost you an opportunity by slowing you down or malfunctioning? If most of your shots are at short range in heavy cover, do you really need xyz-accessory that's only useful for longer shots, or is it hurting you on your shorter shots?

Think of your equipment decisions in statistical terms. If one item might cause you a problem one time in fifty shots, that may be no big deal. If *every* item that you use might cause a problem every fifty shots, you can virtually count on muffing a shooting opportunity before too long.

Strive to use the simplest equipment that you can still shoot accurately enough to do the job for the *majority* of your hunting shots. Wean yourself off of complex, fragile, unnecessary equipment, or at least learn to shoot without these items when necessary.

While I've used Mark and his compound as an example, the same thing applies to traditionalists. You may be using fewer accessories than a compound shooter, but do you really need everything that you're using?

Chuck Adams has long been a proponent of this simple approach. Bob Swinehart, the late-great longbow legend, expressed this same idea when he said that an archer should be able to draw and shoot an arrow as subconsciously as he ties his shoe laces. You don't have to shoot one of Swinehart's longbows, but you should strive for as much simplicity as possible. Adopt the *K.I.S.S principle*. It'll pay off in the long run.

Part 5. The Preparation

A bowhunter can have the best equipment and the most extensive hunting knowledge in the world, but he still has to hit what he's aiming at.

All of history's best archers had to start at ground zero and learn their craft, and they had to practice regularly to maintain it or improve it. Howard Hill, perhaps the best pre-compound archer who ever lived, was known as an extraordinary bow shot. Many people called him "a natural." Yet, Hill spent thousands of hours perfecting and maintaining his skills on the practice range. Chuck Adams, perhaps the best compound hunter alive today, does the same thing, as do all other top modern archers.

Are you living up to your shooting potential? Ask yourself:

- *How well do I shoot? At a tournament? At a deer?*
- *How well do I want to shoot?*
- *How much has my shooting improved in the past month? The past year?*
- *What things did I do to improve and how much did each help?*
- *If I'm not improving, why not?*

If you can answer these questions and give specific details, then you're well on your way to shooting bliss. If not, then some of the tips in this section might help you.

54. Getting Better

Improving any athletic skill has always been a hit or miss affair. Some folks with mediocre strength, speed, or coordination excel in their chosen sport, while others with greater natural talent languish. In the past, no one knew the reasons. Hard work helped but wasn't the only answer.

Today, sports psychologists tell us that continual improvement is a *process*. Practice doesn't make perfect—*perfect practice* makes perfect. There are certain ways that all modern world class good athletes approach their sport.

Know Thyself

Shooting a bow is really a very simple activity—just pull the string back, point the arrow, and let it go. But the devil is in the details. In the real world, a myriad of small things can affect your results by large or small amounts.

To reach your shooting potential, you need to understand all of the intricate cause-and-effect relationships between every element in your setup, draw, aim, and release cycle. Start by going to the practice range and paying detailed attention to every aspect of the way you normally shoot an arrow. No element is too small to consider at this point. Make a written list of each of these items for future reference.

Critical Elements First

Varying some elements of your shooting style will have a dramatic effect on your accuracy and consistency while varying other things will only have a minor effect. Using your list of form elements, identify the most critical items by playing around with different things and noting the results.

After you have a firm feel for what affects what (and by how much), make a short list of four or five *critical elements* to work on first. Your greatest improvement will come here. Later, after they're under control, you can identify the next most critical elements to work on.

Set Goals

Decide what your primary goal is. Is it to bunch as many arrows as you can in the center of the bull's-eye at your weekly archery league; or to kill every deer you shoot at? These are not the same things and demand different approaches.

After deciding on your overall goal, set an initial performance goal on your path to perfection. It should be demanding but *achievable* in a reasonable time. This will provide regular and timely motivational feedback. After achieving that goal, raise the performance bar by setting more aggressive, but still attainable, goals.

Make Plans

Avoid the normal tendency to measure success by the end result of your actions—target scores or individual killing shots. Keep in mind that *you can't directly control your results*. You can only *control the actions* that lead to results. You can't *make* the arrow hit the bull's-eye. Once its in the air, it's beyond your control. All you can control are the things that you do up until the moment of release. This isn't a word game—it's a different way of thinking about things, and making this shift is essential to improving.

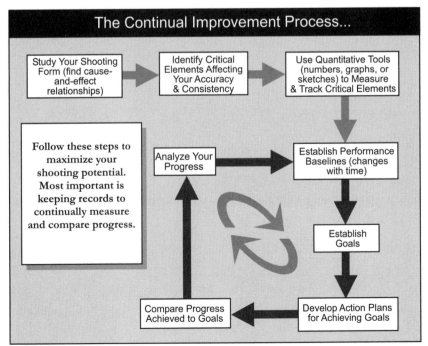

The Continual Improvement Process...

Study Your Shooting Form (find cause-and-effect relationships) → Identify Critical Elements Affecting Your Accuracy & Consistency → Use Quantitative Tools (numbers, graphs, or sketches) to Measure & Track Critical Elements

Follow these steps to maximize your shooting potential. Most important is keeping records to continually measure and compare progress.

Analyze Your Progress → Establish Performance Baselines (changes with time)

Establish Goals

Compare Progress Achieved to Goals ← Develop Action Plans for Achieving Goals

IS YOUR SHOOTING CONTINUALLY IMPROVING? If not, try using the *process* that pro-athletes do.

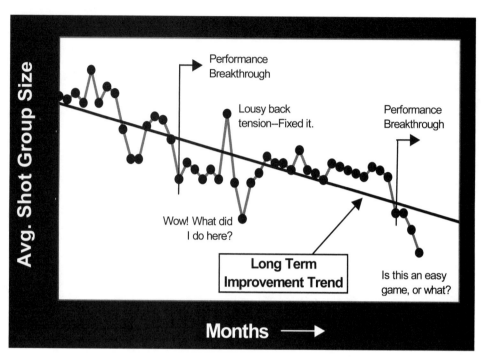

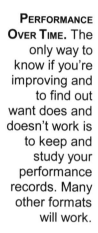

PERFORMANCE OVER TIME. The only way to know if you're improving and to find out want does and doesn't work is to keep and study your performance records. Many other formats will work.

Brainstorm ways to measure the critical form elements that you're working on. Suppose that you have a troublesome release. If you take ten shots, you might give yourself one point for a good release and zero points for a poor one. Train yourself to think of a perfect score for the day as a "10" regardless of the number of arrows that hit the bull's-eye.

If you make a perfect release, but the arrow misses, blow it off and give yourself a point. It may be due to another factor that you're not working on now. If you make a bad release, but accidentally hit the kill zone, consider the shot a failure and give yourself zero points. You'll improve faster by concentrating on the things you can control.

Keep Records

Practicing without something to compare to is like chasing a wisp of smoke. You'll need to find ways to measure your progress along the way. Keep a chronological log of your changing goals, improvement strategies, results, and shooting self-analysis. This is the only way that you can really see what does and doesn't work.

Start each session by formally writing down what you are going to work on and how you are going to go about it. Record all of your results, either in numbers, on a graph, or with sketches of some type—anything that is *objective* and *measurable* and appeals to you. A goal of "Getting Better" is too vague. A goal of "Increasing My *Percentage* of Killing Shots" can be measured with numbers and addressed effectively.

Then, sit down periodically and analyze your long term progress. If you're not improving, ask yourself why not, or what you might do differently. If you're progressing well, study the things that seem to work and brainstorm ways to do them better.

Separate "Work" from "Fun"

This whole continual improvement process isn't fun. It's work. That's what makes it so effective. Balance it with some mindless archery-play. Don't worry about performance; just have fun. But keep the work and play sessions to separate times and places so that you clearly separate them in your subconscious mind.

Lifelong Excellence

Don't get discouraged if you don't progress according to your pre-conceived expectations. Improvement in any area of human performance is rarely steady. Expect mixed periods of improvement, stagnation, or even setbacks. These are all natural precursors to dramatic events that sports psychologists call performance *breakthroughs*. These breakthroughs occur in all athletic endeavors if we give them enough time to happen.

Also keep in mind that this exercise isn't something to try for a few days or weeks and then drop when you get bored with it. It's an ongoing activity—a new lifestyle. Put simply: We may not always shoot as well as we'd like. But we can always *strive* towards that goal.

55. Hunting Practice

It's one of those mornings when it's just good to be alive and in the woods. The first warm rays of sunlight are just breaking over the horizon, the birds are singing, and a cool fall breeze is gently rustling the dew-covered leaves around you. But you don't notice all of this because a beautiful whitetail buck is feeding just 20-yards away. You carefully come to full draw, aim, release, and watch in disgust as the shot sails harmlessly over the 3-D target.

"You stupid idiot! You can do better than that. Now concentrate!" you tell yourself. You go through the scenario again and this time the arrow plunks solidly home behind the deer's shoulder. "Now that's more like it," you say aloud to the trees, "just pay attention to what you're doing."

Re-Think the Problem

If you're like most bowhunters, you probably think that good shooting is being able to stand on the practice range and shoot arrow after arrow into the kill zone. This is nice, of course, but it's not entirely necessary to your primary goal of shooting one good arrow at a deer—perhaps the only one you'll get during the season.

Rather than being able to shoot thirty arrows in a tight group at one time, you should be practicing to shoot a single arrow in the kill zone thirty mornings in a row. This demands a different way of practicing.

The Psychology of Missing

When most of us practice, we make some good shots and some bad shots. The bull's-eyes make us feel good and we remember them. The bad shots make us mad and we tend to repeat them until we get a positive feel-good result. At the end of a shooting session, we may block bad shots out of our minds, or only remember them as aberrations. This can give us a false sense of our capabilities and encourage us to take hunting shots that we shouldn't. What we're *capable* of doing often differs from what we *actually* do.

SPECIFICITY. Sports trainers use a concept known as *specificity.* If you want to get good at an activity, you need to practice that specific activity—as closely as possible.

To get good at taking hunting shots, you need to practice taking them in a realistic way. Use the technique described here to improve your in-the-field shooting in just 30-days.

Dr. Tom Saville, a behavioral psychology professor and bowhunter from Denver, explains it like this: "If we discount our misses by repeating them, we're not developing a subconscious belief that the first shot is the one that really counts. This keeps us from fully concentrating on hunting shots. Also, though we try to forget our misses, our subconscious will remember them and make us more nervous than we should be when shooting at an animal."

Instead of avoiding the psychological pain of missing, Saville advocates using it as a positive element during practice.

Positive Practice

Set up a tree stand and 3-D target in a realistic hunting situation thirty days before the season opens. Don your full hunting garb including jacket, long johns, gloves, day pack, and face mask if you wear them while hunting.

Climb into your stand once each morning before work, and once each evening after work, and sit for a few minutes to settle down and let your muscles start to stiffen. Now imagine that a big buck is walking down the trail towards you. Visualize a past hunting shot or two and try to conjure up all of the normal emotions and excitement that you felt.

Carefully raise your bow while imagining that the deer can see you move.

Move exactly like you would when shooting at a live animal. When your mind says *now*, then carefully go through your normal mental checklist and take the shot.

Now comes the hard part. Regardless of your result, DON'T SHOOT AGAIN! Climb down and go to the house. If you missed, or got a bad hit, live with that frustration and anger until that evening or the next day when you repeat the drill. This pain will make the shot stick in your mind and will force you to concentrate more on your next try.

Our human ego doesn't easily accept this type of failure without a fight, but it's vital to the success of the exercise. Shoot again and you'll delay your improvement. In other words, the pain and frustration of missing will actually make you shoot better, and more quickly, than your accumulation of killing shots.

If you made a good hit, and can do it repeatedly on the first shot, this will reinforce the positive elements of your mental preparation, concentration, and shooting form and make real shots easier.

Vary the position of the target and the types of shots you might have to take when a real deer walks down the trail to you. Find your consistently accurate range and then stick with it in the field.

Separate Goals

Keep in mind that you're not trying to work on good shooting fundamentals here. Instead, you're trying to find your maximum effective range in the field and improve your concentration on your first shots. You can still practice normally. Just do it in other places and at other times of the day so that your mind doesn't confuse the two types of practice. Think of your regular practice as mid-day plinking in hunting camp and this simulated hunting drill as the real thing.

60-Shots

Try this program for at least 30 days—taking no more than 60-shots—before each hunting season (I do it periodically throughout the entire year). At the end of the month, you should have a much better feel for what you can actually do when hunting and much greater confidence that you can capitalize on that that earned shot when it presents itself.

56. Practice Games

Baby predators operate in the active mode. They wrestle, mock-fight, and practice stalking crickets and mice. This increases their chance of survival by teaching them the skills they'll need as adults. They don't consciously set out to practice these things. They learn them naturally by just having fun.

As bowhunter-predators we can do the same thing. Playing regular practice games can help you maintain a healthy zest for the sport and aid in your hunting preparation to boot.

Roving

The time-tested game of roving, or stump shooting, is still one of the best practice games. It can be played alone or with friends. Simply walk through the woods taking turns picking targets—a leaf, shadow, flower, cow-patty, or anything else that catches your fancy—and see how close you can hit to it.

In the spring and summer, stretch yourself a bit by taking hard shots. Learn what you can and can't do. As the hunting season draws near, concentrate on shots that you "know" you can make. This will help you to determine your effective range (can change from year to year), teach you to stay within it, and build shooting confidence. Throw in a few risk-reward shots—such as a kill-zone-sized patch of bare earth that's bordered by rocks—to keep yourself honest.

Pick a Position

Shoot at a fixed target with competitors taking turns specifying *how* the shot has to be made. Shoot while sitting or kneeling, with a twisted stance, with your bow severely canted to the right or left, or anything else you can think of. Find stuff that you can do but your competitor can't, or that will give him a muscle spasm or two in good fun.

PRACTICE GAMES BUILD CONFIDENCE. Practice games are not only fun, but they teach you new skills and quickly tell you what you're capable of doing (and not doing) in the field.

Nocks

This is a favorite of target archers. Find a willing competitor, stand fifteen- or thirty-feet from a practice bale (depending on your nerve), and take turns shooting. The object is bust all the nocks off of your buddy's arrows before he busts all of yours. This is similar to the game of *Cut Throat* in billiards where the object is to remove all of your opponents balls before they sink yours. A word or caution: Play this game with a good friend as losers can get pretty upset.

"Lord of the Ring"

Make a six-inch steel circle from a coat-hangar and attach it to a target bale. Starting at five-yards (or some other distance where you know that you can make the shot), shoot an arrow inside the hoop. That done, move back a few yards and shoot again. Keep moving back and shooting until you miss the ring.

This game does several important things. The steel ring, as opposed to a simple printed bull's eye, has a certain psychic-finality to it. Shots are either *in* or they're *out*. No ifs, ands, or buts. This will force you to concentrate on shooting the arrow as near to the center as you can on every shot. It also identifies, in non-ambiguous terms, just how far you're capable of shooting on your best, worst, and average days.

Done by yourself, this is an excellent way to find your effective range on deer. Done with a friend, it can be an intense competition. The first fellow to miss loses. The game is great fun and a real eye-opener.

The Dark Side

Not enough hours in the day to practice after that long work shift? No problem. Shoot in the dark. Light a candle and practice snuffing out the flame without hitting the candle. It's a real kick when you do it.

Or, lose the candle and shoot at your 3-D target by moonlight using just its dim, partial outline.

Finally, set up a blank target in your garage or basement and shoot in total pitch black from close range. Concentrate on form and the overall feel of the shot. Since you won't be worrying about aiming or the fear of missing, this is one of the best games for grooving your form.

Board Games

Like to play parlor games? Many of them can be played with arrows. The simplest is *Tic-Tac-Toe*. Get a buddy, draw up a few target sized grids and have a tournament. Darts is another favorite. Draw up a large dart board, including the small risk-reward double and triple count areas, and play any of the dozens of standard dart games. Any other card or board game that uses squares or numbers also offer possibilities. Be creative.

Winter Blues

Don't give up those valuable winter practice months just because it's cold and dreary outside. Find some photos or sketches of deer, scale them appropriately on a Xerox machine to a shooting distance of three- to five-yards, paste them on a cardboard back, and practice killing them.

This isn't as easy as it sounds. To be successful, your bow must be precisely tuned so that arrows come off it straight. And your form will have to be near-perfect to prevent flyers that are more common at ultra-short distances.

Flu-Flu Fun

Make up some flu-flus and practice hitting flying branches, cans, cow pies, and other available targets. Learn to aim by feel instead of mechanically. You may be surprised at how well you do when you just let it happen.

57. Think SMALL for Big Game

A good friend called me late one evening a few years ago to complain that he'd just missed the biggest buck of his life. "Not only that, but I missed him by two feet!," he added, obviously in grief. "I have to find a way to get over being so nervous when I shoot at a deer."

"How about if we hit the cottontails heavily this spring," I offered. He rejected this instantly, explaining sagely that rabbits weren't the same thing. "Well, then maybe you should just take lots of shots at record book bucks," I countered. "Yeah, right!" he replied.

This conversation summarizes a dilemma that many hunters face every year. When that moment of truth comes, there's nothing that can calm your nerves better than lots of experience under pressure. Yet this experience doesn't come easily.

Small Game Benefits

Despite my friend's lack of interest, I still contend that small game hunting provides excellent practice that stumps or paper targets don't. Hunters who are consistently good shots on small game usually do well on deer. Conversely, hunters who are erratic on small game are often erratic on big game as well.

Many misses on deer are due to a lack of concentration under pressure. A paper deer will patiently let you setup, concentrate on your form and aiming, and then shoot. But a live one is far less accommodating. They have a nasty habit of taking a step or looking up during the shot which can totally unnerve the best of hunters.

Although rabbits and squirrels may not produce the heart pounding excitement of big bucks, they'll exhibit similar reactions when hunted. Because of this, they can provide excellent practice in maintaining form and concentration under the stress of a hunting shot. The only difference is that

"GOOD EATS" PLUS EXCELLENT PRACTICE. Small game provides better practice than shooting at stumps or paper targets. And... it tastes better!

on a good day you might get two dozen shots at rabbits instead of a few per year at deer.

Small game hunting is also more fun than punching holes in paper or dirt piles. And, or course, a nice side benefit is meat for the pot that you've procured yourself.

Available Everywhere

Small game of one variety or another can be found almost anywhere in the country. Rabbits, squirrels, marmots, and woodchucks are popular targets. Other folks add ducks, geese, grouse, or pheasants to the list. Consistently bagging game birds on the wing requires quick decision making and quick, accurate shots—the same things that are often important in big game hunting.

If you don't have easy access to these critters, there are many species in your own backyard that can help you to develop these same skills. Try shooting at cruising butterflies, dragonflies, or bees with judo-pointed arrows. Hunting bugs may sound stupid, but it's probably no more stupid then hunting leaves or tree stumps.

Give it a try. It may not keep you from missing that new world record buck come fall, but it's certainly a step in the right direction.

Small Game Hunting Tips

If your main goal is rabbit or squirrel stew, that's fine. If your main goal is to improve your deer hunting skills, then keep these tips in mind:

Pick Your Distance. Just because you can walk up and count coup on a bunny doesn't mean that you have to shoot it. Try to shoot at distances that you're likely to encounter when hunting your favorite big game species. If that means stalking backward, then do it.

Pick a Spot. If you shoot instinctively, it's vital to pick a small aiming spot and concentrate totally on it. This is doubly hard on a live animal. Practice picking a spot and keeping your eye on it when the animal takes a hop, scurries towards a burrow, or jumps from one limb to another.

Pick Your Shot. On small game, shot angle isn't important. A broadhead or judo point will usually anchor them firmly right where they sit. But the same isn't true of a deer. Get in the habit of imagining that a rabbit is a deer, or that a squirrel is a mountain lion in a tree, and watch him until he gives you the shot you'd want on these animals. Wait for your quarry to turn his head or move it behind a branch like you would on a big game animal.

Vary Your Shooting Style. Target styles don't always work best on game. Using a mental checklist during shooting may work well on the target bale but not in the field when the animal suddenly moves on check point number 2½. Try different styles. Shoot from sitting or kneeling positions, while twisting your body, or with your bow canted to clear obstructions. Find out what works before deer season.

Part 6. The Mental Game

A commonly repeated adage is that archery is 90% mental. Having watched some of my magnum misses on shots that I paid heavy attention to, I sometimes question this claim. But, whatever the percentage, the mental aspect of archery is clearly a heavy hitter in the accuracy equation.

This subject could fill volumes, and *has* in other sports. In this section, we'll look at a few important mental tricks to consider in your quest for shooting perfection.

58. Concentration

Concentration is vitally important to accurate shooting. Instinctive shooting guru Fred Asbell sums this up succinctly in his excellent series of books and videos on the subject. "How well can you shoot?" he asks. His answer: "How well can you concentrate?" The same might be said of sight-shooters.

And yet, most people in our modern society aren't very good concentrators. It's just not something that we're taught. Older societies often valued the power of concentration much more highly, most notably the Oriental, Asian, and Native American cultures.

When asked to explain the essence of Zen, one master (himself an extraordinary bow shot) responded simply: "When I eat, I eat; when I walk, I walk," referring to his total concentration on the moment. The Japanese word *zanchin* describes a state of total, unbroken concentration. No similar word in the English language captures this idea so economically. Many Lakota Sioux conducted their daily lives according to a simple rule, *Akita Mani Yo*, which translates as "Walk and observe everything that you see."

Compare these examples to your own childhood teachings.

PRACTICE MAKES PERFECT. It's not enough to tell yourself to concentrate. Like any human endeavor, concentration is a skill that must be practiced.

A Quick Test

Take this test. Find a quiet spot and *totally* concentrate your thoughts and visual focus on the minute-hand of a watch or clock. When your focus blurs, or some foreign thought wedges itself into your consciousness, stop and note the elapsed time. Three-to ten-seconds is a common score for beginners.

In contrast, practiced concentrators can spend hours in total focused concentration. Called *meditation* (self-hypnosis uses the same technique), the practice is nothing more than totally concentrating on some element—your breath, a word, or a visual image.

One Age-Old Technique

Find a quiet spot, get comfortable, and totally relax your body. Start by concentrating on the muscles in your scalp, head, neck, chest, arms, and hands. Continue moving downwards through your belly, legs, feet, ankles, and toes. Imagine that the tension is flowing from your body as if it was water seeping out through a drain. Try to feel "light" in the chair.

Now, concentrate on your breadth. Breath in through your nose and out through your mouth. Feel each one as it moves in and out. Or slowly repeat some word, like the number *one*, each time you exhale. As other thoughts wedge their way into your consciousness (as they almost certainly will), gently purge them and continue concentrating on your breadth or a word. Even thoughts like "I need to keep concentrating" are foreign and need to be expelled.

You'll know when you've arrived by the light-headed, muscle-sagging calm that will engulf you and your effortless ability to concentrate on a single thought.

Practice is Essential

This isn't as mystical or geeky as it sounds. Many of the best archers in history have used this, or similar, techniques to improve their shooting concentration. Many Olympic shooters continue to do so today.

Get yourself a good book on meditation or concentration techniques and spend a few hours each week practicing. After a time, you'll only have to call up a trigger phrase or image to mentally turn on maximum concentration.

The main point here is this: You can't just tell yourself to concentrate and expect instant success. Like any human endeavor, you've got to consciously *practice* to become good at it.

59. Visualization

We experience the world through our senses. Our minds process these physical stimuli and converts them into thoughts, words, or feelings. This *state-of-mind* then affects the actions that lead to our subsequent successes or failures.

Going to the Movies

The interesting thing is: We can create artificial sensory inputs with our conscious thoughts and our subconscious minds will perceive them as the real thing. Pro golfers refer to this as "going to the movies." They silently visualize the shot they want to make, the ball's curving right or left trajectory through the air, its landing point and roll distance, and the feel that produces these results. The real shot then mimics the mental movie that they've just watched in their heads.

Some Examples

One Vietnam POW tells the story of how he kept his sanity by mentally playing stroke-by-stroke golf rounds during his imprisonment. When he got home, his actual game improved by a whopping seven strokes, despite his forced inactivity.

You may have seen downhill racers on TV standing at the starting gate, eyes closed, swaying gently back and forth. They are visualizing every turn and mogul on the course, the feel of wind and gravity, and their successful responses to these demands. Then, without waiting for reality to set in, they simply open their eyes and go.

Bowhunting great Paul Shaffer once described a superb shot he made on a desert bighorn. The shot wasn't difficult, he explained, because he had visualized it over and over in his mind and saw the arrow hitting home before pulling the string back.

"GOING TO THE MOVIES." Imagine the results that you want, and all of the actions needed to produce them. Then just let it happen.

Byron Ferguson, a well known exhibition shooter, likes to tell people to "be the arrow." This visualization process is what he's referring to.

Use It You get the idea. Try closing your eyes and mentally visualizing success during your regular shooting practice, during your concentration exercises, and just prior to a real hunting or tournament shot. See the result that you want and yourself successfully doing the things needed to produce it.

It works!

60. Think and Act "Right"

The things that we think about when we shoot, and the ways we respond to good and bad outcomes, affect's our accuracy.

Fear & Anger

People respond emotionally to unspoken cues they give themselves and this can affect their performance, either positively or negatively. Fear and anger are the two most destructive culprits.

You might have a fear of failure—target panic and buck fever are usually caused by this—or a fear of success due to self-induced pressure to keep succeeding in front of your friends. (Fear of success is a rare phenomenon, but does happen in some folks.) Or you might have a fear of looking foolish or inept when you miss.

Fear occurs before a shot and anger after a poorly executed one. Anger then combines with pre-shot fear to make the next shot even worst. Both fear and anger are psychic poisons that destroy concentration. Studies show that these negative emotions release hormones into your bloodstream that physically inhibit performance.

First, be aware of any fears and angers that you have. Then use positive self-talk to counteract them.

Emotional Arousal

Hans Seyle, a Canadian medical researcher, defines two types of stress: good and bad. He likens this to a violin string. Strung too loose, and the sound it produces is dull and listless. Too tight and the string snaps. But with just the right amount of stress, the instrument makes beautiful music.

People are the same. Find the amount of emotional arousal that works for you and then try to cultivate it. If you get nervous at the thought of an important shot, learn to relax. Take deep breaths that start from your belly and expand upward through your diaphragm. Exhale slowly. Do everything in slow motion.

If a bit of stress helps you to concentrate better or feel stronger, learn to create it artificially. Think exciting thoughts. Take short, rapid breaths. Speed up your actions. Either way, find something that works to put you in your optimal state of arousal.

Just Let Go

Time and again, professional athletes relate that they perform at their best when they let go of any conscious thought and just let it happen. When they think too much they develop the much publicized *paralysis through analysis.*

Some describe this as "a peaceful state of nothingness," a "trance-like state," or a "detached dreamlike state." One athlete-poet described it flowingly as "a state where actions happen automatically as if your nervous system is locked unto a radio beam which synchronizes your actions with everything around you." Most just call it being "in the groove," or "in the zone."

Bottom line: For peak shooting success, let go of conscious thought (or as much as possible for your shooting style) and just trust it to happen.

Think and Act "Right"

✓ Recognize your fears
- ? Failure
- ? Success
- ? Looking foolish
- ? Target panic & buck fever
- ? Others

✓ Control your anger over poor outcomes
✓ Cultivate optimum emotional arousal
✓ Trust it to happen

61. On the Practice Range

If the secret to shooting success is to just let it happen, does this mean that there's no place for conscious thought or activity in an archery shot? Not so. Just keep conscious mechanical thinking to the practice range where it's important in developing good shooting fundamentals.

Practice vs. Performance

Learn to separate the *skill acquisition* and *actual performance* phases of archery. Learn to be a perfectionist on the practice range but to let-it-happen on hunting or tournament shots.

Develop a sound pre-shot routine that includes a series of physical and psychological steps that put you in the best possible position to succeed. Incorporate a trigger phrase, thought, or gesture into your routine that will signal you when to turn on maximum concentration (nocking the arrow, for instance). Incorporate another that will signal you when to switch from voluntary control to involuntary action. One guy I know hunches his shoulders towards the target and then goes mentally blank. Another says "Turn it loose [conscious thinking, that is], Mother Goose." And another thinks of "blue nothingness." I don't know what that means, but it works for him.

Find a shooting routine that performs consistently under pressure. It doesn't have to be logical or rational—It just has to work!

Accentuate the Positive

Professional sports psychologists teach their athlete-clients to always remember the positive aspects of their performance and purge the negative aspects from their minds. This breeds confidence.

The following story is told of golfer Jack Nicklaus (who's also a bowhunter!). Jack gave a talk once where he claimed that he had never missed an important ten-foot putt in a major tournament. One guy in the audience took him to task on this statement and a chilly exchange followed.

Sports psychologist Bob Rotella commented on this later: "The question is not whether Jack Nicklaus has ever missed a ten-foot putt. Of course he has. The point is that Jack doesn't *remember* ever missing a ten-foot putt. If you want to play like Jack Nicklaus, then *think* like Jack Nicklaus."

Follow this advise in your shooting. If you're shooting badly, then work on the causes and fix it. But if you just shoot a occasional bad arrow, forget it. Train yourself to think that you will never miss important shots, and you'll improve the chances that you won't.

End on a High Note

Always end your practice sessions after a series of good shots. That way, you'll leave the range with a positive feeling that you'll carry with you until the next session.

Ending on a bad shot can eat on you subconsciously. The problem that most folks make is that they practice until they become fatigued. Then they start shooting badly, and keep shooting to fix the problem. More bad shots result.

Get in the habit of quitting your practice sessions when you're fresh and shooting well. If you suddenly start shooting poorly, continue only long enough to shoot two or three good shots in a row, and then quit for the day.

On the Practice Range

- ✓ Be a perfectionist
- ✓ Develop a sound shot routine
- ✓ Use a trigger phrase or action to turn on maximum concentration
- ✓ Use a trigger phrase or action to switch from voluntary to involuntary control
- ✓ Accentuate the positive
- ✓ Quit on a well shot arrow

A Quick Review

Before moving on, let's briefly review a few key points from the last few chapters:

Consciously practice to improve your concentration. Develop trigger phrases, thoughts, or gestures to signal yourself to relax and enter the concentration and mindless performance zones. Visualize the end result that you want and the actions needed to produce those results.

Focus on a shooting sense rather than mechanical thoughts when hunting. Don't think or reflect, but *feel*. And don't let negative self-talk destroy all of your other efforts.

Keep all of your thoughts positive. Consciously purge negative thoughts from your mind. Be dispassionate about bad results. They're past and can't be corrected. Analyze them rationally without getting upset. Use your analysis to improve the next shot.

Defend your ego. Avoid the tendency to tell yourself you're an idiot after a bad shot. Remind yourself that it's just a bad shot and that you also make many good ones. Talk in the present tense to prevent dwelling on past events.

Decide in advance what you're going to say to yourself when fear, anger, and feelings of inadequacy strike. Find positive self-talk phrases that make you feel good and use them after a bad shot.

Apply a mental tourniquet if you're simply having a bad day. Take a mental timeout: Recall past successes; don't press; care without being obsessed.

Practice these techniques in your everyday life to ingrain them. Carry the right attitude onto the range or into field to start with. Work to cultivate the three-C's—*Concentration, Composure, and Confidence*—that spell success.

62. Target Panic

People who have never experienced the ravages of target panic might read this chapter with curiosity or laughter. It's something that they just can't appreciate until it happens to them. But there are plenty of archers out there who will know just what I'm talking about.

Due to a variety of factors, finger-shooters are more prone to target panic than release-shooters. And traditional archers, who hold more weight at full draw than compound shooters, are even more prone to it. Most of them will experience it sometime during their shooting careers.

But the disease can affect *any* shooter at any time in greater or lesser degrees. Let's look at what target panic is, and at some ways to keep it in check.

Like Alcoholism

In many ways target panic is like alcoholism. It's an insidious disease that starts so slowly that at first you may not even know you have it. Later, as the symptoms become apparent, you try to deny it. When you're forced at last to admit it to yourself, you feel embarrassed and find devious ways to hide it from others. It begins to affect your life.

You start making excuses for your lack of control, quit shooting tournaments, or avoid situations where you have to shoot in front of others. You recede into a shell of self-pity and depression. You pass up shots at deer that you used to take with confidence; or you take them and feel guilty that you did. You reach out for help, but none seems to be there.

You're alone in a wilderness of self-doubt. Finally, you start having thoughts of archery suicide—you seriously consider quitting the sport.

Do You Have It?

In his excellent book, *Understanding Winning Archery*, Al Henderson, defines target panic generically as any feeling that you are not in complete control of a shot. Beyond this, Henderson is at a loss to explain it. This is because the causes and symptoms of the disease are so varied among individuals.

In one of its rarest forms, an archer can't release the arrow. This was the problem that Jon Voight's character had in the movie *Deliverance* (the book's author James Dickey, a bowhunter, may have

Two Faces of Target Panic
<u>Lack of Physical Control</u>
✓ Don't over-bow yourself
✓ Build-up through weight training
✓ Avoid over-practicing
<u>Mental--Fear of Missing</u>
✓ Shoot from close range
✓ Shoot in the dark
✓ Be patient
✓ Aggressively attack symptoms
✓ Use a mechanical shooting aid

known something of this malady first hand). Voight would come to full draw and then freeze. After many long moments of straining, he'd start to shake and tell himself urgently to "release, RELEASE!" Finally, he'd let go wildly in an anguished explosion of movement and breath.

In its more common form, archers are unable to come to full draw, or to hold as long as they want to while aiming. I've seen highly intelligent, successful people almost reduced to tears over their inability to draw their release hand anywhere near their face before letting go of the string.

Release shooters may not exhibit the same outward manifestations of target panic that finger-shooters do, but they might "punch" their releases before they're ready due to the same mental causes that underlie the disease.

Ask yourself these questions: Do I always feel in complete control of my shots? Do I sometimes release before I'm ready? Do I feel like I'm controlling the bow, or does the bow seem to be controlling me? Am I calm when I shoot, or do I involuntarily tense up? Do I intensely focus on the task at hand, or do vague thoughts of missing wedge their way into my mind?

You get the idea. If you have target panic, the first task is to honestly admit it to yourself. That done, here are a few tricks to use to overcome it.

Causes & Remedies

Since the causes of target panic are so varied, it's impossible to give a simple set of answers on how to control them. Your problems may be physical or mental in nature, or a combination of these factors. Attack each cause independently.

Physical Control. Lack of physical control over your bow is often a major cause of target panic among traditional shooters. It's usually a minor or non-existent cause for compound shooters who only hold a fraction of the bow's weight at full draw. But it may still play a part.

Here's what's happening: If you use a heavier bow than you're conditioned for, there's physical discomfort involved. This might not be noticeable on a conscious level but your subconscious mind will recognize it and constantly urge you to shoot to end the discomfort. If you do this long enough, you'll mentally reinforce the habit of releasing prematurely. Over time, you may become so habituated to this bad habit that you might never be able to fully break it.

Hunters who convert from a compound to a recurve or longbow are particularly susceptible to the over-bow syndrome. They just naturally assume that if they were shooting a 70-pound compound, they should be able to shoot a 70-pound stick bow. Then they develop target panic from holding the heavier weight and don't know why.

If you use all of your strength to pull a bow in a hunting situation, you're much more likely to get a short draw or a bad release than if you use one you can handle comfortably. You're also more likely to surrender to buck fever (a special form of target panic) if you feel like the bow is controlling you, instead of the other way around.

The Light Bow Test. There's an easy way see if bow weight is causing part of your problem. If you sense any lack of control with your hunting bow, try one that's significantly lighter and see what happens. If your regular bow is 60-pounds, try using a 20- or 30-pound bow. If your target panic disappears, then the source of the problem is probably physical in nature.

Drop down to a bow weight that you can control completely and then slowly build back up to your hunting bow. During this process, remember to never shoot an arrow that you don't feel in control of. Psychologists tell us that a single bad shot will reinforce your bad habits and might require ten good ones to get you back where you were. If you feel a loss of control creeping in, let the string down and start the shot over. If the problem continues, then drop down again in weight and start building up again.

It also helps to build up your strength through weight training. This way your mind won't associate the stress and discomfort with shooting. A general fitness program probably won't exercise your shooting muscles the right way so pull some heavy bows as part of your training. But don't shoot them. Instead, practice for several weeks just pulling and holding them.

Avoid over-practicing. You only need one accurate shot when hunting. Put all of your concentration into shooting one, or a few, good practice shots and then stop before you get fatigued. Review your practice sessions after you're through. Do you usually start out shooting well on a particular day, during a particular week, and then slowly go downhill? If so, you're probably overdoing it.

Mental Control. If your target panic is only physical in nature, then you're a very lucky person. Most people with the disease aren't in control with any bow. They might be able to comfortably hold a 60-pound recurve at full draw for thirty seconds but can't come to full draw—even for a fraction of a second—with a 30-pound bow when actually shooting an arrow. This indicates that the problem is primarily mental.

If this describes you, then you may have developed a conscious or subconscious fear of missing or of looking foolish in front of your friends. This can be a self-fulfilling prophesy. If you're afraid of missing, you're more likely to "peek" at the shot before it hits the target, or tense up so much before releasing that the arrow never really has a chance to hit where it should.

This fear can sometimes be eliminated by simply redefining your goals and expectations. Concentrate on things you can control and forget about those that you can't. Remember: *You don't have any control over where the arrow goes. You can only control how you shoot it.*

It's also helpful to practice for a few weeks or months from very close range (three- to five-yards) to lessen your fear of missing. Better yet, practice in the dark (or with your eyes closed) so you can't see where your arrows hit.

Be Patient. Finally, keep one important point in mind during your recovery. More than likely, it took you a long time to develop the disease. During this period you probably took many thousands of shots which reinforced your bad habits. According to sports psychologists, building good habits might take ten-thousand well-executed shots. You'll have to work at it for a while before making any real progress. So be patient.

Even after you improve, be constantly aware of target panic symptoms and attack them with a vengeance when they first rear their ugly head.

The Recovering Alcoholic

To return to my earlier analogy: Like alcoholism, target panic can be controlled but it can never be totally cured. I still have occasional bouts with the disease if I practice too much, or at 3-D shoots if I get fatigued. But I've now got the problem pretty much licked.

With an intelligent plan and a bit of hard work, you can do the same thing. And I can assure you that there's no better feeling in archery than to make a comeback from the throes of target panic and once again have confidence in your shooting.

Mechanical Help for Finger Shooters

If these tips don't help, it may be time to take more drastic action. If you're a finger-shooter, try a hunting-type clicker or mechanical release-aid. If you don't like these items for hunting, don't overlook their value as training aids. Using one of them for a few weeks is often all that's needed to re-build a sense of control in your shooting. Then you can go back to your regular shooting style until the panic again rears its ugly head. For a long term cure, work on the physical and mental roots of the problem.

63. Buck Fever

Contrary to popular belief, pain isn't bad. It's good. It's nature's way of warning us to stop doing what we're doing before we hurt ourselves more seriously. The emotional arousal of a hunting shot is a little like this. Some of its symptoms may be uncomfortable, but it's nature's way of preparing us for the task at hand.

Adrenaline is pumped into our bloodstream, muscles fibers tighten and twitch, eyes dilate, heart rate rises, and breathing quickens. All of this is in preparation for our genetically programmed fight-or-flight reaction.

Despite the annoying side affects, there are probably few people who would care to hunt without these things. Lose that magical feeling—a hunter's feeling—and you've probably lost a good bit of joy in the sport. One thing is sure: Every hunter will probably experience the ravages of buck fever some time in their hunting careers.

Part of Being Human

Anthropologists tell us that hunting arousal is a natural part of our evolution as hunting animals. Show a young child a football or toy truck for the first time and there's no immediate response. He has to be taught that these things are fun. Show him a whitetail deer and the response is visceral. His eyes bulge and the little hairs stand up on the back of his neck. In one study, non-hunters (including some avowed anti's) were taken hunting and they exhibited the same physical responses that we do. Despite some modern denials, it's just part of being human.

Is It Really Buck Fever?

Many people refer to normal arousal as buck fever when it probably isn't. While many of the symptoms are the same, buck fever is emotional arousal in spades. It's a nuclear explosion compared to a fire cracker. And it *can* be destructive.

I've known people who were powerless to pull their bows, or even keep their arrows from bouncing off the rest because they were shaking so bad. An *Outdoor Life* article some years ago told of one rifle hunter who jacked his entire magazine of cartridges through the chamber and ejected them without ever pulling the trigger. Turning to his hunting partner, almost in tears, he lamented that he had missed every shot at the buck. These are the ravages of buck fever at its worst.

Give the following tricks a try the next time buck fever grips you. They've helped many hunters get through a stressful situation.

Be Thankful

As mentioned above, emotional arousal isn't bad as long as it doesn't get out of hand. Accept this fact and tell yourself that it could help you make a better

PART OF BEING HUMAN. Emotional arousal during a hunting shot is part of what makes the experience enjoyable. When it gets out of hand, use some of the proven tricks in this chapter to increase your chances of success. They worked here!

shot. Sometimes acceptance alone, or looking at arousal in a positive way, is enough to alleviate the symptoms.

Go With It

Don't fight the symptoms. Denial and fighting will just make them worse. Rather than trying to stop shaking, consciously try to accelerate it. Rather than trying to stifle rapid breathing, breath even more rapidly. Fool your body. Make it think that you're aroused enough and don't need any more help. This may help the symptoms to subside more quickly so that by the time the buck steps into your shooting lane, you're calm again.

"Program" the Symptoms

Muscle shakes and spasms usually don't come in one uninterrupted stream. They occur, then abate, and then occur again a few moments later. If you can't get rid of them, learn to time them, perhaps by trying to accelerate them just before the shot as described above. You only need to be calm at the moment you shoot. Then accept the "big one" that may follow—after you've done the deed.

Kill the Ego

A core element of Zen archery is eliminating the ego. This means that you shouldn't care about how your personal successes or failures are viewed by others. If you miss the buck, don't worry about what your buddies will say. Remind yourself that it's not a life and death situation. It's supposed to be *fun*. If you miss, you're still a good person; still a good bowhunter who will have many other successful days. This can be a tremendous pressure reducer.

Think Calming Thoughts

Identify places, or specific times in your life, when you've been totally and completely relaxed and assign a code word to them. Train yourself to automatically go brain- and muscle-dead when you say the word in your head. And then use it on your hunting shots.

One of those times in my life was on a New Mexico backpack trip with my wife. After hiking seventeen-miles one day up and down steep, oxygen starved mountains, lugging 80-pounds on my back, the relief of a sheltered meadow and its sweet pine scent was an overpowering relaxant. When I say the word *Pine* to myself today, I immediately conjure up the same feeling.

Cure Your Target Panic

People with really bad buck fever might also have a case of target panic which is fueled by a heightened fear of missing. While the two are related, they're separate and treatable maladies. To lessen the buck fever, cure the target panic first. And, unlike buck fever, this can be done at your leisure in your own backyard.

Medicine for Buck Fever
✓ Be thankful for the arousal
✓ Don't fight the symptoms
✓ Program symptoms so that they abate at the right time
✓ Don't worry about poor results
✓ Think calming thoughts
✓ Cure your target panic first
✓ Say a non-tension producing prayer
✓ Practice enough to believe in yourself
✓ Be successful

Say a Prayer

Rather than praying to your maker for help, which can heighten arousal by adding pressure to succeed, try the opposite. My standard little prayer goes something like this:

Lord, thank you for this beautiful morning and for the chance to see such a beautiful creature, wild and free. If I get him, that's fine. And if not, that's fine too. I don't care. I just appreciate the opportunity to be here and have the experience.

As soon as I say this little verse, I immediately become calm. I don't worry about the buck stepping in the right place or turning the right way. I can't control this. If it's meant to happen, it will. If not, then it won't. In short, I don't pressure myself. If all of the necessary ingredients come together, my subconscious just takes over and makes the shot at the right moment.

Believe in Yourself

If you've properly prepared yourself and know you can make the shot, then there's really no reason to be nervous. Tell yourself to *trust your form* and just take the shot. This simple reminder helps many people to calm themselves. If you don't trust your form, of course, this technique won't work. Practice until you *do* trust it.

Shoot With It

Shooting with buck fever isn't something that you can easily practice. Yet, it can be done. Unfortunately, the opportune time is just after you missed a hunting shot. Before the symptoms subside, take a few practice shots from your stand and get used to the different feeling. Do you need to consciously pull the bow back harder? Cant more to keep the arrow on the rest? Aim differently? You may have blown this opportunity, but you can certainly learn what to do differently next time.

Dress Well

Cold weather and buck fever—the really bad kind—go together like peas and carrots, as Forrest Gump might say. If you're on the verge of shivering already, the sudden appearance of a nice buck just might be enough to set off a chain reaction.

Do a few hidden jumping jacks behind a hill if you're stalking, or try tensing and relaxing your muscles in a tree stand to generate some calming heat. Beyond that, just dress warm when its cold. Err on the side of over-dressing when in doubt.

Be Successful

Finally, nothing succeeds like success itself. My buck fever is pretty much relegated to the days when I hadn't killed many deer, wanted to badly, and didn't have enough of a track record to believe that I could do it on purpose. Nowadays, I know I can do it and that it's not an accident. I might get a little nervous on a really big animal, but my pre-rut shots at meat-deer aren't much different than my McKenzie target practice.

If you're just getting started in the sport and tend to get really nervous on a hunting shot, just be patient. The scourges of buck fever *will* lessen with time and your accumulated successes.

64. Bowhunting Goals

The warm summer sun is low in the sky as a young boy, clutching a crude homemade bow and sapling arrow, slowly eases through the field in search of game. He is moccasined and bare chested, as all good Indian hunters should be, and tanned to a golden brown from many previous days spent in this way. Alerted by the slight sound of the approaching brave, a magnificent whitetail buck steps from cover and gives the boy a fleeting ten-yard shot. The shot is high and the deer bounds away to safety. The boy is at once both saddened and elated. "Some day," he says to himself, "I'll kill an animal with a bow like this."

That boy was me and the *deer* was actually a cottontail rabbit. I never did shoot anything with that crude archery gear but the fantasy remained submerged, waiting to surface again at the right time.

Goals are Important

Bowhunting can be enjoyed without setting goals, but hunters who do it tend to enjoy the sport more. They also tend to improve faster than those who don't. In other sports, goals are pretty straight forward—a lower time or higher score. In bowhunting, the great variances in equipment, hunting styles, species hunted, and hunting philosophies make the selection of goals much more personal.

A HUNTER'S LIFE. Most hunters will go through these stages sometime in their hunting lifetimes. Choose your goals appropriately to remain fresh and excited about the sport.

A Hunter's Life

- ✓ **Shooting** Stage--Hunter seeks lots of shooting opportunities.
- ✓ **Limiting Out** Stage--Hunter seeks to consistently fill all of his tags.
- ✓ **Trophy Hunting** Stage--Hunter seeks to take larger and larger animals.
- ✓ **Methods** Stage--Hunting methods and equipment used become the most important aspects.
- ✓ **Mellowing Out** Stage--The kill becomes secondary to the aesthetic aspects of the hunt.

The late Dr. Robert Jackson, a University of Wisconsin researcher (and bowhunter), defined five stages of development that most of us will go through during our hunting careers. Whether we do so consciously or subconsciously, most of us will set goals based on the stage that we're in. The first is the *Shooting* stage. New hunters seek out lots of shooting opportunities. Once they've satisfied this urge, they move into the *Limiting Out* stage. They take great pride in proving to themselves and to their friends that they can consistently fill their tags.

After a hunter has satisfied himself that he has the skills to kill a deer at will, he generally moves into the *Trophy* stage where he shifts his attention to taking larger and larger animals. Next comes the *Methods* stage where hunting

A Little Javelina. The author's first "primitive" kill—a South Texas Javelina—taken using a using a homemade, sinew-backed Osage bow and self-doweled maple arrow. This fulfilled a long suppressed goal.

methods and the equipment used become more important than the size of an animal. Finally, there's the *Mellowing Out* stage where the kill becomes secondary to the aesthetic aspects of the hunt such as observation and appreciation of nature or the camaraderie of a hunting camp.

Not all hunters will go through each of these stages, or go through them in the order that Jackson lists. But if we stay in the sport long enough, most of us will spend some time in each phase. We may also vacillate between phases depending on the circumstances. My interest in taking an animal with a primitive homemade bow was clearly in the methods stage. But if I'm hunting a new species, I may only be interested in filling my tag. Or, if I've taken quite a few animals of some species, I may don my trophy-hunter hat.

Choose goals that are appropriate to the stage that you're in and not due to peer pressure.

Write Them Down

It's important to think about your goals periodically and write them down. This introspective process will force you to think about where you are in the sport and where you want to be in the future. It will help you to realize and abandon outdated ideas and to exchange them with fresh ones.

Whatever goals you decide on, they should have two important characteristics. They should be *sufficiently difficult* to challenge you to work hard and learn. And they should *be achievable* in a reasonable time period so you're continually reinforced and remain fresh and excited about the sport.

Personal Records

Personal records are closely related to goals. They may be the result of consciously set goals or due to some fortuitous circumstance. In either event, new accomplishments are important in keeping us emotionally alive and motivated.

My wife, who's a marathoner, calls these *PRs*. She's observed that while competitive runners talk proudly of their new PRs, many bowhunters don't. I've seen people shoot their first deer and then apologize that it was a doe or spike buck. And I've seen hunters who just shot the largest buck of their lives but were upset because they saw a bigger one that got away.

Enjoy your accomplishments, whether you planned them or not.

**A Little
Javelina**

After my wife pointed this out to me a few years ago, I started thinking about my most satisfying bowhunting accomplishments. Some of them can be appreciated by any bowhunter, like an occasional record book animal or some remote, hard-to-bag species. But most of them represent simpler satisfactions.

Like my first "primitive" kill—a South Texas Javelina taken using a homemade, primitive bow and self-doweled arrow. This goal had sat in the back of my mind for over four decades before I suddenly decided to act on it.

Looking at the animal on the ground as I approached it, I felt a huge personal satisfaction—more than I had felt about some other, very nice trophies that I'd taken in the past. To me, it represented the ultimate in gamesmanship—of a sporting goal carefully decided upon and then achieved. It made me feel very good.

And that's what bowhunting is all about!

Part 7. The Responsibility

Despite its modern technological advances, bowhunting remains a difficult pursuit. This is part of what makes it attractive to most people in the first place. With this difficulty comes an ethical responsibility to the animals that we hunt and to the archers that we hunt with.

If we make a bad shot on a target, we can lose an expensive arrow. If we make a bad hunting shot we can hurt a beautiful animal needlessly. Do it too often and we can hurt the sport that we love.

In this section, we'll look at two ethical issues that are common sources of debate:

❖ Shooting distance, and
❖ Equipment for Women and Youths

65. Shooting Distance

T he subject of shooting distance has always been debated in bowhunting circles. As equipment has become more advanced, it is a more hotly debated issue than ever before.

Evolution of a Sport

Early archers hunted to eat and abstract ethics didn't figure into their game plan. If they had an opportunity to shoot at an animal, they took it. Early twentieth-century archers continued this practice. Howard Hill wrote proudly about an elk that he shot at 185-yards. In one of his films, Ben Pearson arrowed a downhill javelina at an estimated "two city blocks." Saxton Pope and Art Young took frequent 80-yard shots that were near their point-on aiming distance using under-the-chin anchors. They usually classified their first shot or two as "spotters" to get the range before the real shooting started.

By mid-century, this practice was dying as archers began to recognize the practical difficulties involved, their ethical responsibility to the animals they hunted, and the political fallout among non-hunters when they performed poorly. Books and magazines routinely encouraged bowhunters to shoot from close range. Some people still took a long shot here and there, but they didn't talk about it when they did, or brag about the 70-yard heart shot that they made. This attitude prevailed into the 1980s, well after the compound's invention.

Then came more advanced bows and better shooting aids, all promoted as ways to increase shooting distance and hunter success. Hunting philosophies also changed to some degree. With easier-to-use equipment, more people felt pressured to succeed and not lose face in front of their hunting buddies. Hunters have always felt this way, of course, but when taking an

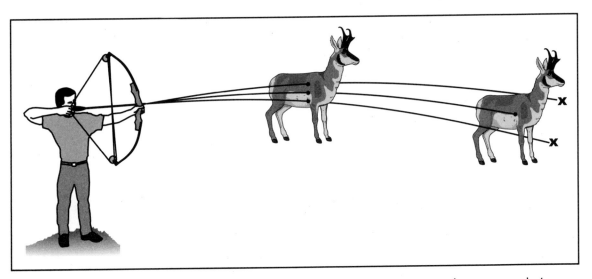

ACCURACY VS. SHOOTING DISTANCE. All of the bad things that can happen to produce a poor shot are magnified as shooting distance increases. Controversy arises over the core question: How far is too far?

animal was an occasional treat during a woodsy outing, they didn't feel as stigmatized when they failed. This, and the increasing emphasis on taking large antlered animals, encourages some people to take marginal shots rather than lose an opportunity.

Today, bowhunters are increasingly divided into two philosophical camps: Those who still feel that the sport should emphasize the skills needed to get close to an animal; and those who openly promote the concept of longer range shooting. "If the equipment can do it," they argue, "then why shouldn't *we* do it?"

The Problem

Philosophy aside, a core problem remains: Almost everything that makes a bowhunting shot difficult—looping arrow trajectory, unknown shooting distance, animal movement, wind, uneven terrain, and others—increase the chance of a poor outcome as shooting distance increases.

The real question is: How far is *too far*? In the next few chapters, we'll look at some actual accuracy data from bowhunter testing.

66. Compound Accuracy

Roughly nine out of ten bowhunters today use compounds as their primary hunting implement. A lot of the argument over shooting distance centers on how good they are. There's no way to tell what this might be on a national basis but the following studies provide some interesting food for thought.

Accuracy at Known Distances

A few years ago I conducted a project for a national bowhunting organization to determine the shooting skills of various classes of bowhunters. Compound shooters were classified into three groups: *Beginners* (less than a year's experience), *Experienced* (experienced hunters who didn't shoot competitively), and *Experts* (placed in the top third of competitors at that year's state shoot). They were also classified into two groups according to their aiming and shooting style: *Sights/Finger* and *Sights/Release-Aids*.

Distance (yards)	Shot Group Diameter* (inches)				
	By Skill Level (mixed shooting styles)			By Shooting Style (mixed skill levels)	
	Beginner	Experienced	Expert	Sights, Fingers	Sights, Release-Aid
20	9.4	3.8	2.5	3.7	2.7
40	>24	8.8	4.8	7.3	5.6
60	>24	16	8.9	14.1	9.8

Circle Diameter	Effective Range* (yards)				
6"	13	28	44	31	39
8"	17	35	55	36	49

* 90% of shots in circle

ACCURACY OF COMPOUND SHOOTERS AT KNOWN DISTANCES. When shooting under ideal conditions at known distances, compound shooters had effective ranges on whitetails (6" diameter kill zone assumed) of from 13- to 39-yards, depending on their skill and shooting style. In-the-field effective ranges would be shorter.

Fifty-six people participated in the tests. All participants were allowed to warm up and check their sight settings. They were then asked to shoot at known distances of 20-, 40-, and 60-yards.

Experts outperformed experienced, non-competitive bowhunters and experienced bowhunters outperformed beginners. Release-shooters outperformed finger shooters. No surprises here. The surprise was that many archers claimed effective ranges (on a pre-test survey form) that were longer than those measured when they were put to the test.

Assuming a six-inch diameter kill zone for whitetails (a safe assumption that will result in solid hits), beginning shooters had an average effective range of 13-yards, experienced shooters had an average effective range of 28-yards, and expert shooters had an average effective range of 44-yards.

For larger western game (eight-inch circle assumed), beginning shooters had an average effective range of 17-yards, experienced shooters had an average effective range of 35-yards, and expert shooters had an average effective range of 55-yards.

The accompanying tables give a further breakdown of the results. Keep in mind that they are based on perfect shooting conditions and precisely known distances.

Range Estimating Ability

Given the importance of accurate range estimation for many bowhunting shots, just how good are we as a group in guessing range? I had an opportunity to answer this question at a state broadhead shoot a few years ago. The tournament was held in heavily wooded terrain and included thirty-five 3-D targets that were set at shooting distances of 15- to 35-yards.

A randomly selected group of experienced bowhunters were asked to estimate the distance to each target and mark it on a data form before shooting. All had at least seven-years of bowhunting experience, had harvested an average of six deer with a bow, and had taken an average of over 1,200 practice shots in the three months preceding the shoot.

The estimates were then collected and compared to the measured target distances. Shooters were able to judge range accurately to within 10% of the actual distance 40% of the time, to within 20% of the actual distance 75% of the time, and to within 30% of the actual distance 90% of the time. In the remainder of cases, they were off by as much as 140%.

Tests conducted by the U.S. Army Gunnery School show similar results. The army found that "skilled" range estimators could estimate range correctly to within plus or minus 15%-17% of the actual distance. Unskilled subjects could only guess correctly to within plus or minus 30%. The skilled subjects could not improve on the 15%-17% figure with any amount of additional practice and had to keep practicing just to maintain it.

Accuracy at Unknown Distances

How do our combination of shooting skills and range estimating skills affect our ability to place killing shots in the field? To answer this, I used a computer to calculate arrow trajectories for every target distance at the state broadhead shoot mentioned above. I used three common arrow speeds: 180-fps to represent a recurve, 210-fps to represent the rating speed of an eccentric-wheeled compound, and 240-fps to represent the rating speed of a high-performance bow.

My initial analysis assumed that every arrow was shot perfectly—that is, if the distance to each target was guessed correctly, that every shot would be a perfect bull's-eye. It included every range estimate (some good and some bad) made during the tournament.

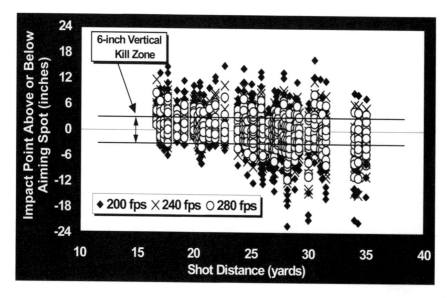

RANGE ESTIMATION VS. ACCURACY FOR "PERFECT" SHOTS. Bowhunters in this study could only guess correctly to within 10% of the actual distance 40% of the time under tournament conditions. Arrow speed had little effect on their ability to place killing shots even though every shot was perfectly executed.

Shooting Skill Level	Kill Zone Diameter (inches)		
	6-inches	8-inches	10-inches
	(1,280 Actual Range Estimates)		
Experienced Hunters	14	15	17
Competitive Shooters	19	24	27
	(Average Range Estimator = +/-30%)		
Experienced Hunters	11	16	18
Competitive Shooters	17	18	23

* 90% of shots in the indicated circle size

EFFECTIVE RANGE* (IN YARDS) AT UNKNOWN DISTANCES WITH NORMAL SHOOTING ERROR AND A 280-FPS ARROW. Shown here are the effective ranges calculated for different classes of shooters when normal shooting errors and normal ranges estimation errors are combined. Slower arrows (not shown) performed just about as well, indicating that accurate range estimation is much more important than arrow speed.

The loss of accuracy due to range estimation error was dramatic for all three arrow speeds. At all distances, the 240-fps arrow resulted in only one additional hit in ten shots over the 180-fps arrow. At 20-yards, archers could only hit an eight-inch kill zone seventy- to eighty-percent of the time. At 35-yards, they could only hit it forty- to fifty-percent of the time.

Next, I added the combined effects of shooting error and range estimation error using data from both previous tests. I eliminated the beginning archers and used a 280-fps arrow speed (speed bow and light arrow) to look at best-case results.

As a group, experienced shooters needed to be within 14-yards of the target to keep ninety-percent of their shots in a six-inch circle. Expert shooters needed to be within 19-yards.

Bowhunting writer Bill Winke has conducted a similar analysis that supports these results. Winke assumed four-inch shot groups, a seven-inch kill zone, and a fixed range estimation error of 13% (an expert range estimator according to the Army). Winke calculated an effective range of 19½-yards for a 280-fps arrow and 17½-yards for a 230-fps arrow.

67. Stickbow Accuracy

Traditional equipment and instinctive shooting are both more difficult to master than compounds and sights. As a result, traditional shooters usually have a shorter effective range than modern shooters. But by how much?

On the Range

Twenty traditional archers were included in the shooting test described in the last chapter. All were experienced, non-competitive shooters and all shot instinctively using their fingers. They had an effective range on whitetails of 26-yards and an effective range on western game of 30-yards. These values are thirty-five to fifty-percent shorter than the effective ranges found for experienced, non-competitive compound shooters who used releases and who knew the shooting distance precisely. Compared to compound shooters who shot with their fingers, they are about twenty-percent shorter.

When compared to the calculated effective ranges of modern shooters at *unknown distances*, the traditional shooters performed about the same.

In the Field

In another test, I directly compared the accuracy between fifteen compound and fifteen traditional shooters in a field setting. The test was conducted for a different purpose and using a different test format than the previous tests which makes a direct comparison of the two sets of data difficult. Still, the results are interesting and are worth mentioning.

Where the previous test was conducted on a target range at known distances that shooters were told to shoot from, this test was conducted with archers picking their own shots from unknown distances. Compound shooters and recurve shooters were randomly pitted against each other, one on one, in a competition. All shooters were experienced, non-competent bowhunters with more than ten-years of experience.

Shooting Style	Known Distances	Unknown Distances
Compound, Sights	37	30
Recurve, Instinctive	26	25

EFFECTIVE RANGE (IN YARDS) FOR DIFFERENT SHOOTING STYLES AT KNOWN AND UNKNOWN DISTANCES. In these tests, compound/sight shooters had 30% longer effective ranges than recurve/instinctive shooters on the practice range at known distances. In a simulated field situation at unknown distances, the effective range of compound/sight shooters was just 17% farther. In terms of total kills, wounds, and misses, both performed roughly the same.

Shooters alternated picking shots. Since the test was staged as a competition, each was encouraged to choose shots that gave him an advantage over his rival. As expected, traditional shooters tended to pick closer shots from more difficult shooting positions, or canted shots through brush that made the use of sights difficult. Compound shooters tended to choose longer, relatively flat shots in uncluttered terrain where they could stand straight and more easily guess shooting distance.

Under this format, the two groups performed similarly in terms of total kills, wounds, and misses. When the results were analyzed by shooting distance alone, the compound shooters were able to shoot accurately at about 17% farther distances than the traditionalists. On the whole, they were effective in making *consistent* killing shots out to about 30-yards. The traditionalists could make consistent killing shots out to about 25-yards.

Tournament Data

Most published 3-D tournament scores tend to support the above findings. The scores of winning compound shooters (the top three places are usually shown) are typically 20% to 30% higher than top traditional shooters. This suggests that compound shooters were accurate at 20% to 30% longer distances than traditional shooters. It doesn't explain what the two groups did as a whole.

Nor do these and the results in the last chapter explain how equipment accuracy translates into hunting success or failure where every archer makes a personal shoot or no-shoot decision. To do that we need to look at actual hunting data.

68. Wounding Loss & Distance

A variety of studies have been conducted on bowhunter effectiveness, many with conflicting results. One thing is clear, though. Bowhunters occasionally lose deer through bad luck or poor performance on their part. Some are due to just plain bad shooting at any distance. But, in general, shooting distance figures heavily into this equation. A marginal, killing shot at close range might be a wound at longer distances.

The Langenau Data

Ed Langenau, a Michigan wildlife biologist, did a study some years ago that underscores the detrimental effects of increasing shot distance. Using survey data from hunts conducted on the Shiawassee National Wildlife Refuge, he looked at recovery rate versus shot distance. Deer hit at zero- to 10-yards showed the highest recovery rate. Those hit at 11- to 20-yards had a lower recovery rate, and those hit at 21- to 30-yards had a still lower rate. The most sobering finding was that not a single deer that was hit at greater than 30-yards was recovered.

Obviously, this is just one study and doesn't suggest that an arrow is incapable of killing a deer beyond 30-yards. Instead, it points out the increasing difficulty of making a good shot as distance increases.

The LSBA Data

Each year the *Lone Star Bowhunters Association* of Texas asks successful hunters to report their whitetail kills on a standardized data form. Information supplied includes the shot distance, trailing distance, and tracking time. Several years ago for a magazine article, I randomly selected three-years worth of LSBA data and analyzed it to see if there was any correlation between shot distance and ease of recovery.

Wounding loses were not asked for explicitly on the LSBA form, so all of the results are for kills only. Still, it's interesting to note that, as a group,

Bow Type	Minimum Value	Maximum Value	Average Value
	Shot Distance (yards)		
Compound	5	50	19.6
Recurve	10	25	16.5
Longbow	7	20	12.2
	Recovery Distance (yards)		
Compound	0	1,000	96
Recurve	0	300	75
Longbow	0	70	58
	Recovery Time (hours)		
Compound	0	16	0.7
Recurve	0	2	0.3
Longbow	0	1	0.5

LSBA Study. Deer shot at shorter range were recovered in shorter distances and less time than those shot at longer distances. This suggests that shorter shots resulted in better hits even though all deer were recovered.

hunters who took the shortest shots had the shortest trails to follow and recovered their animals in the shortest time. These results show, again, that longer shots resulted in poorer hits—even though the animal was recovered.

The Missouri Data

In 1987, Missouri researchers surveyed four-thousand randomly selected bowhunters. They classified compound users as *Gadget Shooters* (their words, not mine) if they used a release-aid and lighted sight-pin, and as *Compound Only* shooters if they used any other combination of accuracy aids. They referred to the traditional shooters as *Primitive*.

Both the number of deer killed and the number of deer wounded went up as archers added more accuracy-aiding devices to their bows. The Gadget Shooters killed more deer, but they also wounded more deer. The Primitive hunters killed fewer deer but also wounded fewer. Compound Only shooters fell in between these two groups on both counts. The ratio of hunters wounding deer versus those killing deer also went up as more accuracy aids were added, with traditional bowhunters having the best performance.

The study's authors explained this curious finding as follows:

The Primitive archers, as indicated by the number of years hunted, were more experienced than modern bowhunters but hit fewer deer that were not retrieved.

Type of Equipment Used (as defined by the researchers)	Percent of Hunters Harvesting Deer	Percent of Hunters Hitting But Not Recovering Deer
"Gadget User"	20.5	17.3
"Compound Only"	18.1	12.0
"Primitive"	16.0	9.9

MISSOURI WOUNDING LOSS STUDY. Both the number of deer killed and the number of deer wounded went up as archers used more shooting accessories. Researchers cited shorter shooting distances as one explanation for the lower wounding rate by "primitive" archers.

The primitive archers, however, are probably unique [in that] they likely know the limitations of their weapons better, take closer shots, and [may be] more conscientious about shot selection.

Four Factors

This finding doesn't mean that recurves and longbows are more effective in terms of wounding than compounds. Certainly they're not. But it also challenges the frequent perception that traditional archers wound more deer. The LSBA data on the previous page seems to support this same point. Rather, the data show that all types of equipment are effective when used skillfully and within their limitations. The traditional shooters just passed up more shots. Stated in another way: EQUIPMENT DOESN'T DETERMINE WOUNDING. HUNTERS DO.

Instead, the following four factors are mentioned by the study's authors:

Knowledge—more knowledgeable hunters are better able to recognize their shooting limitations;

Experience—more experienced hunters have probably taken several deer and may be more willing to pass up marginal shots and wait for better ones on another day;

Conscientious shot selection—more conscientious hunters are more likely to restrict themselves to shots they "know" they can make based on their knowledge and past experience;

Closer shots—all of the above factors result in lower wounding by taking closer shots.

69. Women & Youths

I was at a state hearing a few years ago where game department personnel were soliciting comments on a proposal to limit archery equipment. Among the recommendations was to require arrow weights of 400-grains or more. During the question and answer period, one individual stood up and angrily told the moderator that this was garbage (actually, he was a little more colorful). If the commission adopted this restriction, he explained, his son couldn't hunt.

I've heard similar stories from around the country and it has always mystified me. Certainly, the lad could hunt. He just wouldn't have the flat-shooting trajectory of daddy's bow. Nor, if he were ethical, should he be taking the shots that daddy does.

Forget the emotion for a second. Let's look at the practical realities of the situation.

A Boy's First Buck. Eleven-year-old Lance Fougerat and his first bow-killed buck. Lance used a 40-pound bow and a 550-grain arrow from a distance of 14-yards.

Penetration

Let's say that Mr. X above shoots a 60-pound bow that he pulls 30-inches. It launches a 400-grain arrow (which the state now says he has to use) with 50 foot-pounds of energy. At 40-yards, it still has over forty foot-pounds of energy left to penetrate any animal that it hits.

Junior has been shooting 270-grain

	Mr. X's Bow		Junior's Bow: 270-grain arrow		Junior's Bow: 540-grain arrow	
Shooting Distance (yards)	Energy (foot-pounds)	Momentum (grain-seconds)	Energy (foot-pounds)	Momentum (grain-seconds)	Energy (foot-pounds)	Momentum (grain-seconds)
Launch	50	2,948	23	1,654	28	2,552
20	46	2,823	20	1,545	26	2,468
30	44	2,761	19	1,503	25	2,435
40	42	2,699	18	1,452	24	2,384
50	40	2,637	17	1,402	24	2,351
60	38	2,575	16	1,360	23	2,317

REALITY CHECK. Shooting heavy arrows and keeping shots short can help to overcome the limitations of light tackle for women and youths.

arrows from a 45-pound bow that he draws 26-inches. They are launched with twenty-three foot-pounds of energy and arrive at 40-yards with just eighteen foot-pounds left.

This isn't much punch to get the job done. Not only should Junior shoot a heavier arrow, but he should march right past the 400-grain state minimum to something heavier. Assuming that he used 540-grain arrows (12-grains per pound of bow weight), their launch energy would go up twenty-two percent over his current equipment, and their momentum would go up a whopping fifty-four percent. The arrows still wouldn't have the punch of Mr. X's bow, but they'd do a much better job on any deer that they hit.

Trajectory

Mr. X doesn't like the idea of Junior using heavier arrows since they'd have a looping trajectory that would make range estimates more critical. His own bow has a maximum arrow rise of six-inches for a 40-yard shot. Using the 540-grain arrow, Junior's bow would have the same trajectory at 20-yards, which is a good shooting distance with his equipment.

Practical Decisions

If you shoot a high energy bow, you have penetrating power to spare. You can give up some of it in the interest of flatter arrow trajectory. If your wife or son shoot light equipment, or have short draw lengths, they may not have this luxury. To avoid poor outcomes, they should shoot the heaviest bows *and* the heaviest arrows that they feel comfortable with, and shoot from closer distances.

70. Practical Ethics

It was a beautiful Colorado day and I was coming down the mountainside after a fruitless morning of chasing elk when I saw another hunter mumbling to himself as he walked. When our paths crossed I asked him casually how he had done. "Man," he said, "I just missed three easy shots at big bulls, and all were under 60-yards! I can't believe it. I can shoot arrows into a pie plate all day long at that distance."

As we parted and I left him to his rock-kicking descent down the slope, I reflected on what I had wanted to say but didn't—that his shots apparently weren't all that "easy" since he'd missed three of them in the row, and that maybe he was wasn't quite as good an archer while hunting as he was on the practice range when shooting conditions were perfect. Ultimately, though, these were his decisions to make.

As stated in the introduction to this section, hunting ethics has two faces—ethical responsibility to the animals that we hunt and to the sport of bowhunting as a whole. Here are a few things to consider the next time you face a decision to shoot or not shoot at an animal.

A Few Simple Steps

Shoot Within Your Effective Range. As we've seen in the past few chapters, the modern bow and arrow remains a relatively short range weapon for most people. Somewhere between 15- and 35-yards, depending on the shooter and the circumstances, normal shooting and range estimation errors become so great that even the fastest equipment or the best archer can't *consistently* compensate for them.

Your personal effective range is the distance at which you can consistently place killing shots *in the field under unfavorable conditions.* It will be quite a bit shorter than your consistently accurate range on targets. Find it and stay within it. Chapter 55, *Hunting Practice,* gives one good starting point for doing this. There are others.

Include your past history when determining your capabilities. Sit down sometime and list all of your bowhunting shots in the last few years. Unless you've made the vast majority of them (hopefully, nine out of ten or so), then consider passing up some of those longer shots. When in doubt, err on the side of caution.

Include Your Misses—Avoid the tendency to look only at lethal versus non-lethal hits when assessing your effectiveness. Misses count too. There's an age-old hunter's prayer that says: "Lord, let me kill clean. And if I can't kill clean, then let me miss clean." This is a noble idea but its logic is flawed. A wound is caused by a poorly shot arrow. A miss is a worse shot yet. In other words, every miss is a potential wound that we just got lucky on. If you miss a lot of shots, you're saying, in effect, that your kills are just accidents. This doesn't do much to improve your self-confidence or to favorably represent the sport to the general public as a whole.

Avoid Running Shots—A few highly skilled people have proven that they can hit moving animals, but they are exceptional individuals who have honed this skill through many years of practice. Even then, most experts caution against it on ethical grounds. A standing shot is hard enough. Avoid moving shots unless you've practiced it on targets and, according to one moving-target expert: "You thoroughly and honestly know in your heart that you can pull it off."

The Goal

Wounding loss has been called bowhunting's "Achilles Heel." It may determine our future as hunters through public sentiment. It's unrealistic to think that wounding loss can ever be totally eliminated since, as humans, we learn largely through trial and error. But this should still be our collective goal.

Each of us can move toward that goal by continuing to improve our own bowhunting knowledge, skill, and ethical conduct; and to coach others in a diplomatic way when they use questionable practices or ethics.

All bows used today—compounds, recurves, longbows, and primitive bows—are effective if used within their limitations. Wounding occurs when an individual doesn't recognize, or chooses to ignore, his own limitations and those of his equipment in a field setting.

Part 8. The Future

The Navajo's of America's southwest corner have a word—*horzo*—that expresses the ultimate harmony in nature. Inherent in this idea is that all things in the world are interrelated. Every action has a reaction, and every effect has a cause.

The sport of bowhunting that we learned was the result of decisions that others made for us in the past. And how we bowhunt tomorrow will be determined by the decisions that we make today.

In this section, we'll look at two things that may impact our collective future:

❖ The impact of continuing bowhunting technology, and
❖ The clash of traditional versus modern bowhunting cultures.

71. Bowhunting Technology

The arrival of compounds on the archery scene in the early 1970s drew many new people into the sport and allowed them to become proficient in a much shorter period of time than before. As a result, the bowhunting ranks increased from just under one-million people in 1974 to almost 1.7-million people in 1984. During this same ten-year period, bowhunter success rates increased from about 5% to over 11% nationally, and the number of deer killed increased almost five-fold.

In states that viewed bowhunting as a recreational pursuit having low impact on game populations, some people started to express concern that future hunting opportunities might be lost due to rising success rates. Magazine articles and personal debates on the subject became common.

Recent Trends

In 1980, the average bowhunter used a long-axle-length, 30% let-off, round-wheel compound having a simple sight. He used full-length, mid-weight arrows and released the string with his fingers. In the ensuing two decades, the trend has been towards high-energy-storing cams; 80% and higher let-offs that let archers hold a bow at full draw for long periods; shorter, faster bows; greater use of light arrows that extend shooting range; precision trigger-releases; sophisticated sights and electronics; and laser range finders that eliminate range estimation problems.

Full-draw string locking devices that eliminate holding weight entirely are legal in some states. Another device shoots six-inch steel darts (where the "vanes" also cut) using a barrel-type channel that's attached to the bow riser.

Each of these innovations, and others, have further increased the number of bowhunters (currently 4.6-million according to the *National Sporting Goods Association*) and improved their individual success rates. All of this has acted as a catalyst in keeping the technology debate alive and at the forefront.

Other Factors

To lay rising success rates completely at the hands of equipment technology is unfair. The proliferation of instructional magazine articles, books, and videos in the past two decades have played a heavy role in helping bowhunters to become more proficient more quickly. The ready availability of portable trees stands and blinds, mock scents, game calls, and similar items are other contributors. Perhaps most importantly, bowhunters as a group are more experienced today. Yet, archery technology continues to be the center of attention because it's so visible.

Two Factions

One fact that clearly comes out of any research into the equipment debate is that differences between opposing factions are philosophical rather than technical.

The stated attitude of the pro-technology faction is that the sport should not be difficult. If we can make equipment more efficient and easier-to-use, they say, then why shouldn't we do it? Pressing the technology-envelope becomes a game in itself for this group. And if manufacturers promote archery as fun and easy-to-learn, the industry will continue to grow.

The basic attitude of tradition-conscious individuals and organizations is that bowhunting is not for everyone. It's only for those people who relish its special challenges. If killing is the only objective, they point out, a person should use a rifle. And what's wrong if this limits participants?

In the next two chapters we'll look at this on-going issue in more detail.

72. Technology Issues

People choose their equipment for a variety of reasons and no choice is "right" or "wrong" in a purely philosophical sense. Yet, it's vital to the health of the sport to honestly confront the technology issue that divides bowhunters today.

Public Perception

Studies show that the non-hunting public (not to be confused with anti-hunters) isn't against hunting as long as it's done ethically and responsibly. They recognize their own hunting heritage and show a certain nostalgia for it if tastefully presented.

In one store where I buy western art, paintings of gritty wranglers descending mountainsides with elk antlers tied to pack horses are top sellers. A vintage .30-30 usually protrudes from a time-worn leather scabbard. According to the store owner (himself a hunter): "ATVs and high-powered, scoped rifles would be an affront to most art purchasers, but most of my customers love the historic appeal of these rustic paintings."

Similarly, advertising studies done to determine mass consumer preferences show that the public at large identifies with historical archery equipment but reacts unfavorably to high-tech gear. According to these studies, recurves and longbows are associated more with the respect for nature that Native Americans had; modern gear is associated more with a desire to dominate nature. Traditional gear is viewed as requiring hard-earned skill; modern gear is viewed as an instant means to success.

These perceptions are reflected in mainstream media ads that tend to use recurves and longbows as ancillary props (there are four such ads running on network TV as I write this). Wildlife managers, who try to balance sportsmen's needs with public opinion when setting hunting regulations, wrestle with the same issues.

This doesn't mean that we should all rush out and buy a longbow. It just means that we should be aware of the social impact of accepting ever greater bowhunting technology and the associated image that we portray to non-hunters. These are the folks who may well determine our future as they are increasingly being asked to vote on wildlife issues at the polls.

A Sense of Community

Attend any bowhunting tournament today and you'll likely see pro-tradition and pro-technology shooters segregated into separate groups speaking their own specialized jargon. They frequently cast questioning or suspicious glances at one another and occasionally get into open confrontations over differing bowhunting philosophies. Psychologists tell us that bonds of friendship and a sense of group membership are based primarily on shared interests. As long as radically different attitudes persist within our ranks, the cohesiveness of the sport and the enjoyment that this feeling of brotherhood brings will continue to be damaged.

Equipment Restrictions

More important than the social or philosophical implications above is the possibility of losing future bowhunting opportunities due to ever-rising success rates. As discussed in the last chapter, there are many reasons for this, but equipment technology is the most visible contributor.

The original premise behind liberal archery seasons in most states was a simple one: Bowhunters didn't take much game, so states could give them a lot of time in the field without negatively impacting game populations. Recent years have altered that viewpoint. Rather than being viewed as a recreational pursuit, bowhunting in many states is increasingly being viewed as a management tool due to rising success rates.

In the mid-1980s, Washington bowhunters were among the first to be faced with the possibility of losing some of their hunting season due to increasing bowhunter success. Equipment restrictions were mutually agreed to by the state bowhunting association and the game department and this effectively forestalled any season changes. According to the then-President of the Washington State Bowhunters: "Prior to that time, the attitude of some game officials was that bowhunters were trying to slowly create another long

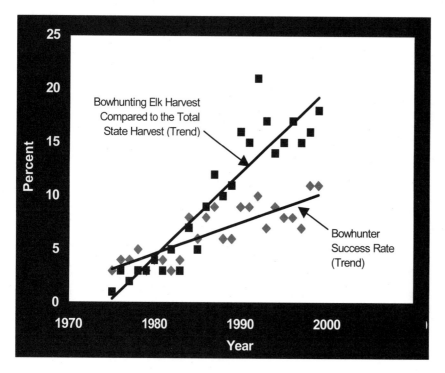

BOWHUNTER SUCCESS IN IDAHO. The success of Idaho bowhunters on elk has more than doubled in the past 25-years and the percentage of bow-killed elk has gone from negligible to almost 20% of the total statewide harvest. During the same time, the average number of days required to harvest an elk with a bow has been reduced from 164-days to just 65-days. Concerns over these trends have caused Idaho legislators to enact stringent equipment and season restrictions. Other states are watching these developments with interest.

range hunting implement[*]. Adding restrictions sent a message that bowhunters in the state wanted to maintain their 'primitive' status. This move was supported by both modern and tradition shooters as being best for everyone. After this, the attitude of wildlife officials towards bowhunting noticeably improved."

Fueled by similar concerns over rapidly rising hunting harvests, Idaho strengthened its equipment restrictions in 1992, and strengthened them

---

[*]According to one source, the Washington game department first became concerned when a high ranking official witnessed a 100-yard bow kill on a bighorn sheep.

further in 2001. Among the current provisions: Arrows must weight at least 400-grains and can't have expanding/mechanical broadheads; electronic or tritium powered sights are not allowed; and compounds must have a let-off of 65% or lower. Montana recently enacted its own restrictions.

Season Restrictions

The effects of equipment restrictions in Montana are too recent to assess. In Idaho, restrictions have proved difficult to enforce (as they are in all states) and legislators recently announced a different policy direction. They defined a new class of *Traditional Weapons*—which include traditionally-styled muzzleloaders and traditional archery equipment—and announced that these will have priority when creating future seasons. Archers hunting in these seasons must use longbows or recurves, wooden arrows, and natural feathers for fletching. Sights will not be allowed.

Legislators stopped short of reducing bowhunter access in existing seasons, but indicated their growing concern over harvest rates by taking this unprecedented new approach to limit hunting technology.

Other States

It should be noted that similar concerns only affect states having limited wildlife resources or heavy hunting pressure. They aren't issues in states that have a "deer problem." My own state of Texas is one of these. It's biggest problem is trying to find ways to get hunters to shoot *more* deer. In contrast to Idaho, Texas' approach has been to legalize additional bowhunting equipment, including full-draw locking devices. So the technology issue remains very much a state-to-state issue.

Implications for Hunters

Depending on who you talk to, the actions of a few states to limit bowhunting technology or bowhunter access are either isolated aberrations or the wave of the future. Only time will tell. Two things are certain, though. First, twenty years ago, when these concerns first reached the national discussion level, no state had acted to greatly limit available equipment technology. Now there are several. And second, other states have expressed similar concerns over rising bowhunter success rates and are watching developments in the western states with interest.

73. The Crossbow Issue

Crossbows are a natural extension of the on-going general technology debate. They are one more step in making the sport easier. Modern hunting crossbows have been around for decades but first emerged as a major national issue in the mid-1980s when manufacturers, intent on adding new converts to bowhunting[*], began to actively lobby state wildlife departments for their inclusion in archery seasons. Various state and national bowhunting groups, concerned that crossbows would further increase success rates and impact hunting seasons, vigorously opposed them.

The situation is currently in a position of near-stalemate with crossbow proponents making inroads in some states, but with organized bowhunting groups slowing significant progress in others.

Crossbow Effectiveness

My own involvement with the crossbow issue started in 1987 when, as part of my engineering consulting practice, I was asked by a major national bowhunting organization to technically evaluate crossbow effectiveness. The study was conducted in four phases over an eighteen-month period and included over two-hundred pages of test rationale, data, and technical analyses. Highlights from this research include the following findings:

Industry Survey. Industry sources were contacted to gather relevant data or opinion on the crossbow issue. All respondents, whether pro-, neutral, or anti-crossbow, agreed that crossbows are superior shooting machines. Respondents differed only in their opinion of whether this is good or bad.

According to the consensus opinion expressed, the primary advantages of crossbows are their ease of learning and use, their ability to be shot from a rest, their rigidly controlled internal ballistics which elimi-

---

[*]By most written state and national definitions, crossbows are not "bows" and hunting with crossbows is not "bowhunting." However, crossbow proponents typically refer to them by these terms.

(Photo courtesy of Gassman's Archery)

A Modern Hunting Crossbow. In terms of speed, crossbows are more like conventional bows than rifles. In terms of use, they're more like rifles than bows. They have rigidly controlled internal ballistics that reduce shooting errors, they can be shot from a rest, they can held in a cocked position while hunting and triggered using minimal movement, and they are easier to use with telescopic sights. Proponents are proposing their inclusion in archery seasons as near-substitutes to today's high-tech archery equipment. Opponents fear that they'll increase archery harvest rates and cause reductions in archery seasons.

nates many common shooting errors, and their minimal required movement for the first shot. In terms of speed and trajectory, they are similar to handheld bows. In terms of use, they are similar to firearms.

Since crossbows can be carried cocked and loaded, they have a much greater potential than handheld bows to injure shooters or bystanders because of accidental discharge. Documented cases support this.

The potential for increased hunter success with crossbows is based on two factors: Increased rates for hunters who switch from handheld bows to crossbows, and an increase in new hunters who are attracted by the promise of long bowhunting seasons with easier-to-use equipment.

Performance. Crossbows are extremely easy to master. In extensive testing, first-time crossbow shooters were given just five-minutes of verbal orientation and allowed to shoot just six practice shots before shooting

Crossbow Shooters (all beginners)	No Firearms Experience	50
	Firearms Hunting Experience	64
	Competitive Firearm Experience	81
	Average	**65**
Handheld Bow Shooters	Less than one-year of archery experience	12
	Hunting (non-competitive) experience	26
	Top competitive archers (state level)	45
	Average	**28**

EFFECTIVE RANGE (IN YARDS) OF 113 CROSSBOW AND HANDHELD BOW SHOOTERS. Crossbow shooters having no firearms or archery experience outperformed top competitive archers. Those having some experience had twice the effective range of average bowhunters.

for record. They had average shot groupings that were better than top competitive handheld bow shooters who participated in the tests.

For typical hunters—those having firearm[1] or handheld bow experience but who were not competitive shooters—crossbow shooters had an effective range of 64-yards compared to 26-yards for handheld bow shooters. When used for hunting, this means that they could accurately shoot almost 2½-times farther, cover over six-times the area around a stand, and theoretically kill over six-times[2] the number of deer as handheld bow shooters under the same circumstances.

Crossbows have a greater potential for improvement than handheld bows, which are currently near their performance limit. This would increase their relative advantage over future handheld bows.

The New Push

Crossbow manufacturers have recently expanded their efforts to get them legalized in archery seasons. They are spending heavily to achieve this end, believing that this will create a whole new class of purchaser—folks who aren't interested in or capable of shooting a compound but who would welcome the benefit of an extended hunting season.

---

[1] There were no experienced crossbow shooters in the study area so shooters were classified according to their experience with firearms: Competitive firearm shooters; experienced firearm hunters who did not shoot competitively; and beginners who had never shot a firearm of any type.

[2] Hunters can accurately shoot anywhere within the circle defined by their effective range as its radius. If one hunter can shoot accurately at twice the distance of another, he could theoretically cover four-times the area around his stand. If he could accurately shoot at three times the distance, he could cover nine-times the area. And so forth.

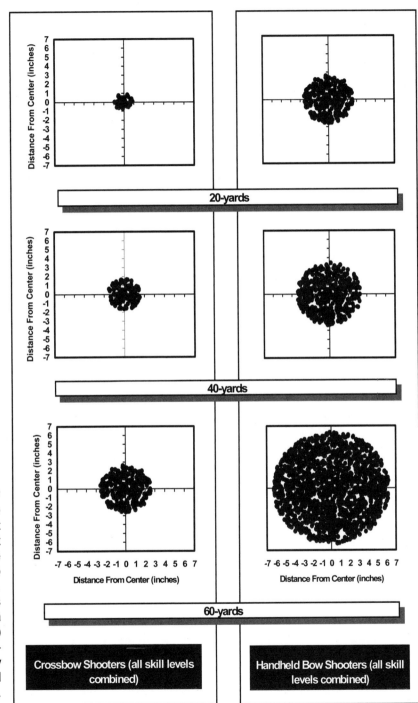

SHOT PATTERNS OF CROSSBOW AND HANDHELD BOW SHOOTERS. The shot patterns at the right represent circles where shooters could group 90% of their shots. Crossbow shooters (none had ever shot a crossbow before) significantly outperformed handheld bow shooters at all distances.

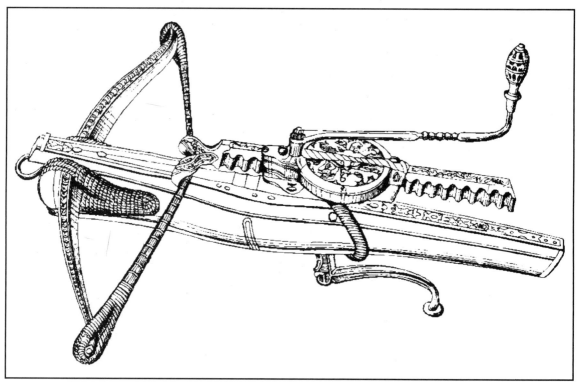

1,200-POUND MEDIEVAL CROSSBOW. Although crossbow designs have advanced significantly in the past few years, they're still not as potent as many historical designs. The technology currently exists for 500+ feet-per-second crossbows which suggests that (given marketing demand) future crossbows will be much more effective than at present. Handheld bows are currently near their technical performance limits.

At a recent archery trade show, a session speaker described how the industry should go about increasing crossbow sales:

We need to market them as direct substitutes to today's compound bows and mechanical releases. There is very little difference in speed, the ability of a user to hold either implement at full draw for long periods of time, or to release it cleanly with a trigger. We need to convince wildlife managers of this and show them that excluding crossbows, while allowing current equipment, doesn't make sense[*].

---

[*] This isn't a direct quote, but a synthesis of several minutes of discussion. It does, however, capture the essence of the speaker's proposal. It should also be noted that (according to one industry insider) this is not the opinion of the majority of mainline archery equipment manufacturers, who are against crossbow use in bowhunting seasons.

Implications
for
Bowhunters

Whatever the actual future performances of crossbows and crossbow hunters, common sense says that harvest rates will increase by some amount. In states having limited wildlife resources and large numbers of bowhunters, the result may be shortening of bowhunting seasons. In states having an over-population of game animals, or few bowhunters, seasons will probably remained unchanged. Any concerns regarding crossbow use will have to be addressed on a state-by-state-basis.

CROSSBOW HUNTING IN OHIO. In Ohio—the state with the longest history of crossbow use during archery season—the total deer harvest almost doubled in the first ten years after their inclusion in bow season. This was due to crossbows' greater ease-of-use and to a large influx of new hunters.

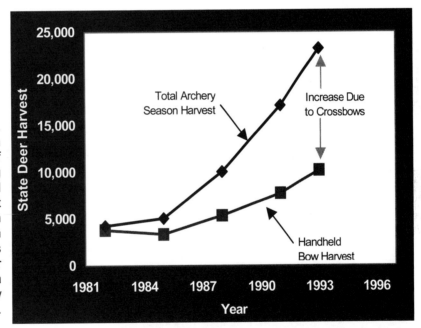

Weapon	Year				
	1982	**1985**	**1988**	**1991**	**1993**
Handheld Bows	3,782	3,339	5,322	7,708	10,155
Crossbows	446	1,689	4,716	9,401	13,055
Total	4,228	5,028	10,038	17,109	23,210

(Data source: Professional Bowhunters Society website)

74. A Clash of Cultures

At a 3-D shoot recently, I overheard an interesting conversation between two bowhunters. One, a recurve shooter, was explaining to his compound-toting counterpart that traditional bowhunting is harder than compound hunting; and, that because of this he had to be a better hunter to kill a deer. His companion wasn't buying it. "You're not better than me," he countered. "you're just an elitist with some outdated sense of challenge. We owe it to the animals we hunt to shoot the most effective equipment that we can, and that means compounds."

This conversation is typical of many that I've heard over the years, though some haven't been as jovial as this one between friends. These attitudes, widely held by both camps, serve only to drive a wedge between bowhunters. Let's examine them more closely.

Compounds More Effective?

We've looked this question previously so I won't dwell on it here. To summarize the main points briefly: All archery equipment is effective in the right hands. Compounds work better in some situations and traditional gear works better in others. Most people use compounds because they're easier to master initially and take less time to maintain hunting proficiency. Given the extra time and effort, however, some hunters actually feel that they are more effective with a recurve or longbow. Statistics show that the greater difficulty of mastering traditional equipment doesn't translate into greater wounding. For ethical shooting, it may just translate into fewer shots taken. On the whole, then, neither bow is more or less effective than the other for everyone.

Traditiona-lists More Skillful?

Although many people naturally associate difficulty with skill, they're really two separate issues. The *difficulty* of taking an animal involves three things: Time to develop needed shooting skills, time needed to maintain shooting

DIFFERENT STROKES. Any equipment will do the job in the right hands. Who cares which way is harder? Use the equipment that you can shoot effectively and that "rings your bell."

(Photos courtesy of Idaho bowhunters, Roger and Pat Stewart.)

skills, and the number of shooting opportunities available to a hunter due to his effective range.

It's more difficult to master traditional equipment and traditional archers may have to pass up more shooting opportunities. They might also lose more opportunities since they have to draw and release the arrow in a few seconds when a shooting opportunity presents itself compared to compounds that can be held at full draw while an animal is moving into position for a shot. This gives them a greater chance of being spotted at the moment of truth.

But this added difficulty doesn't mean that traditional archers are automatically more *skilled* than modern archers. They may just be longer suffering.

Who's Better?

If traditional archery is harder, does this make traditional archers better hunters? Maybe yes and maybe no. Consider this case: One guy uses a primitive all-wood bow and another uses a modern compound. Both hunt the same area for the same number of days under the same conditions and both consistently take 140-class bucks each year. Few people would dispute that the primitive hunter was probably more skilled. He likely had to find more shooting opportunities on trophy animals or get much closer to make a shot.

In the real world, however, the primitive hunter would probably be very happy with a doe or small buck—or may not score at all. So who's better in this case? Who knows? We can't prove it objectively one way or the other. It's a case of apples and oranges. How many does and small bucks could the modern shooter have taken if he were trying for them?

The point here is that buying a recurve or longbow doesn't automatically make you a better bowhunter overnight. Their limitations may force you to become a better hunter over time; but, then again, maybe they won't.

Archery Elitists

Rather than who's better, or which is harder, a larger question might be: Who cares? Most bowhunters took up the sport for its increased challenge. Yet, challenge can be found at many different levels. This doesn't make anyone good or bad—just different. Elitists (on both sides of the fence) aren't created by their choice of equipment. They're created by their attitudes towards other archers.

What's important is for each of us to enjoy our hunting experiences and to get a special thrill each time we take an animal. When people ask me what equipment to use, I tell them to think about what they want out of the sport and to choose accordingly. Who cares which way is harder, or who's better? Choose the equipment that "rings your bell." Do it your way whether or not you fill your freezer every year.

Our Collective Future

The next time you're drawn into a meaningless debate like the one mentioned earlier, don't bite. Point out to your protagonist that we are all kindred spirits—all part of a larger brotherhood of hunters. While we might have different personal interests in equipment and shooting technique, our collective future may ultimately hinge on our ability to stand together and face the outside threats to our way of life.

Epilogue

Just Have Fun!

This book as been a pretty intense exploration of the *hows* and *whys* of contemporary bowhunting. Its purpose was to give serious bowhunters serious information to use, or to just think about.

I've tried to present the sport in a way that would allow readers to make informed decisions based on their own desires and needs. If I tended to lean to one side or another on an issue, this was based on hard technical considerations and nearly 40-years of practical bowhunting experience. Or, in the case of personal shooting ethics, it was based on my belief that this is vital to the future health of the sport. Mostly, I've just tried to present a broad portrait of the sport and its many pros and cons.

It's easy to become wrapped up in all of the modern technical wizardry, the pressure to succeed, or the sport's ongoing political controversies, and lose sight of the real reason that we started in the first place: *To have fun!* Bowhunters drift out of the sport at a higher rate than in many others and this is a frequent cause.

My early hunting camps were filled with humorous tales of deer seen but left untagged, squirrels that tried to climb a hunter's motionless leg, or birds that landed on a camouflaged hunter's hat. In the age before instructional books and videos telling us in clinical detail how to waylay a trophy buck, we learned through trial and error. A downed deer was cause for real celebration instead of the bored "congratulations" that's muttered in many modern camps. Noontime was spent in lively stump-shooting contests and every hunter had a handful of battle scarred utility arrows that were put to all types of ingenious tests.

In contrast, many modern hunting camps are filled with serious hunters huddled around a video viewfinder looking at this buck or that and somberly assessing whether its spread or G-2 tines are large enough for him to "make the book." If you find a hunter shooting a bow at all during midday it's usually only for a shot or two to check a sight-pin setting.

Time marches on and there's certainly nothing wrong with all of this, but I can't help but feel that some of the early spontaneous joy of archery and bowhunting has been lost in the process.

Ask yourself this question: Are you having as much fun as you used to? If not, then figure out why. Science concerns itself with *how* to do things. The parent branch of philosophy tells us whether or not we *should* do them. The world needs both. Consider these purely philosophical points when making your own shooting and equipment decisions.

"Roots" My own interest in bowhunting was sealed after first reading Saxton Pope's *Hunting With the Bow and Arrow* as a teenager. My mother had randomly chosen it at the local library (without knowing the course it would set my life upon) in the hopes that it would calm by youthful hyperactivity on a cold, wet winter day. It worked wonderfully. I was spellbound by it then; and I'm renewed and re-energized each time I pick it up today.

Read or re-read Pope's books (which include his African adventures in *The Adventurous Bowmen* and other lesser works), Maurice Thompson's *The Witchery of Archery*, Roger Ascham's *Toxophilus*, Howard Hill's *Hunting the Hard Way*, or any of the other old time archery texts. In contrast to many modern books (this one included) which deal primarily with sterile hunting or shooting techniques, the old texts have few modern equals in capturing the timeless spirit and excitement of bowhunting. Use them to remind yourself that the mechanics of shooting a bow and arrow or stalking an animal and the joy that you derive from them are separate things. Continually strive to maintain that simple childish glee that you felt when you released your first arrow or took your first deer.

A Common Bond The sport of bowhunting has always been fractured and divisive. The great variety of shooting equipment and hunting methods used, types of animals sought, and different personal hunting philosophies almost demands it. As previously discussed, much of this destructive divisiveness has always centered around technology issues. In the 1930s and 40s it was about sights. In the ensuing decades, it was successively about manmade arrow materials, compounds, ledge releases, mechanical trigger releases, electronic sights and tracking devices, and laser range finders. Today, it's about crossbows. Tomorrow it will be about the crossbow's successor.

All of this begs the question: How much technology is appropriate in a "primitive" sport? Every hunter has to answer this question for himself. We also need to answer it as a group in an effort to recapture some of the cohesiveness that we've lost in the sport and to restore the common bond and joyous feeling of brotherhood that all bowhunters once felt.

As with so many things in life, the answer may lie in compromise. The sport of golf offers one alternative case history. Like archery, golf is an equipment-oriented personal pursuit that involves as much mental as technical skill (hence, my use of several golfing analogies in the book). In contrast to archery, however, golf has taken a much more unifying approach to its own equipment disputes.

Golf's ruling body in this country, the USGA, has historically accepted material advances that have made equipment more durable and efficient but has steadfastly disallowed technological improvements that would have altered historical shot-making skills or the historical form, function, and method of use of its equipment. It has allowed graphite shafts, metal drivers, and better golf ball materials, but has set limits on golf ball size and weight, standardized launch-speed, and the efficiency ("spring-like effect") of clubs. It has prohibited all use of form-molded grips, laser sighting aids, clubs with moving parts, and all mechanical helps for ensuring more consistent swings.

Each time some item has been disallowed, there have been objections from inventors, manufacturers, or consumers—even lawsuits—but the USGA has stood firm. The result is a unified, rapidly growing sport. Not every golfer agrees with these decisions, but they do feel a clear sense of community and brotherhood when they step onto a golf course.

If not for this approach, it's not hard to imagine that two sports of golf might have evolved—one practiced by traditionalists using hickory-shafted clubs and hand-stitched "Featherie" balls; and another practiced by high-tech proponents using elaborate mechanisms designed for the sole purpose of getting the ball into the hole in as few "ball-strikes" as possible.

Following golf's example won't be easy. Bowhunters have tried before to develop national organizations to address technology concerns, and they've routinely failed. Squabbles inevitably erupt and the organization atrophies and dies. But we still need to keep trying to achieve this lofty end. We need to ignore earlier failures and continue trying to develop a national consensus organization that can gather inputs from manufacturers, state wildlife departments, and mainstream bowhunters; synthesize it; and then force solutions that everyone can live with.

It isn't as important where this compromise is made as it is that we just make one—and then stick to it! Any sport is simply more fun when everyone is playing the same game in the same way.

Re-Assess Your Goals

Recall from an earlier discussion that bowhunting goals, whether consciously or subconsciously expressed, are moving targets. Beginning hunters just want to succeed as quickly as possible. As they gain experience, their emphasis increasingly shifts towards greater challenge and, ultimately, to the simple joys of a hunting camp.

I see too many people today who have lost some of the joy of archery and bowhunting due to peer pressure. I've seen compound shooters who really want to use recurves, and recurve shooters who really want to use compounds, once you get to talking to them in depth. But they don't for fear that they'll become outcasts in their shooting club. And I've seen hunters sitting forlornly in tree stands for days on end waiting for a whitetail buck to walk close—because books and magazine articles routinely tout this as the easiest means to success—when they really want to be on the ground sneaking up on critters. Then they grow bored with the sport and don't know why.

I also believe that the increasing emphasis on trophy hunting has caused some people to stagnate in their personal development as hunters. Certainly, this is a rich part of the challenge in the sport, but it's not everything. In her hugely popular book, *Passages—Predictable Crises in Adult Life*, author Gail Sheehy says that the most unhappy people that she identified in over sixty-thousand surveyed were those who single-mindedly pursued financial success throughout their lives. The happiest people were those who successfully balanced financial and career goals with personal and spiritual growth.

I believe that hunting is a little like this. Some hunters just substitute bucks for "bucks." Common themes among disenchanted hunters are: "I've already shot all of the animals that I ever care to shoot" or "I've already shot the biggest buck that I'm ever likely to shoot, so what's left?" Incapable of moving beyond this stage (what Sheehy calls a passage), they drop out.

In their competition with other hunters to bag the biggest (or most) animals, some hunters fail to recognize some of the non-tangible benefits of hunting: The spiritual joys of trying new things, setting new goals, and experiencing the sport in a variety of ways.

To get the most enjoyment from the sport, get in the habit of periodically re-assessing your own bowhunting goals and updating them when required.

Choose Your Own Challenge

Most people want their bowhunting activities to be challenging. But they also want to score a certain percentage of the time. Note that one half of this equation—challenge—involves adding difficulty to the hunting process while the other half—success—involves reducing difficulty. Everyone makes their own tradeoff at a different point, but most people seek an element of both. Optimum satisfaction with the sport involves making an optimum personal tradeoff between these conflicting goals.

Dr. Dave Samuel, a well known former wildlife biology professor and prolific bowhunting writer, has suggested this decision-rule in a speech he once gave entitled "Draw Your Own Line:"

Every bowhunter should choose and use the most basic equipment with which his proficiency level will allow him to harvest game, while maintaining the maximum challenge and enjoyment of his sport.

He then explained that if someone has the time and dedication to accept the challenges of simple equipment, then that's what they should use. If they don't have the time or inclination to put in this effort, then they should choose the minimum equipment that they feel lethal with.

The happiest hunters know what they want out of the sport and then pursue it. Perhaps your buddy needs to kill three deer every year to be happy, but you'd be satisfied with one every three-years if you did it your way. Different strokes for different folks. Choose your level of challenge, not someone else's.

| "Timeless" Bowhunting | In closing, let me suggest one extension to Samuel's rule: Maximize your shooting and hunting enjoyment by using all types of equipment and shooting styles. Learn about your fellow archers. Rekindle the fellowship, based on a common understanding, that all archers once felt towards one another. |

If all you've ever shot is a release-aid and sights, try releasing an arrow with your fingers or experiencing the age-old joy of seeing an instinctively aimed arrow centering the bull's-eye. Breakaway, if only as a diversion, from the rigid mechanics that some gear demands and let your spirit soar.

Industry statistics suggest that this is a fast-growing trend as the bowhunting population continues to age demographically and to seek more internal pleasure rather than outward success from their hunting activities.

A few examples. My extended group of bowhunting friends include a number of eclectic fellows who routinely buck prevailing bowhunting "wisdom." One shoots a recurve with sights; another a compound instinctively; and a third uses an old ledge-release with both his stickbows and compounds, adding or removing sights on a whim.

Several use recurves as their primary bows but still enjoy the thrill of shooting a dozen arrows into a styrofoam cup at 40-yards with a fast, flat-shooting compound. Others use compounds for their serious hunting but get a huge off-season charge when they take a bristling javelina at hand shaking distance in tight brush or pluck a flying quail from the air with their stickbows. In the process, each of these people have become better informed, more well-rounded bowhunters who continue to enjoy the sport immensely.

Whatever your equipment and hunting persuasions, I hope that this book has expanded your archery horizons a bit and given you information that will help you practice the sport more effectively and more knowledgeably. Above all. I hope that it will help you enjoy it more.

Index